To Margo
with the
Bo

"*Standing on High Ground* powerfully captures the spirit and resilience of those who stood up for the land, water, and climate against a toxic pipeline the planet can't afford. This anthology is a testament to the bravery and commitment of the many individuals who put their lives on the line and is a stirring reminder that when we stand together, fueled by love and a fierce dedication to our planet, we can challenge even the most daunting of adversaries."
Mike Hudema, activist and author of *An Action A Day: Keeps Global Capitalism Away*

"*Standing on High Ground* is an important read for many reasons. The succinct history of the struggle against TMX at Burnaby Mountain (with timeline and maps) is very useful. The resisters' powerful stories provide important insight into how people become land defenders motivated enough to undertake civil disobedience and get arrested. Their courage and the creativity of their actions is inspiring."
Joan Kuyek, author of *Unearthing Justice: How to Protect Your Community from the Mining Industry* and *Community Organizing: A Wholistic Approach*

"These moving and powerful stories of resistance, civil disobedience, and incarceration are infused with a passionate love for the earth and a desire to take this world to a better place. These resisters, Indigenous and non-Indigenous alike, are truth tellers: their courage and sacrifice are inspiring. Their activism is a challenge to those who are indifferent to the urgent struggle against the environmental racism, ecocide, and corporate greed that is ravaging the planet."

Pierre Coupey, RCA, founding editor of *The Capilano Review*;
professor emeritus, Capilano University

"The reflections in this book offer insight into why fellow citizens would risk incarceration to engage in illegal, though peaceful, opposition to an oil pipeline. Rebecca Solnit has observed that activists are motivated not by anger but love. The authors of each chapter share not only their understanding of what is at stake in the climate crisis, but also their deep respect and love—for Indigenous nations defending their unceded lands, for our children and grandchildren, for those who have already lost their lives and homes to extreme weather, and for natural places and the species in them."

Kathryn Harrison, professor, Department of Political Science; Brenda and David McLean Chair in Canadian Studies, University of British Columbia

STANDING ON HIGH GROUND
Civil Disobedience on Burnaby Mountain

Edited by
Rosemary Cornell, Adrienne Drobnies,
and Tim Bray

Between the Lines
Toronto

Standing on High Ground: Civil Disobedience on Burnaby Mountain
© 2024 Rosemary Cornell, Adrienne Drobnies, and Tim Bray

First published in 2024 by
Between the Lines
401 Richmond Street West, Studio 281
Toronto, Ontario · M5V 3A8 · Canada
1-800-718-7201 · www.btlbooks.com

Library and Archives Canada Cataloguing in Publication
Title: Standing on high ground : civil disobedience on Burnaby Mountain / Rosemary
    Cornell, Adrienne Drobnies, Tim Bray, eds.
Names: Cornell, Rosemary, editor. | Drobnies, Adrienne, editor. | Bray, Tim, editor.
Description: Includes index.
Identifiers: Canadiana (print) 20240381815 | Canadiana (ebook) 20240381890 | ISBN
    9781771136631 (softcover) | ISBN 9781771136648 (EPUB)
Subjects: LCSH: Climate justice—Canada. | LCSH: Civil disobedience—Canada. | LCSH:
    Protest movements—Canada. | LCSH: Political activists—Canada.
Classification: LCC GE220 .S73 2024 | DDC 363.7/0523—dc23

Cover and text design by DEEVE
Printed in Canada

We acknowledge for their financial support of our publishing activities: the Government of Canada; the Canada Council for the Arts; and the Government of Ontario through the Ontario Arts Council, the Ontario Book Publishers Tax Credit program, and Ontario Creates.

*We dedicate this book to all those who stood up to TMX
and were willing to face arrest.*

Contents

"It's often assumed that anger drives such work, but most activism is driven by love, a life among activists has convinced me."

From *Recollections of My Nonexistence* by Rebecca Solnit

"Yes, it's true you can't solve the climate crisis alone, but it's even more true we can't solve it without you."

From "Here's Where You Come In" by Mary Annaïse Heglar in *Not Too Late*, edited by Rebecca Solnit and Thelma Young Lutunatabua

PREFACE:
How This Book Came to Be

Your editors, Rosemary Cornell, Adrienne Drobnies, and Tim Bray, live near each other in Vancouver, BC. In response to a call to "Protect the Inlet" and stop the Trans Mountain Pipeline Expansion (TMX), they marched up Burnaby Mountain with thousands of others on March 10, 2018. One week later, on St. Patrick's Day, Tim joined a group of resisters who defied the injunction to stay away from the TMX construction site and was arrested at the project's front gate.

Rosemary, who had been active in the 2014 protests against TMX on Burnaby Mountain, was spurred again into action by Tim's arrest. She began attending vigils and rallies supporting resisters who were occupying trees to block pipeline work in 2020 and 2021. When members of a prayer circle, Janette McIntosh, Ruth Walmsley, and Catherine Hembling, were arrested in the fall of 2021 and faced jail time, Rosemary was dismayed that their moral action was to be met with imprisonment. What could she do to honour their courage? Was anyone trying to record for posterity the historic events taking place on the ground? She reached out to Adrienne, who was active with the Save Old Growth environmental group, and to Tim.

The three of us, in a series of kitchen-table meetings, began to explore the possibility of an anthology recounting the arrestees' experiences. But a challenge loomed: How would we collect the material?

In 2020, playwright Mairy Beam had obtained many transcripts of arrestees' statements to the court, offering their motivations for civil disobedience. Mairy wove these into a play, *Irreparable Harm?*, which was performed at the Vancouver Fringe festival later that year. Mairy generously shared those transcripts with us. We found more court statements on the Protect the Planet: Stop TMX website (stoptmx.ca). Then we contacted other arrestees, inviting them to participate, in part to tell the world about their conscientious opposition and nonviolent resistance to a misguided action of the Canadian government, but also to preserve their stories and to encourage everyone to join the fight against climate change.

This anthology features testimonies from twenty-five arrestees, preceded by a historical overview of the pipeline project and resistance to it, and followed by an essay by Professor D.B. Tindall about the history, theory, and practice of civil disobedience.

Most of the arrestees are middle-aged or older. They were following Bill McKibben's callout to seniors whose careers are over or winding down to "go get arrested and let the young people go to university and get their lives established." But four arrestees are in their twenties. They represent Generations Y/Z and exemplify the response of youth radicalized by their sense of a tenuous future not of their own making. We are grateful for the compelling accounts offered by Indigenous arrestees Jim Leyden (Anishinaabe), April Thomas (Secwépemc), Billie Pierre (Nlaka'pamux), Tawahum Bige (Łutselk'e Dene), and Maya Laframboise (Red River Métis). Other Indigenous resisters did not offer written testimony, but rather spoke to the court extemporaneously, in keeping with their traditions. We recognize and honour their presence in this fight.

We have edited the arrestee testimonies with the goal of making the writing accessible to readers while preserving the contributors' unique voices.

The resister-contributors are a remarkably diverse group and, overall, were gracious and eager to co-operate in the process of birthing this book. Now, six years after the grand march up the mountain, their testimonies are in your hands, woven together into a fabric that is rich in human colour and texture.

INTRODUCTION
AND BACKGROUND

The email arrived with the subject line: Kwekwecnewtxw! The message was from Will George, of the Tsleil-Waututh Nation (TWN), and it was brief: "Protect the Inlet: On March 10th, Coast Salish members are launching an ambitious project to stop Kinder Morgan, starting with a mass protest march up Burnaby Mountain." The resistance against the Trans Mountain Pipeline Expansion (TMX) had seemed quiet in the preceding months of 2018. But behind the scenes, the Tsleil-Waututh and their allies had been planning feverishly as the pipeline company, Kinder Morgan, began to prepare the site on Burnaby Mountain, BC, for expansion of the oil storage facility, known as the "tank farm."

March 10 arrived, mild and with blue skies. All morning, protesters spilled out of packed SkyTrain cars into the late-winter sunshine at the transit station at the foot of Burnaby Mountain. Thousands of people joined the crowd, the air abuzz with the sounds of chanting and drumming. First Nations Chiefs and Elders from as far away as Haida Gwaii, in traditional regalia, led the march up the hill to the site where Will George and his crew were just finishing the construction of Kwekwecnewtxw (pronounced "Kwe-kwek-new-tukh"), the Watch House, only metres from the TMX tank farm fence. Speeches by Elders and Chiefs followed on a nearby field, and a call went out for any and all to step up for civil disobedience training and action. Kinder Morgan had been paying attention and had already obtained an injunction to keep protesters away from the work zone. This day was the launch of an intense campaign of civil disobedience to stop TMX.

The first actions and arrests began seven days later at TMX's front gate on Burnaby Mountain; co-editor Tim Bray was among them on that first day. Most of the arrests narrated in this book happened on or near Burnaby Mountain. Another three accounts

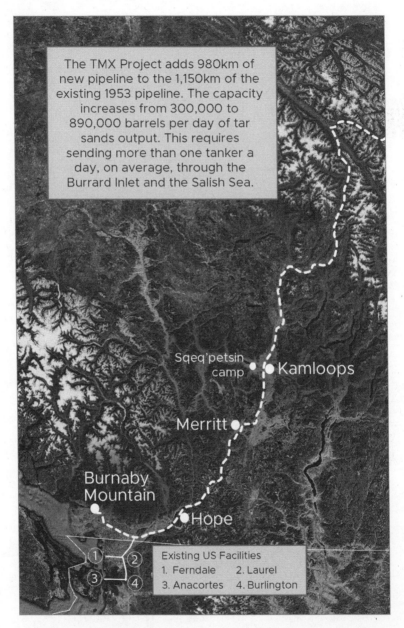

The TMX Project adds 980km of new pipeline to the 1,150km of the existing 1953 pipeline. The capacity increases from 300,000 to 890,000 barrels per day of tar sands output. This requires sending more than one tanker a day, on average, through the Burrard Inlet and the Salish Sea.

Sqeq'petsin camp · Kamloops

Merritt

Burnaby Mountain

Hope

Existing US Facilities
1. Ferndale   2. Laurel
3. Anacortes   4. Burlington

Route of the Trans Mountain Pipeline from Edmonton, Alberta to Burnaby, British Columbia, and refineries in Washington State.

Maps by Tim Bray, based on data from Google Maps, OpenStreetMap, and TMX regulatory filings.

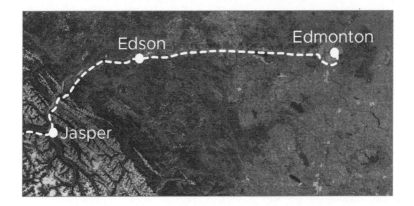

are from people arrested on the banks of the Thompson River near Kamloops, part of a group of Secwépemc and allies who resisted drilling under the river for the pipeline, which trespasses through their territory.

Who are the people that committed to this level of action? What would make them willing to go to jail? This book gives their testimonies in answer to these questions.

Pressure for Pipelines

The 2018 resistance and arrests were just one battle in a larger conflict against TMX that started in 2013 and continues today. How did the TMX project come to be? Why and how did a resistance movement grow in response to it?

To prevent catastrophic global warming, climate scientists have been unequivocal that we must immediately reduce our reliance on fossil fuels and reject fossil fuel infrastructure projects such as TMX. TMX also inflicts a multitude of environmental and cultural harms on the peoples and landscapes it traverses in transporting bitumen from the tar sands.[1] It puts all of us at risk in both the short and long term, and shows blatant disregard in particular for the Indigenous populations and their territories.

Given all this, what can be the case for proceeding with the project?

The raw product of the Alberta tar sands is bitumen, a tar-like substance that is much too viscous to ship through a pipeline. It is combined with other petroleum products to create diluted bitumen ("dilbit"), which is pipeline-friendly.

Map of the Vancouver region; sites of TMX Resistance labelled

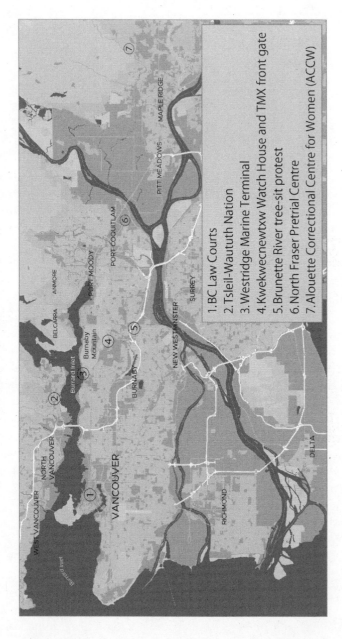

1. BC Law Courts
2. Tsleil-Waututh Nation
3. Westridge Marine Terminal
4. Kwekwecnewtxw Watch House and TMX front gate
5. Brunette River tree-sit protest
6. North Fraser Pretrial Centre
7. Alouette Correctional Centre for Women (ACCW)

Burnaby Mountain and its environs; sites of TMX Resistance labelled

1. Westridge Marine Terminal
2. Site of 2014 resistance camp
3. Simon Fraser University
4. TMX tank farm
5. TMX front gate
6. Kwekwecnewtxw Watch House
7. T-Rex badminton court

Alberta tar sands operators have long complained of a lack of pipeline capacity to export their bitumen. In recent decades, they have aggressively lobbied governments in Canada and the US for construction projects including Northern Gateway, Keystone XL, Energy East, Line 3 replacement, and TMX. The first three have been cancelled. The new Line 3, from Alberta to Wisconsin, has been operational since October 2021. TMX is the last tar sands crude oil pipeline to be constructed.

This pipeline fever is taking place in the ongoing context of rapidly expanding bitumen production: 2.4-fold between 2005 and 2015, and threefold between 2005 and 2020.[2] And the tar sands outfits are banking on even more expansion.

The TMX project was born in 2013 when Texas company Kinder Morgan (KM) applied to twin the existing Trans Mountain Pipeline. That pipeline was constructed in 1952–1953 and Kinder Morgan purchased it from the Canadian government in 2005. The 1,150-kilometre pipeline connects a bitumen loading station east of Edmonton, Alberta, to a storage depot and ship-loading station at the Westridge Marine Terminal in Burnaby, BC. (See map, Route of the Trans Mountain Pipeline).

Burnaby Mountain (Lhuḵw'lhuḵw'áyten), which is at the centre of this story, is fifteen kilometres from Vancouver's downtown. Its peak elevation is 370 metres; just a hill by local Coast Mountain standards. Simon Fraser University (SFU) and a residential neighbourhood are at its top. Forest covers the rest, much of it a protected conservation zone. The north slope is a sheer cliff plunging into the salt water of the Burrard Inlet, which also hosts Vancouver's harbour. Directly across the inlet is the Tsleil-Waututh Nation's home. That community's view of Burnaby Mountain is marred by the Westridge Marine Terminal on its northwest flank, where tankers are pumped full of tar sands dilbit. (See maps of Metro Vancouver and Burnaby, showing sites of TMX resistance.)

The new pipeline, a larger iteration of the existing one, runs to a tank farm on the mountain's southern flank. From there, it passes through a tunnel being drilled through the mountain, under the residential community that has grown in the seventy years since the first pipeline was laid, and ends at the salt water's edge.

The pipeline has multiple endpoints and carries multiple

products.[3] It forks at Sumas on the BC/Washington State border, one branch continuing to Washington refineries at Cherry Point, Ferndale, and Anacortes, and the other continuing to Burnaby. The pipeline can carry dilbit, ordinary crude oil, or synthetic crude refined from bitumen. There is a refinery in Burnaby that can process the synthetic crude. But the main payload—93 percent of the total after the expansion project—will be dilbit, some to be refined in Washington State, most to be sent by tanker out of Burnaby.

When the new pipeline is finished, the system will carry 890,000 barrels/day of these products, tripling the current capacity. From the Burnaby Westridge Marine Terminal, the dilbit would be shipped to the US and, potentially, Asia.

Kinder Morgan abandoned the project in May 2018 in the face of mounting opposition and construction costs. Controversially, the government of Canada, led by Justin Trudeau, bought the existing pipeline and the expansion project on August 31, 2018, for $4.5 billion. You will find a scathing account of this transaction in Elizabeth May's contribution in part 3.

To justify TMX, Trudeau and his ministers are fond of offering enthusiastic statements that jobs and economic growth are compatible with environmental protection. Let's consider jobs. Building the pipeline has indeed created employment. As of December 2023, the Trans Mountain website claimed that 34,590 people had been hired to work on the project since its inception.[4] According to one source, however, there will be only about ninety permanent operations jobs once the pipeline is running.[5] Projected job growth in Alberta's tar sands depends on the profitability of Canadian bitumen. Pipeline boosters claim that it will enable export of the crude product to Asia (currently it is only shipped to the US), and are banking on 16 percent growth in oil extraction in Alberta over the next twenty years.[6]

How can increased production be justified in the face of a directive to cut emissions? A 2021 analysis in the journal *Nature* showed that Canada's "budget" for oil production, to keep global heating to 1.5°C, is six billion barrels.[7] The TMX project alone plans to ship this much oil by 2040. Despite Trudeau's claims, TMX seems profoundly incompatible with the 1.5° goal specifically and global climate stewardship generally.

Pushback against the Pipeline

There are four immediate negative impacts from the new pipeline:

- The first concern is with greenhouse gas (GHG) emissions, which will contribute to global warming. The annual GHG emissions associated with this project include 9–15 megatonnes (Mt) carbon dioxide equivalents (CO_2e) for the extraction and transport of the bitumen.[8] This amounts to 6–10 percent of the emissions for the entire oil and gas industry in Canada (150 Mt in 2020).[9] In addition, 1 Mt of annual emissions is directly linked to the construction of the pipeline and its terminals.

  The government has argued that the pipeline construction will not weaken Canada's GHG reduction commitment, as the emissions linked to TMX expansion have already been accounted for in their submitted plans.[10] But it should be pointed out that the government's arithmetic does not include emissions due to burning the fuel outside Canada, which are 71 Mt, or 85 percent of the total. All in, the yearly emissions from all aspects of this project are equivalent to adding an extra twenty million gas-powered cars to the roads each year.[11]

  How can this be justified? Canadian government environmental commissioner Jerry V. DeMarco presented his assessment in November 2021 with these words: "Canada has become the worst [climate] performer of all G7 nations since the landmark Paris Agreement." His report pointed out that there are "a host of recent decisions by the Liberal government that are incoherent with meeting Canada's climate commitments, such as investing in the Trans Mountain Pipeline Expansion." The report also stated that "Canada's growing oil and gas production remains a key barrier to meeting its climate targets."[12]

- The second concern is increased tanker traffic in the Salish Sea. Huge tankers will go in and out of the Burnaby Westridge terminal at a rate of more than one per day, a minimum seven-fold increase. These behemoths must navigate a narrow passage through Burrard Inlet, threading the needles of multiple busy bridges,[13] past Vancouver and its suburbs, the Gulf and San Juan Islands, and navigate the Strait of Juan de Fuca on their way to open ocean. (As we prepare this book for publication, a huge ship that lost power has wrecked a key piece of big city infrastructure, the Francis Scott Key Bridge in Baltimore.) These waters are subject to strong tidal currents and are already busy with shipping traffic, since Vancouver is the fourth-largest west coast port.[14]

There is concern that increased noise from tanker traffic will impact marine life. A major dilbit spill from a tanker could devastate the local economy. It could kill half a million sea birds,[15] as the fertile waters of the Salish Sea host huge numbers of migrating geese and ducks for many months of the year. Juvenile salmon, forage fish including herring and anchovies, marine mammals such as killer whales, harbour seals, sea lions, otters, and mink, and billions of shellfish would also be at risk.

- The third concern relates to expansion of the Burnaby Mountain oil tank storage facility (the tank farm) and Westridge Marine Terminal. Prior to expansion, the tank farm contained thirteen storage tanks with a total volume of 1.6 million barrels.[16] The project removes one tank but adds an additional fourteen, for a 2.3-fold increase in storage volume. At the same time, it expands the number of berths at the marine terminal from one to three.[17] This infrastructure presents major fire and spill hazards for the surrounding area, as the tanks will be wedged in between protected forests, Simon Fraser University, and residential neighbourhoods.

- Finally, this project lacks consent of many First Nations through whose unceded territory it is being built. This includes 518 kilometres of Secwépemc territory in the BC Interior[18] and much of the BC southwest coast. The Salish Sea tanker route crosses the territories of more than thirty First Nations in BC and Washington State.[19] Indigenous law mandates protection of the land and waters for future generations. This requirement is at the heart of the fierce opposition to the pipeline by Indigenous land defenders. The right to uphold their responsibilities to future generations is recognized in Article 25 of the United Nations Declaration on the Rights of Indigenous Peoples (UNDRIP).

Pipeline Politics

A project of this magnitude, with so many potential community, economic, and environmental impacts, must have been subject to public scrutiny. What did this look like for TMX?

National Energy Board review in 2015. Alberta governments, both Conservative and NDP, have ardently supported the pipeline. The federal government under Stephen Harper started pushing the project in 2014. This book's contributions from Elizabeth May and Robert Hackett (part 3), and Tim Takaro and Ruth Walmsley (part 4) describe the flawed National Energy Board (NEB) review process, which imposed egregious limits on public participation and topics that could be raised. It excluded, for example, discussion of the climate change impacts of the project. This led to the resignation of expert intervenor Marc Eliesen, the former CEO of BC Hydro and Ontario Hydro, and deputy minister of energy for Ontario and Manitoba, who stated that the process was rigged in favour of approval.[20]

Review by ministerial panel in 2016. In May 2016, the newly elected Liberal government ordered an additional hearing. More than 90 percent of the hearing's intervenors, emails, and online survey responses opposed the project, and the surprisingly discerning report prepared by the panel raised a multitude of cautionary questions, including: "Can construction of a new Trans Mountain Pipeline be reconciled with Canada's climate change commitments?" "How might Cabinet square approval of the Trans Mountain Pipeline with commitment to reconciliation with First Nations and to the UNDRIP principles of 'free, prior, and informed consent'?" and "How can Canada be confident in its assessment of the project's economic rewards and risks?"[21]

The Liberal cabinet of Justin Trudeau brushed aside these concerns and approved the project on November 29, 2016, subject to 157 conditions. Nonetheless, in 2018 the federal government was forced by a federal appeals court to redo consultations with affected First Nations. Despite steadfast opposition from the Tsleil-Waututh and Secwépemc Nations, on whose ancestral lands the pipeline is being built, the federal cabinet again approved the project on June 18, 2019. Ironically, the previous day the government had declared a climate emergency. It is impossible to reconcile the pipeline approval of the Liberals with their platform and promise to be climate leaders. TMX is one of Canada's dirty dozen "carbon bombs."[22]

Trudeau himself has openly stated that cabinet granted pipeline approval in exchange for Alberta premier Rachel Notley's support for a national carbon price and a cap on tar sands emissions.[23] In May 2018, Kinder Morgan stopped work on the project in the face of strong First Nations, local community, and BC provincial opposition, demanding assurance that the federal government would remove roadblocks. Within days Finance Minister Bill Morneau announced the federal government's decision to buy the pipeline and expansion project from Kinder Morgan. In this book, Elizabeth May's contribution digs deep into the political machinations that led to the TMX approval and purchase by the federal government.[24]

Pipeline Economics: Boon or Boondoggle?

How much is TMX costing, and will it ever make money for Canadians? Kinder Morgan estimated in 2013 that the TMX construction costs would be $5.4 billion. In 2018 it sold its operation to the Canadian government for $4.5 billion. Costs estimates rocketed to $21 billion at the start of 2022, when the work was only about 50 percent complete. At that time, Minister of Finance Chrystia Freeland stated that no more public funds would support the project, but two months later she abruptly reversed course and offered it a $10 billion loan guarantee.[25] As of February 2024, estimated costs for completion have again ballooned to over $34 billion.

The government claimed that TMX would rake in $73 billion in revenues for industry and $46 billion for government over twenty years of operation.[26] Other financial analysts differ: the Parliamentary Budget Officer voiced skepticism that the pipeline would ever turn a profit.[27] Also, Trans Mountain's model assumes an operational life of a hundred years,[28] which flies in the face of Canada's "net zero" commitment within thirty years. Moreover, Jonathan Wilkinson stated, when he was Canada's minister of environment and climate change, that the pipeline would operate for only thirty to forty years.[29] It is very difficult to see TMX as anything but an environmental *and* financial disaster.

Resistance to the Pipeline: First Nations and Other Voices

The Tsleil-Waututh Nation has been at the forefront of the resistance against the pipeline expansion since its inception, with strong collaborative efforts from the Squamish Nation on the coast and Secwépemc Peoples in the BC Interior. The Tsleil-Waututh Nation has never ceded its ancestral land or waters, rich in marine life, which include the Burrard Inlet (səlilwətaɬ). Tsleil-Waututh have been nurturing the shoreline back to health for decades, and recently celebrated a limited clam harvest, a practice intrinsic and of great spiritual significance to their culture.[30] All this progress could be easily ruined in one disastrous spill.

The Tsleil-Waututh have mounted an enormous effort to stop TMX. They created the TWN Sacred Trust and launched an independent assessment of the Trans Mountain Pipeline and tanker expansion, grounded in Tsleil-Waututh's unextinguished law and contemporary policy. The assessment consisted of expert scientific analyses on issues such as oil spill risk. It also included analyses of the impact of the project on their right to practise their culture and ceremony, and to safely harvest shellfish.[31] TWN leaders have spoken at Kinder Morgan shareholders' conventions,[32] the Toronto Dominion bank AGM,[33] and numerous local town hall meetings and public rallies. They launched a successful legal challenge in 2018, based on lack of consent, Indigenous rights, and title infringement.

The Tsleil-Waututh Nation took the lead in organizing public protests in alliance with environmental nongovernmental organizations (ENGOs). They organized kayak/canoe paddling protest events across Burrard Inlet to the marine terminal while it was under construction. They built the Watch House (Kwekwecnewtxw) near the gates of the tank farm and were deeply involved in organizing the 2018 civil disobedience protests there, and helped set up the tree-sits near the Brunette River in Burnaby in 2020. Most of the stories of resistance found in this book emerge from the inspirational, energetic leadership of the Tsleil-Waututh.

Several bands of the Secwépemc Nation near Merritt and Kamloops have mounted opposition campaigns that have included intervention at Kinder Morgan shareholder conventions and civil disobedience and arrests. The arrests included that of Secwépemc Hereditary Chief Saw-Sês and Matriarchs April Thomas and Miranda Dick in October 2020 during a ceremony at an ancient village site (Sqeq'petsin) on the Thompson River. This book includes three stories from participants in this action at Sqeq'petsin (parts 1 and 3). In 2023, Secwépemc again resisted TMX drilling a path for the pipeline under sacred sites at Jacko Lake (Pipsell) in violation an earlier agreement.[34]

Prominent Indigenous voices have tirelessly and passionately spoken out at every opportunity for the last decade against TMX. They include Sundance Chief Rueben George; former Chief Judy Wilson of the Neskonlith First Nation and former secretary-treasurer of the Union of BC Indian Chiefs (UBCIC); Grand Chief Stewart Phillip, president of UBCIC; and his wife Joan Phillip, who as we write is MLA for Vancouver–Mount Pleasant.

Community groups and leaders have also been key opponents of the TMX project. Chris Bowcock, chief of the Burnaby Fire Department, voiced his strong opposition to the number and density of tanks at the Burnaby Terminal for failing to meet the minimum mandatory standard for fire truck access, and because of the risks posed by their location.[35] About 230,000 people live and work within a 4.2-kilometre radius (the evacuation zone),[36] including three high schools, ten elementary schools, and Simon Fraser University. In the event of a fire, the firefighters would not be able to manoeuvre their trucks within the site and more than 30,000 people could be trapped on top of Burnaby Mountain. The tank farm is situated just below the intersection of the two exit roads. It is highly unusual to locate an oil tank farm within a population centre.

Simon Fraser University's administration, the Cities of Burnaby, New Westminster, Vancouver, North and West Vancouver, and Victoria, as well as the Province of BC and the State of Washington have been opposed to this project, and representatives from some of these bodies intervened as opponents in the NEB hearings (2015–2016).[37] In the 2017 BC election campaign, the provincial NDP said it would use every tool in the toolbox to fight TMX. Once the NDP formed government, they attempted but did not win their case at the BC Court of Appeal and the

Supreme Court of Canada to block the pipeline based on the right to regulate transport of toxic materials.[38] Similarly, court cases to impede construction pursued by municipalities such as Vancouver and Burnaby have been unsuccessful.

Not surprisingly, the project has been opposed by many non-profit organizations focused on climate action, the Salish Sea ecosystem, wilderness preservation, fish conservation in rivers, and water pollution.[39] A few groups participated as intervenors in the NEB hearings (2014–2015), presenting analyses of the impacts of a bitumen spill on Salish Sea marine life.[40] The board concluded that the project would have *significant adverse effects* on the Southern Resident killer whales, and on Indigenous cultural practice associated with these iconic whales.[41] There are only seventy-four whales in this resident population, and they face extinction pressures due to lack of Chinook salmon, shipping noise that interferes with their communication, marine toxins, oil spills, and inbreeding. ENGOs have collaborated with the Tsleil-Waututh in organizing rallies, marches, educational events such as webinars, letter-writing campaigns, phone-banking, and even organized a group hug of Burnaby Mountain.

The Road to Civil Disobedience
Acts of resistance against the Trans Mountain Pipeline Expansion began in 2013 and continue to the present day. The TMX project has become the line in the sand for the thousands of resisters who have committed to action to stop expansion of the Alberta tar sands.

When the residents of Burnaby discovered in 2013 that Kinder Morgan planned to submit an application to "twin" the pipeline, they formed the group Burnaby Residents Opposing Kinder Morgan Expansion (BROKE). Several arrestees featured in this book were BROKE members: Robert Hackett (part 3), Ruth Walmsley (part 4), and Elan Ross Gibson (part 5).

Then, in the fall of 2014, Kinder Morgan employees were caught cutting trees in a conservation zone on the west side of Burnaby Mountain without the permission of the City of Burnaby. The local community, including many from SFU, mobilized, establishing a protest camp next to Burnaby Mountain Park and occupying it continuously throughout a rainy and often snowy November. Local First Nations women maintained a Sacred Fire at the camp. People began hiking into the forest to monitor the activities of the Kinder Morgan workers.

In an attempt to intimidate and silence the activists standing up against Big Oil, the company sued five individuals for a total of $5.6 million. They included SFU professors Lynne Quarmby and Stephen Collis, along with BROKE member Alan Dutton and two other young camp organizers, Mia Nissen and Adam Gold. These were SLAPP suits (strategic litigation against public participation) intended to suppress public opposition. The five protesters appeared in courtrooms overflowing with supporters during the first week of November 2014.[42]

On November 14, 2014, Kinder Morgan obtained an injunction from the Supreme Court of BC, prohibiting protesters from interfering with their work on Burnaby Mountain.[43] Police marked the injunction line with tape at the protest camp site. Civil disobedience against the injunction began immediately.

The last two weeks of November 2014 were chock full of high-intensity action. Every other day a different group would show up to step over the injunction line and be arrested. One day it was BROKE members, another it was faith groups, another it was Indigenous leaders—including Tsleil-Waututh Matriarch Ta'ah George and Grand Chief Stewart Phillip. To boost their spirits, the crowds sang to the arrestees as the police loaded them into transport vans. On November 27, a group of academics gathered including volunteers for arrest, but at the last minute, word came that the charges against the approximately 120 people already arrested had been dropped because the injunction line GPS coordinates submitted by Kinder Morgan were incorrect.[44] A joyous celebration erupted as helicopters flew equipment away from the KM site. Messages of support and news of solidarity rallies poured in from other countries. The world was watching!

When the Conservative government of Stephen Harper was replaced with that of Justin Trudeau's Liberals in 2015, there was optimism among TMX resisters. Trudeau had promised to add climate concerns to the NEB consideration process. One of Trudeau's early actions was to ban tanker traffic on the BC north coast, effectively cancelling the Northern Gateway Pipeline that would have transported bitumen to Kitimat. Would TMX be next? A new set of TMX public hearings ensued in early 2016.

But despite the overwhelming negative public feedback, and the many reservations of the ministerial review panel,[45] the federal government approved the project in November 2016. Robert Hackett has more to say about this in his contribution in part 3.

It was time to take the government to court. The Tsleil-Waututh Nation took this on with several other First Nations, arguing that the previous NEB hearings (2014–2015) leading to the project approval in November 2016 were negligent with respect to Aboriginal consultation. They won their case in 2018 in the Federal Court of Appeal, the first litigation win against TMX. Resister morale surged again. But then the appeals court ruled that it would not hear additional arguments on topics that had already been covered in previous hearings. Tsleil-Waututh, Squamish, Coldwater, and Stó:lō Nations challenged that ruling. Ecojustice, an environmental law nonprofit organization, also challenged the approval of TMX on behalf of Raincoast Conservation Foundation and Living Oceans Society, on the grounds that it violated Canada's Species at Risk Act with respect to protection of endangered Southern Resident killer whales. These cases were pursued all the way to the Supreme Court, but the court ruled on March 5, 2020, that it would refuse to hear arguments from First Nations and Ecojustice.[46] Meanwhile, the federal cabinet had already approved the pipeline on June 18, 2019.

By 2018, it was understood that the legal actions alone were not likely to stop TMX. Another tactic remained—civil disobedience. It had a history of success on Burnaby Mountain just four years earlier. What happened then, and in succeeding waves of resistance up to the present day, is illustrated in the graphical Timeline of Events.

In the fall of 2017 and early 2018, resistance moved to the gates of the Westridge terminal in Burnaby, where work to build the new tanker berths was ramping up. Kayak-tivists tied themselves to a pile-driver float and five were eventually arrested. On land, a group of protesters staged blockades at the terminal gates, arriving well before dawn and ahead of the TMX workers, with the goal of delaying work. On the very first morning, the resisters shivered in freezing conditions and fretted about the annoyed workers stalled in their trucks as they waited for the police to arrive. Then, a gift: a TV news helicopter flew low overhead looking for a story. Just

Timeline of Events: Trans Mountain Pipeline and Resistance

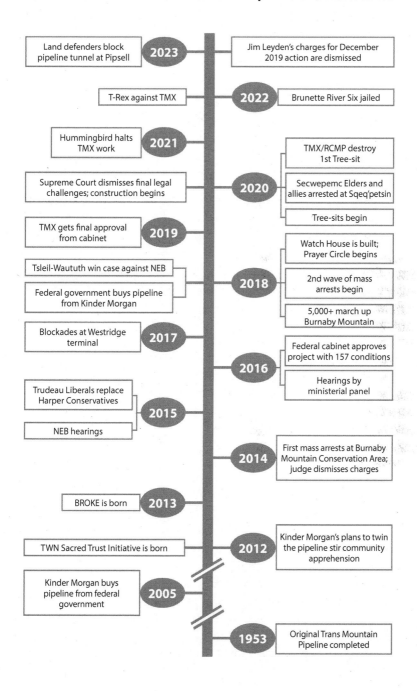

Land defenders block pipeline tunnel at Pipsell

2023

Jim Leyden's charges for December 2019 action are dismissed

T-Rex against TMX

2022

Brunette River Six jailed

Hummingbird halts TMX work

2021

TMX/RCMP destroy 1st Tree-sit

Supreme Court dismisses final legal challenges; construction begins

2020

Secwepemc Elders and allies arrested at Sqeq'petsin

Tree-sits begin

TMX gets final approval from cabinet

2019

Watch House is built; Prayer Circle begins

Tsleil-Waututh win case against NEB

2018

2nd wave of mass arrests begin

Federal government buys pipeline from Kinder Morgan

5,000+ march up Burnaby Mountain

Blockades at Westridge terminal

2017

Federal cabinet approves project with 157 conditions

2016

Hearings by ministerial panel

Trudeau Liberals replace Harper Conservatives

2015

NEB hearings

First mass arrests at Burnaby Mountain Conservation Area; judge dismisses charges

2014

BROKE is born

2013

Kinder Morgan's plans to twin the pipeline stir community apprehension

2012

TWN Sacred Trust Initiative is born

Kinder Morgan buys pipeline from federal government

2005

Original Trans Mountain Pipeline completed

1953

then, their "STOP KINDER MORGAN" sign caught the wind so that the helicopter got a clear shot. The story got a spot on the morning news, reaching more potential resisters. The action continued almost daily for months during the cold, dark winter. Fifteen of these protesters were sued by Kinder Morgan, and those suits remain active.

One large group of resisters walked all the way from Victoria to the Westridge terminal, and met a rally at the gates. Five of them chained themselves to the terminal entrance gates and refused to leave for two days, after which the police cut their chains and arrested them. After marching the 110 kilometres from Victoria, they weren't about to return without making good trouble.[47] They were prepared for the cold, but sleeping on the ground without toilet facilities took plenty of determination. Still, for two days they had stopped the black snake pipeline with their bodies.

On March 10, 2018, the March up Burnaby Mountain launched a new wave of mass arrests. To keep an eye on the proceedings during this time of expansion of the tank farm, the Tsleil-Waututh Elders gave their blessing to the construction of Kwekwecnewtxw. They appointed Jim Leyden, a contributor to this book (part 1), as Watchman. Over the next months, groups of resisters would visit the Watch House in the morning and assume a blocking position in front of the TMX front gate. Some of them fastened themselves to the fence with plastic zip ties. Each day the Burnaby RCMP detachment dutifully arrested all of those blocking the gate. Arrestees included public figures such as Green Party leader and contributor to this book Elizabeth May (part 3), former Vancouver City Council member Jean Swanson, and Kennedy Stewart, who has been a federal MP and mayor of Vancouver.

The Watch House also served as a place of refuge and spiritual grounding for protesters, including arrestees. Jim tells the story of how, despite being assured by police that he could carry out his spiritual and cultural activities at the Watch House without interference, he and fellow Anishinaabe land defender Stacy Gallagher were arrested off-site in December 2019. None of the nonindigenous protesters present at the "contentious" ceremony were arrested. Jim and Stacy received extraordinarily harsh prison sentences.

Judge Affleck offered the first set of arrestees a choice of a fine or community service. When this failed to stop the protests, in mid-April he changed the charge from civil contempt to criminal contempt of court, and in June he changed the punishment to jail time. The arrestees charged with criminal contempt of court were nonetheless tried in civil court, and none has a criminal record for civil disobedience, even those who were imprisoned.[48] The sentences since then imposed by Justice Kenneth Affleck and his successor, Justice Shelley Fitzpatrick, have ranged from seven to ninety days.

In August 2020, a group called Protect the Planet created an aerial camp in the path of the pipeline in the Brunette River corridor in Burnaby. The goal was to prevent tree felling by TMX for the installation of pipes bored through Burnaby Mountain to the sea. The Canada Energy Regulator (CER), successor to the NEB, had dismissed objections from the City of Burnaby, and the federal fisheries minister deferred to CER to permit chopping 1,308 mature trees next to salmonid-bearing streams. Resisters built a rough cabin twenty-five metres above ground on the limbs of a cottonwood tree. TMX workers destroyed the first tree fort, but the team speedily built another, as well as three skypods.

A dedicated group of volunteers succeeded in keeping the tree-sits continuously occupied twenty-four hours a day, seven days a week, for many months. A hardy fellow from Quebec did the lion's share of tree sitting that winter, which included a full week of −10°C and strong winds in February. At the same time, a Prayer Circle Action Group, dedicated to taking nonviolent direct action, emerged from a multi-faith affinity group that had been meeting on Burnaby Mountain next to the Watch House since July 2018. This group was integral to the support network that brought food and supplies to the team of rotating tree-sitters.

In April 2021, tree cutting was halted by a hummingbird.[49] Expert birder volunteers found several hummingbird nests among the trees slated for clear-cutting. They called in a wildlife enforcement officer, who observed a nest in a tree being sawed down in violation of a law prohibiting destruction of migrating bird nests. His report shut down the entire operation along the Brunette for five months.

After tree felling began again in September 2021, three members of the Prayer Circle were arrested for blocking access to equipment.[50] These three—Janette McIntosh, Ruth Walmsley, and Catherine Hembling—along with student activist Zain Haq and two tree-sitters, Dr. Tim Takaro and Dr. Bill Winder, became known as the Brunette River Six. All six tell their stories in part 4 of this book.[51]

In the summer of 2022 two young women, Emily Kelsall and Maya Laframboise, disguised in inflatable T-Rex suits, climbed over the fence to the TMX site on the southern flank of Burnaby Mountain. They proceeded to set up a net and, in a hilarious stunt, played badminton for fifteen minutes or so until security ordered them out. They were arrested on the spot, and were later tried and sentenced to twenty-eight and twenty-one days in jail. They relate their experiences in part 6 of this anthology. These individuals followed in the steps of more than 250 people arrested since 2018 for opposing the TMX project.

The harsh treatment of TMX protesters, particularly Indigenous resisters, has drawn international attention. Between 2019 and 2022, the United Nations Committee on the Elimination of Racial Discrimination sent three letters to the Canadian representative to the UN in Geneva raising concerns about Canada's escalated use of force, surveillance, and criminalization against land defenders and peaceful protesters and for Canada's failure to obtain the free, prior, and informed consent from First Nations for the Coastal GasLink project and the Trans Mountain project.[52] Amnesty International also denounced Canada's record on Indigenous Peoples' rights and climate justice in its 2022/2023 annual report, citing violation of the rights of the Tsleil-Waututh Nation in the construction of TMX.[53]

This introduction has covered a brief history of how and why TMX came to be, and how and why it was resisted. We turn now to the testimonies from people who became convinced that the tar sands pipeline project was, and is, lethally irrational. Living in the pipeline's path, they felt it their duty to resist. In twenty-first-century Canada, that resistance got them arrested, tried, convicted, and fined (if lucky) or jailed. They tell how they were caught up in the machinery of a criminal justice system weaponized by those who profit from confiscation, extraction, and destruction.

Part 1
Resistance from Turtle Island

Kwekwecnewtxw, the Tsleil-Waututh Watch House on Burnaby Mountain. The tank farm is visible through the break in the trees.
Photo: Tim Bray

JIM LEYDEN,
Watchman

Biography *(in Jim's own words)*

Jim Leyden is my adopted name—my spirit name is Stehm Mekoch Kanim, which means Blackbear Warrior. I was born in 1952 on the Six Nations land, but my mother is Anishinaabe. I was part of the Sixties Scoop (but was scooped in the fifties). I think I joined the resistance because throughout my life, everything was taken away from me. My family! I'd get into one foster home and start getting attached, and then I'd be moved to another and then another. When I was finally adopted, into a white family, I remember standing with a suitcase on the steps of the Brantford, Ontario, farmhouse I'd been living in, next to an apple tree—a little apple tree I had grown from scratch. Standing there I just felt lost and couldn't understand why I wasn't going to be staying with this family anymore. I was asking myself, What is wrong with me? In foster care I'd gone through a couple of families that were abusive. In the family that I lived with as an adoptee, the father was an extremely angry, abusive man. He taught me that I could never be anything. I know my real dad has died, and I am still searching for my mother, brothers, and sister.

I got involved in activism beginning in my early teens in the California grapes boycott fight, the underground press, the fight against the Vietnam War, and human rights committees. I ended up out here in BC, working in the Downtown Eastside for about twenty years. I was an Aboriginal Program Coordinator at Oppenheimer Park, where 80 percent of the population was Indigenous but there wasn't a single Indigenous program at that time. I managed to pull together multiple Indigenous programs.

I've long been mentored by Elder Robert Nahanee to carry out Sundance and Sweat Lodge Ceremonies. I take the commitments and the conditions of the Sun Dance Ceremony seriously. My TMX action started when the Tsleil-Waututh and Squamish Peoples started fighting against the pipeline. I was asked by my Elder to join in the fight and bring our teachings as a pipe-carrier to the camp near the Burnaby Mountain tank farm. I answered that call.

———————

Jim was arrested in August 2018 for breaching the injunction. He was sentenced to twenty-eight days, a portion of which he served in October 2020. His case was appealed and he was released, but the appeal was denied on June 19, 2024, and he was re-incarcerated on that day along with Stacy Gallagher. They planned to appeal to the Supreme Court of Canada. Jim was also charged in December 2019 and sentenced to sixty days' incarceration. The sentence was appealed and the case was dismissed in July 2023.

Narrative: Confronting the Legal Face of Racism

I was appointed in early 2018 as an Elder at the Watch House, our traditional Watch House on top of the pipeline, which has the right to exist according to the injunction.

A Watch House is a traditional Coast Salish building that used to be found all up and down the coast. They would be set up near the village where the Watchman could oversee the territory where an enemy could enter. The job of the Watchmen was to watch the coast and see if there are people coming—in canoes or whatever—and determine whether they were friend or foe. If they were friends, Watch House family members would go down and tell the village and the village would start cooking up a feast. If they were foes, the people would arm themselves and get ready to fend off the invaders.

As Watchman I was asked to follow the seven teachings, which include to keep peace, talk with truth, and walk with humility. I went to the protests at the Trans Mountain Pipeline site to have Pipe Ceremonies with people. I started teaching there about the Indigenous ways to the people from the four directions.

At the big rally Chief Judy Wilson was speaking and suggested that we should step up and get arrested. We did that in August 2018—the three of us—Stacy Gallagher and Tawahum Bige and myself. While we were waiting to go to court, we got arrested again. I was convicted and sentenced. That sentence was appealed, but I did a bit of time in jail waiting for the appeal to be accepted. I will tell more about that later.

The role of a Watch House, and the duty of the Watch People, is to keep an eye on the land and report to the people. That's what I was doing when we saw that TMX workers were shipping out from the tank farm what we believed, because of a strong petroleum smell, to be contaminated soil. They did a really good job of hiding what they were doing. So we called a meeting for the media and the people protesting the pipeline, to come to a gathering where we would discuss the shipping of contaminated soil off of the property there and into Coquitlam. That's within the statutory duties of the Elder of the Watch House.

That was why on December 2, 2019, I showed the media all the pictures we had, and it was lucky we did because that stopped the dump trucks. Not one showed up on December 2 or 3, even though they'd been coming in solid for several days before. Anyway, we showed them the pictures of the trucks and aerial shots of Trans Mountain's work on Burnaby Mountain.

At the end of the day I participated in a Pipe Ceremony. We moved over to one end of the crosswalk where people were blocking the road and held the ceremony. The police officers came and joined us in the Pipe Ceremony. Nothing was said about shutting down the ceremony. I had pre-emptively warned the police, told them that we would have this finished in a few minutes and then clear away, because it was at the end of the day for us.

At that time, the police were friendly to our ceremonies. They've always been invited because we are inclusive. We invited the police and also the Trans Mountain security guards—all ex-Mounties, it seemed. The security guards never came, but the cops quite regularly came into our ceremony. I remember one ceremony at the Burnaby TMX site where we thought we were in big trouble when somewhere between twelve and twenty uniformed RCMP officers came up to us. The commanding officer advised me that we could go ahead with our ceremony, and said these were new officers who were just learning how Indigenous ceremony works.

Anyhow, we had our ceremony on December 2, then on December 28, my lawyer called me: "What have you been doing? They've issued a warrant for your arrest!" The distance between the 2nd and the 28th still baffles me. They have the right to make arrests, but this was the first case where they didn't issue an arrest immediately upon violating the injunction. The other strange thing is that there were ten people there, but they only arrested the two Indigenous people. That seemed bizarre, but it's known as selective arrest and prosecution: when they only take in the people who are visible minorities.

There were people named on the injunction who were there on December 2—I was never named on the injunction—and the police officers and security guards referred to them in their statements justifying the arrest, but didn't arrest any of them. They were not Indigenous people. That just makes you shake your head, you know? At the end of the day, the RCMP just turned around and arrested us out of the middle of nowhere, because they decided it was time to arrest a couple of Indians, I guess.

Stacy Gallagher and I were charged with criminal contempt of court and violating the injunction. We're appealing that right now, saying that on December 2 I was carrying on my duties as a Watchman and that the Pipe Ceremony was part of that, and there was no intention whatever to block traffic. My intention on the day was just to hold the ceremony and keep the peace. If you read the arrest transcripts, they said Stacy and I were the only ones they recognized. We think we have a really good chance at winning the appeal based on the fact that I was not blocking traffic and I was not involved in the larger blockade that went on there that day.[1] I was carrying out my statutory duties as a Watchman and as Elder at the Watch House.

Now I want to talk about my time in jail, which seriously affected my health. When I went to jail I went in with the attitude that it's only a prison sentence if I accept it as such, so I put myself in a vision quest. I kept myself on vegetarian food and could make my own soups out of stuff that I got from the commissary or from jailhouse meals. So I was cooking up my own meals in the microwave oven, and was doing quite well with it.

What stands out for me is the stupidity and incompetence of the jail system. I have pancreas meds and I have heart meds, and it was three days before I finally got any of them. I have a heart condition. When my cardiologist put me on new meds, he said, "If you miss these meds even for one day it reduces your heart and lung capacity. If you miss blood thinners even for one day, you could die from blood-clotting." Without the pancreas meds, my intestines were not working properly because I don't have what's needed to digest food well.

One day a nurse comes up and says, "Leyden." I come to the door and she says, "I've got insulin for you."

I say, "I don't take insulin."

She says, "Yes you do." I say I don't.

"Yes you do."

I say, "I'm not diabetic."

"Yes you are."

I say, "Can you recheck?"

So she yells downstairs, "Is this insulin supposed to be for Leyden?" They say yes, then they say "No, no, hang on, it isn't." They were trying to give me insulin, which could have killed me on the spot. And I wonder what would have happened to the person the insulin was intended for.

That's the incompetence of that system. It's a mutual admiration society where they tell themselves the courts are doing well, and they tell themselves the people in jails are well protected. And it's just not the case. My point is really simple. It was not by the grace of the corrections system or court that I survived. It was by the grace of God (I'm a spiritual person) that I got through prison without croaking. And then at the end of it all, they were supposed to give me one more refill and they didn't have that ready either. The medical system in the jail is absolutely inadequate and incompetent.

Two other prisoners from our land protectors who had gone to jail also had trouble getting their meds. One woman had a heart condition, and they gave her the wrong meds. She told them, "These are not the meds I'm supposed to take." They basically said, "You take them or nothing." That's the medical system there, I believe it's called "wilful blindness" in the courts. They look away so they don't have to see the ramifications of what they are doing.

They talk about COVID protocols, but they have great big holes in them so they may as well not have any at all. We share the phones and they are not sterilized between use. There are no masks available to prisoners.

Near the end of my time in jail, I ended up getting a spider bite and got really sick. I got released on bail the day after the bite.

I went to a clinic and they wouldn't deal with me because it was too close to closing time. I was going to walk home, but the bus was right there so I jumped on. Long story short, I ended up later that day at St. Paul's Hospital. I was not conscious and was vomiting. I had peed myself and everything. The staff at St. Paul's found out I had a major bacterial infection, and I stayed there for almost two weeks. I was on feeding tubes and a ventilator. They couldn't put in a vein access device because the infection was so bad the IV would have become infected by the bacteria.

I came close to dying from that. What I saw in jail and what happened to me there had really affected me a lot. But when I was in front of the court for my next case, Judge Shelley Fitzpatrick's logic was, "Oh well, you're still alive so jail didn't affect you that much." I had letters from my doctor saying they couldn't send me back to jail because I was so sick, but Judge Fitzpatrick sentenced me to go back anyhow for the second charge.

Let me talk about Judge Fitzpatrick. The first judge was Kenneth Affleck. When he retired, Shelley Fitzpatrick became the judge. We had one case with Judge Affleck, with Kat Roivas. Kat said she was smudging people, and he ruled that was why she was there at the ceremony, that she wasn't there to block traffic. He threw her case out, with good reason. We referred to that decision in our later cases, but it went nowhere with Judge Fitzpatrick.

I had originally gotten them to exclude the Watch House from the injunction because of my duty there. When Judge Fitzpatrick sentenced me, her comment was to the effect of, "So much for surveillance. You are now no longer allowed to be at the Watch House, and the five-hundred-metre exclusion applies to that as well." We ended up going to court and getting that overturned, so I do have the exemption as an Elder of the Watch House. That means the appeals court has recognized my statutory role as an Elder at the Watch House.

We have an understanding that when we do surveillance we don't touch the fence, which is alarmed, and we don't harass the workers. We're only doing static surveillance; we're not engaging with anybody. We're there to take photographs and to see what's going on.

We've caught TMX doing a lot of things that were wrong, so we know we had a very important role at the Watch House. I would argue that it was an important role within the injunction as well. We were the only ones upholding the integrity of the injunction. For example, when we saw they weren't using proper equipment, we'd report it. When we saw that they were contaminating the salmon streams, we would report it. We even reported it to the proper bodies when workers were put in dangerous situations by the contractors. I would argue that we were protecting the integrity of the court at that point. We were making sure these TMX guys weren't running totally roughshod over laws and rules. So for us to no longer be allowed to do that is to take an important component out of the guardianship of the area and the protection of the area against abuse.

I sit in on almost all the TMX arrest cases as an Elder, with all my ceremonial gear, feathers, and my pipe. In one instance Judge Fitzpatrick sentenced Will George, one of our traditional family, to jail. People were muttering "shame" as she was leaving. As Fitzpatrick got out the door I expressed my feelings about her attitude toward Indigenous people. About three appearances later, after the people in the courtroom had been boisterous the afternoon before, she walked in and told me to leave, with a message along the lines of, "There'll be no more of that here. Mr. Leyden, you can leave. I did not appreciate your comments the other day." I smiled and I left. In a racist system, I guess you're not allowed to sit in a courtroom and speak the truth.

She sent health-compromised people like me to jail, saying, even if my health had suffered, I survived, so nobody else should have to worry about their health in jail. She refused to read the letters from my doctors and the hospitals. She just absolutely refused to look at them. That's more wilful ignorance. We thought Affleck was bad, but never felt like we were experiencing racism.

My story shows how we ran right into the legal face of racism and colonialism by engaging in resistance to this pipeline.

Statement to BC Supreme Court Justice Shelley Fitzpatrick, June 2021

I would be remiss to not express my concerns over the apparent arrogance and prejudice of this court when dealing with Aboriginal litigants.

The failure to show any respect for, or even a modicum of consideration to the Gladue report guidelines[2] on sentencing of Indigenous persons, the recommendations of the Truth and Reconciliation Commission, the United Nations Declaration on the Rights of Indigenous Peoples, the Assembly of First Nations report on "Dismantling the Doctrine of Discovery," and even the non-indigenous-specific recommendations of the Prosecution Service bears witness to the vicious prejudice of this local court.

While any one of these reports on its own could be ignored or considered less significant than the desires of the local prosecutors' office or the judge's bench, the prevailing recommendation against incarceration should have led to the seeking of options other than incarceration in sentencing. These reports represent the considered conclusions of Canadian and international experts, and have been endorsed by a massive body of Canadian legislators and independent judiciary bodies. The lack of respect for these legal directives is not surprising, considering the atmosphere of racist queries and innuendo which has been allowed to permeate this courtroom.

But I must be careful not to confuse things that are understandable with things that should be unacceptable. As a traditional warrior, I must speak out against racism and supremacy however it expresses itself, be it in a white supremacist rally or in a courtroom—thinly camouflaged and legitimized by the black veils of civil authority. Not because I do not respect the court, but because I must stand up to defend it and protect its integrity. Because it is indeed the only thing which stands between those who would pillage, rape, and anarchize our society. Yet, Edmund Burke once noted that bad laws are the worst form of anarchy. And even Andrew Jackson, the white supremacist and ethnic cleanser of Indigenous lands, pointed out the only thing between justice and tyranny is the people who would stand up against it. And when the court fails to meet the standards reflected by our Lady Justice in the people's hall outside the courtrooms, then it sadly befalls the public to stand up against institutionally endorsed tyranny.

APRIL THOMAS,
Secwépemc
Matriarch

Biography

April Thomas is a Secwépemc Matriarch from Tsq'escenemc, "The People of Broken Rock" (aka Canim Lake Band) in Secwépemc'ulecw. The Tsq'escenemc are members of the Secwépemc (Shuswap) Nation, with a population of about 11,000.

April's formal education includes a BA with a double concentration in Political Science and English from Thompson Rivers University (TRU) in Kamloops, BC, as well as a degree in General Studies and a certificate in Aboriginal Studies and Management for Supervisors. She also obtained a certificate in First Nations Public Administration from the University of Northern British Columbia. April and her husband, Jamie Thomas, own a forestry company, Secwepemc Silvaculture.

April has been a land protector and human rights advocate and activist since 2010. Before that, she learned the ins and outs of the colonial system and its impacts on her people through her experiences in education and employment with many Secwépemc organizations and bands. She has extensive knowledge in the Secwépemc language and the culture and history of her people, including Secwépemc laws, the United Nations Declaration on the Rights of Indigenous Peoples (UNDRIP), the BC Declaration Act committing to recognize its framework, and promises made with regards to Truth and Reconciliation.

April has been involved in many campaigns, including the fight against a modern-day treaty that would extinguish allodial Secwépemc'ulecw rights and title,[3] downgrading the Secwépemc to the fourth level of government on their own unceded territory; the outcry after the Mount Polley Mine spill disaster in 2014; and the delegation to the United Nations Committee on the Elimination of Racial Discrimination in Kelowna and Geneva, Switzerland, where she spoke against the Trans Mountain Pipeline (TMX). She works on the political and legal landscape to stop corrupt bands, corporations, and government from making decisions that affect collective rights and title on Secwépemc'ulecw and that cause harm to the people and territory.

———————————

April was arrested on October 15, 2020, and sentenced in May 2023 to thirty-two days in jail. As of spring 2024, the sentence is being appealed.

Narrative: My Ordeal in Canada's Justice System

In the days leading up to my arrest, I was busy trying to upgrade my degrees to bring my political science up to being a major at TRU. However, due to the lack of housing, COVID, and the un-foreseen stress of representing eight defendants in the TMX case, I was not able to complete the needed courses. However, I have not given up on this, as well as my goal to attend law school in upcoming years.

It has been and will always be the way of the Secwépemc'ulecw (Shuswap Nation territory and people), as with many other Indigenous Peoples, to protect and care for our land and people. We believe in leaving the land as we found it when we are out hunting, fishing, and gathering, as we are one with all beings who depend on Mother Earth. And we always give thanks by making an offering to Mother Earth for what we are taking as well.

I am from Tsq'escenemc, one of the six out of seventeen Secwépemc bands whose band councils signed an agreement with TMX without proper consultation with or the consent of our members, whose interests they are required to uphold. When these elected Chiefs sign agreements and give consent to projects such as TMX, they do so illegally, as they have never obtained what they call "free, prior, and informed consent" from the very people they claim to represent. They not only break their own colonial laws, but they also break our sacred Secwépemc laws as well.

We, the Secwépemc, have never ceded, surrendered, sold, or signed away our lands and waters. We have not lost them in war;

we have always lived on these territories we call Secwépemc'ulecw, and we will always be here.

Sqeq'petsin Camp

The Sqeq'petsin camp (colonially known as Mission Flats) was formed by Secwépemc in response to the ongoing plans to drill under the Thompson River (Secwépemcetkwe). Where they planned construction is where our fish have to travel to get to their spawning grounds. The Secwépemc Elders Council had passed a resolution before the camp was set up to direct our Secwépemc warriors to protect the water and stop the TMX pipeline. Hereditary Chief Saw-Sês (colonially known as Henry Sauls) and Matriarch Miranda Dick took this directive very seriously and put all of our Elders' love and wishes into the work and ceremony to ensure the Sqeq'petsin camp came to be. The site of the camp is very sacred to our people, as it was once one of thirty-three sacred village sites which pre-existed settler contact. It was a place of gathering for our Secwépemc, and the water that flows through it is the lifeline, just like bloodlines, of our Nation and all that depend on it.

The Sqeq'petsin camp was in ceremony and prayer daily by the fire that was lit on the ancient sacred village site. There was so much industrial work being carried out in this area that the smell caused the people at the camp to get sick, but they stayed and maintained their unwavering commitment to protect the water and land no matter what they suffered. Up to this point, hundreds of people from across Secwépemc'ulecw and neighbouring Nations came to offer many prayers and ceremonies on both sides of the river.

Our Secwépemc believe that caring for the land is a sacred responsibility given to us by Tqelt Kukpi7 (the Creator) and Chief Coyote and that we must fulfill this responsibility by any and all means necessary, as we have always done. Our responsibility to uphold Secwépemc laws are for our Ancestors, all living beings today, and for the next seven generations to come.

Former environmental engineer Romilly Cavanaugh visited the camp and confirmed that directional drilling could cause silt and chemicals to be spilled into the Thompson River. According to Cavanaugh, pipeline companies obtain government permits for this work, but are rarely inspected, so they are essentially self-regulated. This brings great risks to our water and our wild salmon. Given this information we felt a sense of urgency to do something.

I personally have seen the devastation to the land and water should such a disaster occur, as I was there firsthand to witness the Mount Polley Mine disaster, so I very much understood this urgency. After all the mass destruction that occurred as a result of one the world's biggest tailings pond spills, there was no real effort done to clean it up; all they did was cover it up with sawdust and plant some trees.

The camp delivered a cease and desist order to TMX at the landing pad and the core drilling site. They were asked to cease construction immediately as they were trespassing on unceded, unsurrendered Secwépemc'ulecw and contravening Secwépemc law to care and to protect the land, language, culture, people, and water, and the work would risk disturbing our Ancestors at our sacred village site, Sqeq'petsin. However, the order was ignored and construction continued.

The night before the arrests took place, Matriarch Miranda Dick, of Neskonlith te Secwépemc, tasked me to attend a ceremony to spread the ashes of the sacred campfire which held the prayers of all the people who came to the fire. This was to take place the next day. I agreed to be there to support her and to be the legal observer for the ceremony in case it got interrupted by the TMX security, the RCMP, or the RCMP's CIRG (Community-Industry Response Group) unit.

Arrests

Eight water defenders were arrested on October 15 and 17, 2020, while conducting ceremonies. On the first day of arrests, we delivered a cease and desist letter to TMX corporation for the second time. Again, the Secwépemc order was ignored. Chief Saw-Sês, his daughter Gwa (Lorelei) Dick,[4] Billie Pierre, Romilly Cavanaugh, and I were all arrested at the TMX drill pad sites. On October 17 the arrests happened while a Hair-Cutting Ceremony was underway. Miranda Dick cut her hair in ceremony to show she was grieving for Sqeq'petsin. Miranda was arrested along with three nonindigenous allies, Heather Lamoureux, Susan Bibbings, and Laura Zadorozny.

All of us were originally charged with mischief, which was later changed in 2021 to civil contempt of a court order and then changed again to criminal contempt.

Court Proceedings

For most of the case I was representing all eight arrestees in the many court appearances. On March 1, 2021, Miranda and I demanded a third-party adjudication over our case on the grounds that the Canadian government's purchase of TMX puts the courts in a direct conflict of interest, as the prosecution and judge also work for and are paid by the Canadian government. Since the Canadian government is also obligated to act in the best interests of the First Peoples, specifically over our unceded lands, how can it do that while acting in the interests of the TMX and taxpayers as well? Nonetheless, Judge Fitzpatrick ignored our request.

We later put in applications for a stay of proceedings and Charter violations; however, Judge Fitzpatrick denied these as well. We put forward numerous points as to why our charges should be dropped, including the issues of Canada's lack of jurisdiction over unceded land, an illegal injunction, RCMP misconduct, conflict of interest between judge, prosecutor, and TMX—with the "Corporation of Canada" paying for all three, and abuse of process and mistreatment regarding information disclosure and court proceedings. We made these arguments over two days, and Judge Fitzpatrick made her decision in ten minutes, making it very clear that she does not respect us or Secwépemc law.

The case dragged on with numerous adjournments. Twice it was delayed because I had COVID; another postponement came because I lost a brother and sister due to COVID complications, along with possibly over one hundred relatives and community members. Even Crown prosecutor Neil Wiberg had to adjourn because his best friend died. Other delays of proceedings were (ironically) due to natural/climate disasters including wildfires, floods, mudslides, and extreme winter conditions shutting down roads everywhere. On October 6, 2022, during the trial for all eight defendants, I collapsed in the Kamloops Supreme Court room and our trial got adjourned. I was diagnosed with severe noncardiac chest pain due to extreme stress. There were so many unforeseen delays in the court, and Judge Fitzpatrick had the nerve to later blame all these occurrences on us.

Our new trial date was December 5, 2022. I was planning to present the case on behalf of the other arrestees—discussing Secwépemc law, cases, and history, and intended to have Elders and Chiefs provide oral testimony. But my sister passed away a few days before the trial date. This time Judge Fitzpatrick decided to proceed to trial without me even being present, citing that she would not tolerate any more excuses from us. Our Charter rights to a fair trial were violated.

On February 21, 2023, at the sentencing trial for Miranda and the other October 17 arrestees, Judge Fitzpatrick denied the findings of children's remains at residential schools, including the more than 215 children found in a mass grave at Kamloops Indian Residential School in May 2021. Defence lawyer Benjamin Isitt, who had been hired for this court appearance, had mentioned the children as being buried and she felt the need to interrupt, calling the graves of the children "potential remains," as though their bodies don't exist until they are unearthed.[5] No respect, no compassion for our people at all! Indian Residential School survivors and others attending court were shocked and cried out against the callousness of the Judge Fitzpatrick. In response, courtroom sheriffs forced survivors to leave the courtroom.

The four women—Miranda Dick, Heather Lamoureux, Susan Bibbings, and Laura Zadorozny—were each sentenced to twenty-eight days in jail. Chief Saw-Sês (a survivor of the Kamloops residential school) received the same sentence two days later; Romilly received thirty-two days. Billie and I were sentenced later, in May 2023. Billie received forty days of house arrest (as she has a daughter in her care) and I was given thirty-two days in jail. Heather, Susan, and Laura served their prison sentences. Saw-Sês, Miranda, Billie, Romilly, and I have filed appeals, based on a number of injustices. However, recently, Saw-Sês and Miranda have decided to serve their time in jail.[6]

Throughout the almost three years of TMX hearings, we have been consumed by countless deaths, tragedies, and grief. However, each of us had our own unique strengths and wisdom to contribute to seeing this court case through, and I couldn't have done it without them all. Regardless, Judge Fitzpatrick continues to impose the highest sentencing she can, especially on those of us who are Indigenous. Fitzpatrick appeared to display on numerous occasions that she had already made a judgment on Secwépemc members even before evidence and arguments were presented in court. Her remarks in court felt inflammatory, harassing, and paternalistic. Fitzpatrick repeatedly interrupted defence counsel while assisting the Crown's submissions, and characterized the women in court as criminals, saying, "The only people they should blame is who they see when they look in the mirror," while she herself refused to do the same.

Although we were found guilty by Judge Fitzpatrick, I still feel like we won! Now on to BC Court of Appeal.

For too long the question has been, what is the legitimacy of this Indigenous claim to sovereignty in the face of the Canadian state and not the more just and appropriate question—what is the legitimacy of the Canadian state in the face of this Indigenous claim? There has always been a reasonable apprehension of bias in the decision-making process of any Canadian or provincial judge when asked to consider land claim matters in court, and this TMX court case was no different.

We are witnessing genocide in action. Hereditary Chiefs and Matriarchs remain unwavering in their commitment to protecting their territories, saying they won't back down to "Canada" and its illegal jurisdiction. We plan to continue to fight for Secwépemc land and title rights and plan to take this case all the way to the UN.

I am thankful, and say Kukstsetsemc, to all who have come to the camp, who attended court, who have offered their prayers, ceremonies, and love to the land and the land defenders; to all those who supported the land defenders by way of funds, camp supplies, and needs; and most of all those who took the time to attend, organize, and stay at the camp.

Statement to the BC Supreme Court: Excerpts from an Affidavit Deposited on March 14, 2022

Background

Jamie Thomas and I have three children, three grandchildren, and many nieces and nephews. Jamie and I continue to take in many of our family needing a home, especially the youth. I am an upstanding citizen, I do not have a criminal record and do a lot to contribute to the safety, health, and overall well-being of my family, community, and our Nation, Secwépemc'ulecw. Our forestry company, Secwepemc Silvaculture, mainly contracts to our local bands, the city of Williams Lake, and local forest industry companies. Our company does firefighting, fire mitigation, silviculture, fire wood, and logging on a small scale. I do the office management and Jamie Thomas takes care of the operational duties and responsibilities. We have been operating for five years and manage up to twenty employees a year.

My tribe originated up from the Rocky Mountain Jasper area, one of the most eastern villages of the Secwépemc; we were called the Snare Tribe. We were forced to leave that area and were displaced to Tsq'escen, where I grew up. I come from Hereditary bloodlines, and as one of the remaining tribe members I now stand as the representative for our people, the Snare Tribe.

Secwépemc'ulecw (Shuswap People and Territory)
The Secwépemc traditional territory spans over 185,000 square kilometres with approximately 11,000 members; we are seventeen Indian Act bands and have three original sacred village sites.

For the colonial court record, I stand in solidarity with and under the authority of our Secwépemc in exercising and asserting allodial rights and title to our unceded, unsurrendered Secwépemc'ulecw. The land and rights of the Secwépemc te Qelmucw[7] have been stolen and have never been reconciled with the Original People of this country you call Canada. I have not, cannot, and will not swear any allegiance to the Crown in right of what is now called British Columbia, or Canada, or to the Imperial Crown of Great Britain.

The reality is that the Original People of Secwépemc'ulecw have been systematically forced to live under a colonial structure that is not of their own construct, which is built on systemic racism and the theft of our lands and resources while our people are forced to live and suffer in the worst conditions of poverty and despair. These oppressive policies of genocide have systematically targeted Indigenous lives.

Trans Mountain Pipeline
In 2012, the Trans Mountain (a.k.a. Kinder Morgan) Pipeline Expansion project was granted to the proponents without "free,

prior, and informed consent" of the Secwépemc. In fact, when the original pipeline was put in (back in 1951), it too was done so without proper consent from the Secwépemc. As well, due to the Indian Act, it was illegal to seek legal counsel and organize around land rights from 1926 to 1951. Again, history is repeating itself and Canada is ignoring international human and Indigenous obligations to seek consent from our people.

All proponents involved in the TMX project are in a conflict of interest. Canada is in a conflict of interest because it owns the Trans Mountain Pipeline. The Chiefs and Council members who signed agreements are in a conflict of interest because they are being paid to sign this agreement by both Trans Mountain and the government. Under colonial law both Canada and the band councils have fiduciary and human rights obligations they are supposed to uphold on behalf of our people as they are to act in our best interests. And yet, neither Canada nor the elected Indian Act Chiefs and Councils have the authority of the people to make such decisions on our behalf. The six bands who signed agreements did so without the consent of the entire Secwépemc Nation, which constitutes seventeen bands and approximately 11,000 members.

The TMX Pipeline is a threat to all of Secwépemc'ulecw as it passes through 518 kilometres of our traditional territory, crossing over rivers and creeks, drilling under the river, crossing over and under many roads, and it is built alongside many major roads, rivers, and waterways, and many residents' homes. Secwépemc'ulecw is not just our home to which we sustain our culture, practise our ceremonies, and exercise our rights; it is also home to our land animals, birds, water creatures, the air, the water, the plants. These are all living beings that are equal to us and a part of who we are as Secwépemc; it is our duty to speak for and protect those that can't do so for ourselves; this is our way. It is also home to many of our guests and relatives who are all welcome as long as they respect and uphold Secwépemc'ulecw laws and authority. This pipeline is a major threat to our very being, especially if there are more wildfires, floods, and mudslides.

Arrests, Detentions, and Proceedings
On June 1, 2018, Justice K.N. Affleck of this court granted an injunction to Trans Mountain ULC. The injunction was granted

without proper consultation and/or consent from the people of Secwépemc'ulecw. My co-accused and I were illegally arrested and unreasonably forced into a colonial court system under duress. During my arrest, detention, and prosecution I personally have been met with the following violations of my rights:

1. Unlawful detainment and physical assault by the RCMP on Oct. 15 who physically restrained me from leaving the area by placing me back of police vehicle for over an hour then transported me to the police station where I was detained for another eight hours and was unreasonably forced to sign documents upon release from custody which consisted of a Promise to Appear in Court.
2. Did not have my rights read to me upon my arrest.
3. Did not receive or have any injunction read to me.
4. While in Ceremony, my right to peaceful protest was interrupted and denied.
5. I was forced to attend court several times under duress.
6. The prosecutor failed on numerous occasions to provide me with transcripts requested, although he was ordered by Judge Fitzpatrick to do so.
7. The prosecutor failed to provide us full disclosure of our police reports; it took him almost a full year to provide it to us, thus further delaying the process. We are still waiting on many of these requests as well as additional requests.
8. Unlawfully charging me for trespassing on my own traditional territory, unceded Secwépemc'ulecw, to which I am a title holder and am obligated to uphold my roles and responsibilities as a Secwépemc Matriarch. This includes protecting the people and territory. They did so with an illegal injunction that violates Secwépemc'ulecw rights and title.

Throughout this entire experience, I never felt that we were being treated fairly or equally under the law. The RCMP kept changing what we were being charged with from mischief when being arrested, to civil contempt of court order when being released from the RCMP detachment, to criminal contempt of court halfway into our court proceedings, making it very unclear to us as to whether it was criminal or civil proceedings. We did ask for clarification on many occasions but were left with even more confusion. I also feel this court violated its own colonially imposed laws by not upholding our Charter of Rights and Freedoms throughout our court proceedings.

Serving Notice

I am serving notice to this Supreme Court of BC that under the written terms of King George III's October 07, 1763 Royal Proclamation and in the absence of any internationally binding Treaty of Cession, Purchase or Surrender of Secwépemc'ulecw, specifically with our Secwépemc Nation's Matriarchs & Hereditary Chiefs, the Province of British Columbia, through its judicial system, is knowingly and illegally imposing its deceptively obtained jurisdiction on Secwépemc te Qelmucw, friends, guests and allies. This arguably constitutes Misprision of Treason in an International Court of Law.

Furthermore, under Section 35.1 of the Canadian Constitution 1982, I am filing a constitutional challenge to the effect that British Columbia courts do not have jurisdiction to impose their judge-made laws on our Secwépemc Sovereignty in what you now call the Province of British Columbia.

BILLIE PIERRE,
Nlaka'pamux
Land Defender

Biography

Billie Pierre is a mother, student, and editor at the Media Co-op. Growing up, she witnessed the Coquihalla Highway being built through her territory as a showcase item for Expo 86, an international transportation and communication fair. But the real purpose of the highway was to facilitate the export of "resources" stolen from Indigenous territories through the Vancouver ports. She's witnessed the mass clear-cutting of her territory, as winters get increasingly warmer.

In the mid-1990s while still in her teens, Billie moved to Vancouver and became active with organizations by and for Indigenous youth. First, with the Vancouver Native Youth Movement, she campaigned to oppose illegal BC treaties, protect Aboriginal Title, and keep territories unceded. She helped create and run *Redwire Magazine*, an uncensored Native youth magazine, which was a much-needed avenue for the Native Youth Movement to promote their struggles and political concerns. She helped organize an international Indigenous youth conference in Vancouver, realizing the common links of tribal people globally, who value their land and way of life, and who struggle with displacement, racism, and political repression. In the 2000s she supported campaigns to protect St'at'imc and Secwépemc territories from mega-tourism projects.

During this time she learned more about who she was as a Nlaka'pamux native and moved back home to Merritt to be on her own territory. There, she has witnessed too many Nlaka'pamux people dying before their time. In the past ten years, her people have experienced the impacts of ruptured mining dams and unimaginable natural disasters linked with climate change. Billie has stepped up to protect water, forests, wildlife, and the traditional way of living that is key to the survival of the next generations.

———————

Billie was arrested on October 15, 2020, and sentenced to forty days' house arrest on May 19, 2023. As of spring 2024, the sentence is being appealed.

Narrative: Defending My Ancestral Territory and Values

In July 2020, I joined a small group of Nlaka'pamux people to hold an Elders' Sacred Fire on the north side of Britton Creek along the Coquihalla Highway. Secwépemc Elders Saw-Sês and Miranda and some other of their family members held ceremony with us. Shortly after, the Secwépemc Elders lit a Sacred Fire at Sqeq'petsin (sacred site on the Thompson River), on their territory, and I began to visit and show my support.

September 30, 2020, marked the first day that TMX had scheduled to log at Falls Lake, one of the most lush areas of my own territory that I've seen affected by the TMX project. I drove up the Coquihalla Highway to the Falls Lake turnoff and parked my vehicle in front of the heavy machinery. I arrived at the site before any workers were present. Although about a dozen showed up throughout the day, they kept a distance from me. My action blocked logging that day. I was eventually detained after the RCMP arrived later that same day and I was released away from the work site. Support again came from Saw-Sês, Miranda, and their family.

In the following weeks, I spent more time at Sqeq'petsin, taking part in the ceremony, praying for the salmon and water. The Thompson (Secwépemcetkwe) goes through Nlaka'pamux territory and is the river that most of my people from the Nicola Valley rely on for salmon. Anything that takes place upstream of this river impacts us. In the immediate years following the Mount Polley Mine tailings dam rupture in 2014, the number of fish we caught dwindled by over 90 percent. A second bitumen pipeline being tunnelled under the river is yet another direct threat to our salmon if it ruptures.

The intention behind my actions that led to my arrests has

been to go on my own territory and to hold ceremony with traditional allies. We've been forced into a colonial capitalist system and have been paying with our own blood, our forests, and animal relatives to survive in this foreign, imposed system. We're forced to live a lifestyle that's in conflict with our natural way. We need to make our own way back to our rightful path and take care of each other, our territories, our animal relatives, and our water. Walking the path our Ancestors walked is in conflict with this capitalist system; my own actions doing so have led to two arrests. And yet I sleep well at night knowing I'm doing something right, and I pray that I planted some seeds.

Excerpts from Statement to BC Supreme Court Justice Shelley Fitzpatrick, December 6, 2022

I am from the Nlaka'pamux territory, which is west of Secwépemc'ulecw, and our Nations are traditional political allies. I'm thankful to have been able to take part in ceremonies and pray for the protection of the water and salmon at Sqeq'petsin.

We've been hit hard in the past ten years, losing much of our salmon in the Thompson and Fraser Rivers, linked to the 2014 Mount Polley Mine tailings dam rupture on Secwepemc Territory. This impacted traditional sustenance fishing for all the Nations along the Fraser River. In June 2021, the temperature at Lytton, the heart of Nlaka'pamux territory, reached an all-Canadian record of 49°C during the epic heat dome that followed an uncharacteristically early forest fire season. The town ignited and burned to the ground in fifteen minutes. Five months later, the flood of Merritt and mudslides along the Coquihalla Highway and throughout the Fraser Canyon were brought about by an atmospheric river and the inability of the land to absorb the excess precipitation because so much of our forest has been logged.

We've been hit hard by the negative impacts of mining, logging, and climate change, and yet Trans Mountain is drilling a second bitumen pipeline under the so-called Thompson River upstream from Nlaka'pamux territory. This puts our fishing at further risk downstream on my territory. An expansion of the tar sands would bring about increased temperatures, and the Nlaka'pamux territory cannot afford to be put further at risk of hotter and drier summers.

The Nlaka'pamux Nation has not ceded our Aboriginal rights and title, and we have not lost it through war. When gold was discovered in the Fraser River in the 1850s, the Nlaka'pamux were negatively impacted by the sudden overwhelming influx of gold prospectors, and when several Nlaka'pamux women were raped, Nlaka'pamux warriors decapitated the rapists and threw their bodies in the Fraser River. This action led to the 1858 Fraser Canyon War. Our traditional allies, the Secwépemc, Syilx, and St'at'imc warriors, came to help fight in the war, though we eventually decided to make peace with the prospectors. Years later, in 1910, Nlaka'pamux, Syilx, and Sta'at'imc representatives gathered in Kamloops with Secwépmc people and presented a joint letter to the prime minister Sir Wilfrid Laurier, affirming that our territories rightfully belong to us.

Here in Secwépemc'ulecw, I stand under the authority of the true and rightful title holders, the Secwépemc, and am subject to their laws. Section 25 of the Canadian Constitution guarantees certain rights and freedoms shall not be abrogated that have been recognized by the Royal Proclamation of 1763 and any rights or freedoms that now exist by way of land claims agreements.

The Royal Proclamation of 1763 explicitly states that Aboriginal Title has existed and continues to exist and that all land would be considered Aboriginal land until ceded by treaty. The Royal Proclamation sets out that only the Crown can buy land from First Nations. It forbade settlers from claiming land from the Aboriginal occupants unless it had been first bought by the Crown and then sold to the settlers. Without treaty, purchase, or surrender with the Secwépemc Nation and under the terms of the Royal Proclamation of 1763, the Province of BC is illegally imposing its jurisdiction on the Indigenous people.

Further, in the Delgamuukw ruling of 1997, the Supreme Court of Canada observed that Aboriginal Title constituted an Ancestral right protected by Section 35 of the Canadian Constitution and that the provincial government has no right to extinguish the Indigenous Peoples' rights to their ancestral territories. This ruling outlined a test to prove Aboriginal Title, where Indigenous people seeking to prove their title to ancestral territories must provide evidence with the following requirements: the Indigenous Nation must have exclusively occupied the territory before the declaration of sovereignty by the British Crown in 1846,[8] and prove a continuity between present occupation and occupation before the declaration of sovereignty.

The Shuswap by James Teit and *Notes on the Shuswap People of British Columbia* by George M. Dawson both share numerous accounts of Secwépemc occupation of their traditional territory from the early 1800s. Additionally, a map from 1845 with Secwépemc names of locations on their traditional territory has been provided. A current map of Secwépemc territory outlining that no treaties have been signed proves current Aboriginal Title and also continued occupation of their own territory to the present time. The video submitted clearly shows Prime Minister Justin Trudeau's very public acknowledgement that Canada has no deed to Secwépemc territory. Thus colonial and Secwépemc laws affirm the same history and reality—we stand here today on unceded territory, and Secwépemc rights and title to this territory have never been extinguished.

Adding further insult, recently TMX has been charged with disturbing a historical site, which was close to where we did our ceremonies. BC Prosecution Service spokesperson Daniel McLaughlin told *Kamloops This Week* via email, "The allegation is that they did damage, excavate, dig in or alter a site that contains artifacts, features, materials or other physical evidence of human habitation or use before 1846."

The Crown seeks to convict us for violating a TMX injunction which clearly states that anyone having notice of the injunction is "restrained and enjoined from physically obstructing, impeding or otherwise preventing access by Trans Mountain, its contractors, employees or agents, to work in any of the sites as set out below." However, I was arrested in an area that had no TMX injunction sign, work site sign, or gate while I was in the middle of my ceremony. I chose an uninhabited location well away from the people to have my private prayer ceremony undisturbed. The five-step process that police are supposed to follow was not done, so my arrest was an illegal one. I did not have notice of the injunction prior to my arrest. Video evidence submitted to this trial clearly shows the injunction being read to me when I was already handcuffed and on the ground. Then I was not given the opportunity to freely leave the area. Instead, Constable Portman said he "started" the five steps, but he did not indicate that he finished them.

The CIRG and RCMP officers called to testify are not credible witnesses; they either do not recall events accurately or are not being forthright. CIRG officer Samarasinghe claimed there were forty people protesting, but the submitted video in Exhibit 8 shows approximately six land and water defenders present, most standing well back from the machinery. Samarasinghe stated that there were lots of signs on the hillside where I was arrested which indicated that the area was a construction site and that he entered past injunction notices. The footage (again, Exhibit 8 from the start to minute 1) proves there were no signs, injunction notices, or fences present. The statement of Samarasinghe was contradicted by a TMX security guard, Crown witness Karen Deloroy, who stated that TMX didn't have signs or injunction notices near where I was arrested and that you couldn't see the drill site signs from where I was arrested because they were too far away and obstructed by trees.

Constable Samarasinghe stated he did not go through the five-step process of the injunction. Samarasinghe stated that excess force was not used during my arrest, but the video submitted in Exhibit 8 shows an officer using a deliberate pain compliance technique on my left ankle by violently hyperextending the joint repeatedly while I was handcuffed and in the custody of several officers. I am heard repeatedly calling out in pain that an officer is bending my foot and causing me pain. This technique was also used on my wrist, resulting in injury, as confirmed by the medical report I submitted (Exhibit 6).

Constable Chung also said there were work site and injunction signs visible. The submitted evidence shows that there weren't any. He stated on the stand that he is aware that an "individual must be given the opportunity to leave after the injunction is read." Yet he did not give me a chance to leave (as shown in the video footage submitted by the Crown).

CIRG officer Portman stated on the witness stand that he originally arrested me for mischief and then changed the charge to violating the injunction, but in the police video we hear, "You are under arrest for breaching the injunction." The video at no time shows an officer stating I'm being arrested for *mischief*. So his testimony on the stand is inconsistent with the video evidence (Exhibit 2). The five-step arrest process for the injunction was also not followed by Portman. In the video, you can hear a woman's voice saying, "You are required to read the injunction." The video shows after reading the injunction, I was not given time to leave and that I was already on the ground in handcuffs. Exhibit 8 documents that Portman groped my breast. Portman stated he wanted to take me down the hill with as much dignity as possible. But he also admitted that he did at one point see that my pants were sliding off as I was carried down. Yet he did not offer the courtesy to let me attend to that. He also testified that I was yelling that I was being raped. Nowhere in any of the videos submitted did we hear me say those words. Again, this shows inconsistencies between his testimony and the videos and stills submitted as evidence. He claims that he doesn't recall people yelling that I was in a ceremony.

In conclusion, the prosecution has failed to show beyond a reasonable doubt that I participated in a public breach of the injunction. As such, I should be acquitted of this charge.

Part 2

Resistance from a place of spirit

Prayer Circle activist Christine Thuring meditating at the TMX staging grounds near the Brunette River with a red dress hanging on the earth-moving equipment. Photo: Donna Clark

TAMA WARD,
Storyteller
and Educator

Tama at the Climate March,
October 2019

Biography
Tama Ward is a theologian, storyteller, educator and Minister of Children, Youth and Families at Canadian Memorial United Church in Vancouver. She writes widely on topics of life and faith and has published in the *Sun Magazine*, the *Globe and Mail*, and the *Messenger of St. Anthony*, and has been long-listed twice for CBC's Creative Nonfiction Prize. Links to her work can be found on her website (tamaleighward.com).

Tama lives along the condo-stacked banks of the Fraser River on the unceded ancestral land of the Halkomelem-speaking peoples and the Qayqayt First Nation in current-day New Westminster. She is grateful to share life with her steadfast husband of twenty-six years, Loren, their two adult children, Abigail and Oliver, cockapoo, Mocha, and golden-eyed cat, Badger.

Tama was arrested on March 24, 2018, outside the gates of the Kinder Morgan tank farm. She was sentenced to twenty-five hours of community service on June 26, 2018, by Justice Affleck.

Statement to BC Supreme Court Justice Kenneth Affleck, June 26, 2018
Your Honour, I want to tell you about the day in March that I stood at the gates outside of Kinder Morgan attempting, as the evidence has accurately established, to block access to the construction of a pipeline that I oppose.

The police records and the Crown's argument tell one side of the story. I'm grateful for your willingness to hear the other.

To be honest, I had rather heroic ideas about my actions. I have a fifteen-year-old son, Oliver, and a seventeen-year-old daughter, Abigail, and they had become discouraged about their future. It seemed that every day on the news there was another development (you know the headlines): the collapse of the bee population worldwide, the demise of the Great Barrier Reef, the breaking up of the polar ice caps, extreme weather destroying homes and neighbourhoods, the anticipated extinction of orangutans within the next ten years. And so on. There are many things a parent can endure, as I'm sure you can appreciate, Your Honour, but watching your kids lose hope is not one of them.

So, simply put, rather than sit passively by, I decided I would do something to empower them to reclaim their future. I had read recently that the civil disobedience toolkit has been lost to a whole generation in the west where hard-won liberties are now so taken for granted we naively presume right will prevail. So I set out the morning of March 24 to demonstrate nonviolent protest in action (though, truth be told, I hardly knew what I was doing myself.)

Yet isn't it the way with life: just when you think you are way out in the lead, you discover that there are others with a knowledge and experience base who have been there long (sometimes centuries!) before you ever appeared on the scene.

We were a big group that day (fifty or sixty, I believe). It was biting cold and then it started to snow: huge flakes, the size of saucers (you've probably seen the footage). The snow caked on our heads and soaked through our clothes to the bone. No one had come dressed for snow.

And that's when a man by the name of Stacy, a self-identified Anishinaabe ally of the Tsleil-Waututh, began walking back and forth in front of us in his toque and grey sweats and work boots, like an unlikely commander of a legion. And he started to play his drum for us and sing us the resistance songs of his people. And when our teeth began to chatter, he told us jokes and laughed with us. And when we could no longer feel our fingers and toes, he walked among us passing out warm soup and bread.

And the day dragged on and as our spirits began to flag, an Indigenous woman, whom I believe you have met, stood up on a ledge just to the right front of where I was. She needed a cane to balance her frail frame. Yet with her free hand she held up an eagle feather high into the air above us. I can't tell you what she meant by this gesture, but I can tell you how I experienced it: as an act of protection, as though to care for us and give us the strength we would need for the stand we were taking.

And when the police arrived, they positioned themselves in a line in front of us to begin their arrests. It was at this point that an Indigenous man wearing a felt bowler hat stepped out from the crowd of supporters. I learned later that he is an artist and activist who goes by the name Ostwelve. And he planted himself eye-to-eye in front of each of the officers in turn and urged them to reconsider their options: "History doesn't have to unfold like this," I overheard him implore. "None of us, not me, not you, has to follow the script life has handed us."

As the hours passed I was worried about my daughter who had come to support me and as far as I knew was standing by herself lost in the crowd in the snow and the cold. I asked for news on her and word came back to me that she had been invited by the Tsleil-Waututh youth leader, Cedar George-Parker, to join a group of Indigenous youth for a special youth-focused ceremony in the shelter and warmth of the Watch House. And I thought "Who *are* these people?" From what I know of the historic record, all we've ever done is swindled, robbed, bribed, and used whatever means available to us to take their land out from under them.

In the days following my arrest, it became my quest to find an answer to this question. I went to the Tsleil-Waututh camp by the Watch House on the soccer field to find out. If you haven't already done so, I hope you get the chance to visit the Watch House, Your Honour. I think you'll be surprised as I was surprised to discover that this protest-based surveillance camp, before it is anything else, is a place for spiritual grounding.

The first thing you'll be invited to do on entering the camp is to offer prayer at the Sacred Fire. It's an act that starts you down the road of reaffirming your connection to the Creator and to all living things. And the more time you spend at the camp, the more you will remember what it means to put human relationships before personal acquisition and the health of the earth before material comforts.

I won't take any more of your time, Judge Affleck. My account has come full circle. I crossed the injunction line not to bring discredit to the court but to bring hope to Abigail and Oliver.

I believe we found the hope we were looking for, though not as we expected. It comes from the knowledge that at the forefront of the struggle there are Indigenous leaders, not only here in our city, but across our country and around the world, who understand that caring for the earth is a sacred duty and comes at a great cost.

Regardless of the penalty you have assigned me today, my actions will have cost me little more than a sliver of my white privilege. In contrast, the cost to the leaders I met on the mountain that day is incalculable. They have laid everything on the line for the sake of the struggle. They are the true heroes. It has been an honour to stand with them.

Narrative: My Subversive Community Service Hours

In the days following my sentencing, I contacted a nonprofit organization called RAVEN (Respecting Aboriginal Values and Environmental Needs), whose mandate it is to raise funds in support of Indigenous legal challenges. They agreed to supervise my twenty-five hours of community service and suggested I meet the terms of my probation by organizing a fundraising event in support of their Pull Together campaign with 100 percent of proceeds going toward covering the costs of challenging the expansion of the Trans Mountain Pipeline in court. The irony was lost on no one!

I called the event the Service Hours Cabaret, and the September night turned into a soulful celebration of community, solidarity, and resistance. The people of Canadian Memorial United Church offered the use of the great hall for the coffee-house-style gathering. Earnest Ice Cream, where my daughter was working, donated three tubs of ice cream. Local writers and artists gifted books, jewellery, pottery, and paintings as door prizes. Tsimshian/Nuu-chah-nulth SFU professor Clifford Atleo brought words of gratitude and perspective as a RAVEN board member. Vancouver musicians offered up their time and talent, including a breath-taking clarinet solo by fellow arrestee and event coordinator Johanna Hauser, the toe-tapping music of Fraser Union, a sing-along with Earle Peach and the Solidarity Notes choir, and songs of allyship and resistance with Stephen Tanner and friends from Music on Main.

But the most soulful part of the night was when Stacy Gallagher stood with his drum and taught those gathered the Anishinaabe water song.[1] We all sang while Stacy drummed. I recognized it as the song he had taught us on the morning of our arrest. The same song he had sung to warm our spirits as we stood shivering in the falling snow, waiting for the police to arrive.

He had us turn in the four directions—toward Burrard Inlet, toward the snow-capped North Shore mountains, toward the Fraser River, toward the Salish Sea. With each turn we recognized and honoured the water of our lands as a sacred trust. Watching the movement and the energy in the room that night, I wasn't sure if we were encircling the song or the song was encircling us.

Four months later, the youth group from Canadian Memorial United was inspired to undertake a fundraiser of their own for RAVEN. Six teenagers raised over $2,000 toward the Heiltsuk legal challenge seeking to toughen oil spill regulations along the whole Pacific coast and set a precedent for Aboriginal Title to the foreshore and seabed.

Such are the ripple effects of taking action. Concentric rings of awakening, growing ever outward.

HISAO ICHIKAWA,
Activist, Musician

Photo: Tim Bray

Biography

Hisao Ichikawa was born in Japan in 1940, the youngest of eight children in a family of farmers. He was the target of bullying and abuse at school. At age twenty-nine he left Japan to find a better life, eventually settling in Canada in 1969. He tried his hand at many seasonal jobs: a chokerman at a logging camp, then a cook on a fish-packing boat, where he had to read *The Joy of Cooking* every day to cook western meals he had never eaten. As a fish buyer he travelled the BC West Coast from Vancouver Island to Prince Rupert. Between jobs he hitchhiked the world. While travelling in South America he met Luz, a Peruvian woman, and they resettled together in Canada. They were married in 1991 and their two daughters were born in 1992 and 1996.

As the chief caregiver for their children, Hisao had little time for activism until their youngest daughter turned eighteen. Then in 2014, he began to volunteer for environmental and political causes and travelled many times to the Unist'ot'en camp to help with building a healing lodge and preparations for winter. He also adopted a lifestyle of radical conservation. Activism became a full-time job for Hisao, one that now includes busking for donations regularly at the SkyTrain station at Cambie and Broadway where he speaks to passersby about the joy and freedom of simple living with respect for all life and the harm of overconsumption and waste.

Hisao was arrested in front of the tank farm in early July 2018, and sentenced to jail in September 2018 for seven days, serving five.

Statement to BC Supreme Court Justice Kenneth Affleck, September 2018

I am originally from Japan, but I left that country forty-nine years ago. I am grateful to live on this beautiful unceded First Nation territory, which was kept pristine until the settlers from Europe came and looked for money to make from any natural resources they found. The colonialism has caused much pollution. The water in many rivers is now polluted and fish are dying and the people drinking it are getting sick. The government is making one of the most serious mistakes in Canadian history, but all of us are also responsible. As long as we keep buying new things and wasting, we are asking industries to produce more. Whatever we use, clothes, furniture, gas, food all come from Mother Earth. The more we use and waste, the more we pollute our environment.

Right now my wife is dying, with cancer spread all over her body. As the air, water, and soil get polluted, more and more people and other living beings will get sick. We cannot buy health with money. We are standing at a very critical moment in our history. To slow down global warming and pollution, we must slow down, make less money, buy less, and waste much less than now. We don't need economic growth. We need to step on Earth much more gently for the generations to come and all other living beings.

Narrative: Fighting for Nature with a Loving Heart and Light Footsteps

I am an uninvited visitor to Turtle Island since 1969. I emigrated from Japan because I wanted to start a new life in Canada. I am grateful to be on the unceded First Nation territories and I feel responsible for the environmental crises we are facing. In 2014 I started collecting signatures to stop Enbridge's Northern Gateway and Kinder Morgan pipelines, and began visiting the Unist'ot'en camp near Houston, BC, to support the Indigenous effort to block Enbridge's Northern Gateway and Coastal GasLink construction through their territory.

Whatever I do to protect or restore Nature, I do it with love, not out of a sense of obligation. I may have only a few years left in this life, so how should I spend that time? I write and rewrite my own life story as a healer of Earth and people, and I play the role as faithfully as possible. I give holistic macrobiotic healing workshops, advice, and shiatsu massages to the people in need in the protest camps. As much as I can, I go to protest rallies and camps where I am surrounded by friendly people I can trust.

I also adopted a lifestyle of radical conservation, which includes dumpster diving to recover usable food. I also eat vegetables grown in my own large garden, and so I don't need to buy much. I regard soil and water to be sacred. I gave my car to my daughter and I use my bike or transit. Overconsumption and waste of nature's provisions are the cause of all the environmental problems. And I believe it is impossible to stop climate change, if we, consumers, keep fuelling industries to produce more oil and short-lived products. Everything we use comes from Mother Earth and the more we use, the more we pollute. We cannot stop the climate-destroying projects just by protesting. We need to face arrest with acts of civil disobedience, and then fill up the jails with protesters. Also we must educate everyone, especially children, not to waste things, to step more gently on the earth for our survival.

So in response to the callout by the Tsleil-Waututh Elders, one day at the end of June 2018, about six other protesters and I blocked the entry to the tank farm on Burnaby Mountain. The police came and arrested us in ten minutes. I did not resist. I am simply a conscientious objector to tar sands expansion projects but was treated like a criminal. I was charged with criminal contempt of court. I pleaded guilty because I did not want to waste the legal fund to fight the corrupt court system that was created by a colonial government for the protection of elite settlers. On the way to the prison, the police treated me like a drug smuggler. Was it really necessary to check for drugs in my private parts? When I was in jail I needed dental floss, so I asked the guard for some, but was refused. I managed to take a thread from the bed and cleaned my teeth.

I always strive to use any situation in a positive way. So on the day before I was released, I gave an origami workshop, which was a good entertainment for the bored inmates. The prison guard was kind enough to provide some used paper for the lesson on creating cranes. I was in jail for only five days. The time in jail did not give me any inspiration, but neither did it dampen my spirit for further activism, including direct action and civil disobedience. Since my 2018 arrest at the gates of the Burnaby Mountain tank farm I have been arrested five times: two times at the Fairy Creek old-growth logging protest and three other times for TMX resistance, including gluing my hands to freeways and chaining myself to the entrance door of the Royal Bank of Canada, one of the largest funders of the fossil fuel industry in the world.

I busk with my guitar and a big banner, my attempt to stop the pipelines and save the old-growth forests. I go out in snow and rain, as long as it is not pouring. I usually put the banner where the drivers can also see. I sometimes talk to people, hoping to educate as many as possible. I don't get much money, but what I receive, I send to environmental groups, protest camps, and protesters in need.

What impact have my actions had? I sing my songs at whatever protest rally I go to. So now many people can sing them without me. One day at Fairy Creek, a police officer told me he taught his family "Save the Old Growth" and sang it in front of me. Another police officer recorded it as sung by me and my Fairy Creek friends. If the police can sing my protest songs with their family, it might soften their hearts. I do not wish for the police to hate me; rather, I wish for them to like me and my songs, so they might understand how important our protest is. My weapon is love, love that includes everyone.

Stop the Pipelines

*(A song Hisao wrote and sang at innumerable rallies,
as a call and response to the tune of "La Cucaracha")*

> Stop the pipelines
> Stop the oil tankers
> We don't want them here
> Because they pollute
> Because they kill
> All the life on the Earth
>
> Save the old growth
> Save the ecosystem
> For our kids' future
> United together
> Standing together
> Stop the cutting forever
>
> Save the sky for eagles
> Save the water for salmon
> Save the forest for bears
> Let us all live in peace

EMILIE TERESA SMITH,
Anglican Priest

Emilie Smith (right) with Will George at Vancouver Law Court, 2018

Biography

Emilie Teresa Smith is an Argentine-born Anglican priest and a writer. She serves as rector of St. Barnabas parish in New Westminster, BC. She has spent many years living and working in Abya Yala (Latin America), particularly in Ixim Ulew (Guatemala). In 2012 she was elected co-president of the Oscar Romero international liberation theology network (SICSAL). Since then, she has visited every region of Abya Yala and the Caribbean, coming alongside numerous community struggles for the protection of sacred land and water. Emilie is deeply indebted to numerous teachers, including poet Julia Esquivel, liberation bishop jTatic Samuel Ruiz, and visionary Anglican priest and Cree-Dene Sundancer the Reverend Vivian Seegers, who have shaped and guided her life. She is mother of three, grandmother of five, and married to choir director Patti Powell. She now lives in what is called by some Vancouver, Canada.

Emilie was arrested on April 20, 2018, and sentenced on August 8, 2018, to one week of incarceration, serving 4 days.

Abridged Statement to BC Supreme Court Justice Kenneth Affleck, August 8, 2018

Esteemed Judge Affleck,

It is with much consternation that I find myself before you, charged with contempt for your court. Let me begin by apologizing. Never at any moment have I, nor do I now, hold you in contempt. I see you. You are my brother, a fellow child of God.

I am grieved that my actions have been interpreted as a sign of disrespect. My intent was to engage in urgent dialogue. The need to speak with one another is so great it caused me to behave in ways that are out of the ordinary.

Our world, the planet we all live on, our Holy Mother on whom we all depend, is in peril. We humans have caused this earth-wide devastation, because the dominant worldview has named greed as the central good of our human community and has forgotten the cost of such selfishness. We have forgotten the virtues of moderation, co-operation, harmony, balance, generosity. The result of this forgetting is the accelerating destruction of fields, forests, mountains, rivers, fish, caribou, lichen, cedar.

Somehow—bizarrely—many of us have accepted this greed-based worldview. We have, reluctantly perhaps, agreed that there is no other way to achieve a good life for ourselves and our children, but by destroying the earth. Maybe we think someone else will clean up the mess, or that some miracle technology will come and scoop our poisons out of the sky and water and earth. Or maybe we just can't imagine another way, and we have given up trying.

One of the very specific ways that the world has gone wrong is in this plan to expand a corroding pipeline that carries bitumen and winds its way from the contaminated boreal forest of the Cree and Dene people, through the mountains and then the dry lands of the Interior, alongside the great salmon river almost to the sea, where it plans to cut through a low mountain to the ocean inlet that nestles into the great green-blue mountains to the northeast of this courthouse. It was on a road, between the weirdly named tank farm—as if something good were alive and growing there—and the marine facility of this pipeline, that I found myself one morning last April, kneeling with a handful of my beloved brothers and sisters, praying and singing.

There are other ways of seeing and being in the world that are desperately trying to communicate with the greed-based worldview. For example, my ancestors' traditions, which emerged over two thousand years ago out of a small, dry country on the eastern side of the Mediterranean Sea, say these things:

"The earth is God's and all that is in it, the world and all who dwell therein." (Psalm 24)

"God so loved the world, that God sent a Son into the world to save the world." (Gospel of John)

"Woe to you who sell the poor." (Prophet Amos)

The founder of my tradition, Jesus of Nazareth, was often at odds with the legal authorities of his time. Yet he said, "I did not come to abolish the law, but rather to fulfill it." Humbly, we too, the followers of this way, do not mean to destroy any law, or to act with contempt for your court, but rather we mean to stand up for a deeper law, the essence of all law which says that protecting life matters more than profit. I hope that I am not speaking out of turn, but it is time to demand respect for this other law. I am sorry if at times we have appeared to be angry, but these things are urgent. Last year my first grandchild was born.

He arrived during the swirling smoke storm of summer, caused by unprecedented wildfires, yet another terrifying manifestation of our rapidly changing climate. For his first week he couldn't go out into the world. His soft newborn lungs breathed the filtered air in a sealed-off room. Outside the sun hung menacingly orange in a thin grey sky. Now I await with joy for my second grandchild to be born this coming October. I am scared too. Honestly, I don't know what world we are leaving to them. I am furious that greed seems to trump well-being for the generations to come. But then I remember: my tradition also has something to say about righteous anger.

There was one time remembered in all four of the gospels when Jesus was incandescent with rage. This is when he cleanses the temple. Making a whip of cords, he drives the money-changers out, those who prey on the poor.

"You have made my Father's Holy House a market-place!" he roars.

All of Creation is God's Dwelling Place. All of Creation is sacred and lovely and not to be used for the transient accrual of trinkets for a precious few. Earth is not a product, not a resource to be developed. Earth has a body, a spirit, a life, a soul and memory.

Tragically, our Christian teachings were used as weapons in the process of colonization, assimilation, destruction, yet in their heart they proclaim a different way. There is a core teaching of profound love and worship of God's world, and a teaching about brothers and sisters and neighbours, about caring for vulnerable ones. Above all, we are to honour in humility the Life Force of the Universe.

When the colonizers came to these lands, they did not bring these teachings. The colonizers brought fear and power, greed and violence.

Recently, we in the church realized, with shattered hearts, that in our full collusion with state power, with what was then "the law," we betrayed the very message of what Jesus came to reveal to us. We had forgotten about love. We looked back and saw the trail of destruction laid behind us, that lay on our altars. We have said that we are sorry—more than we could ever say—for the harm done in our collaboration with the state in the horrific Indian Residential School system. These things were perfectly legal then—and horrifically wrong.

We as a country have preached reconciliation, have signed on to UNDRIP and the International Labour Code Convention 169.[2] Through all these renewed statements and promises, we hope to be new kinds of people. We intend to move away from a dominating position, where we are always right, to a place of humility—a place of true reconciliation. Not just pretty words: but stepping back, stepping down, and allowing other cosmo-visions to have power.

In separate canoes, in the same direction.

We have heard the report of how the authorities, the police, and the company security officials viewed the events of the morning of April 20, 2018. I would like to tell you about how I experienced that morning:

We arrive at Kwekwecnewtxw, the Watch House, the night before, as darkness is sinking down onto the mountain. It has been raining all spring, but this night is clear enough that a slip of yellow moon hangs in the west. It is misty yet two stars burn through—they watch us like the eyes of a great owl, discerning, curious, and noble. We sit by the sacred, roaring fire, and it speaks to us. And we retire to rest in the cedar house that stands on the hill.

We are here at the invitation of Will George. I would leave if he asked me to; of course I would. But I will not leave because the court of Canada has granted an injunction to a Texas oil company, saying they can do what they want on this place which is not theirs.

Oil companies have been on this mountain, in these waters, for some sixty years, practically my lifetime, but that does not mean they actually own it. They don't own anything.

We wake before dawn. We are shivering cold in the house, on the mountain. We eat hot oatmeal, down in the camp kitchen, and drink hot water. The chill begins to fade. Some of my oldest friends are here: Vikki, Vivian, Laurel, Ron, and some very new friends, Rachael, Steve. And my sister-in-law, Lini. We head out. Before dawn we are blocking the gate. Slowly the sun rises over the oil facility. The tanks glow eerily in the pale green morning. It smells like a gas station, and my stomach feels soft inside. On the other side of the fence birds scatter-sing in the trees that are left, but as the sun rises, a clearing can be seen, freshly mown alongside of us. Trees have been cut, making way for the tail end of the pipeline. There are a few trees left; the tallest one flashes strangely. A cone has been placed there to prevent eagles from nesting. We say those eggs and eagles matter. We have come to be an interruption.

Will George comes to stand with us, drumming and chanting. His song sinks, rises and covers us, pressing us, pinning us to the land. We cannot move. The song is so loud the mountains across from us hear and are glad. The little mountain where we stand—so carved and damaged already by human greed—breathes and says thank you. The drum echo shivers up the inlet, roars back filled with the promise of the ancient ones, the ones who have been here forever. The echo is a song of gratitude, an invitation and—finally—a command.

Listen to me, says the drum, the song, the echo, the water, the mountains, the inlet, the sea, the ancient ones, the ones whose hearts were broken when this land was taken, the ones who watched when this land was murdered for the first time. Listen to me, says the drum. In humility, in sorrow, in reverence. Listen.

And so we stand, we kneel. I kneel. With all that I am, I am sorry.

What was done here was so thorough that hardly a sign remains of the original inhabitants, their communities, their sacred places, their way of being with Earth. It has become ordinary to not see it. One can grow up without ever seeing, and then to normalize as inevitable this not-knowing way of being. Residential schools, anti-Potlatch laws. Stamp. Stamp. Destroy. The Anglican Church first among the colonists. Assimilate, diminish, destroy.

The companies came and made this inlet their slag heap, their garbage dump, their toilet. The railway bosses came, the mining bosses came, the forest-felling bosses came. My ancestors came along with them, working men and women. We brought our religion, our state, our laws, our courts, our roads, our houses, our city, our entire way of being, which made no room for others, but smothered, suffocated, ripped, and destroyed. And then we pretended that nothing else was ever here.

But they are here still. The eagles, the trees, the bears, the whales, and the Original Peoples. The crucifixion of this land, the genocide of the Coast Salish People, did not work. Though the bosses try again to say this land is theirs, we kneel and say no. This land belongs to the One who made it. We turn in obedience towards those who have promised in truth to care for it. We will not leave.

The only authority that speaks here is the drum.

Narrative: Letters from Alouette Women's Correctional Facility

I have paper! I have a pencil! I'm in jail! The world is sharply divided. There is a here and a not here, a yes and a no. Mostly, the women in green sweats are broken and hurt. The women in uniforms watch us for transgressions. I sleep, eat, try to phone out, but can't make things work, so I settle and I wait.

August 8, 2018

Yesterday was a strange dream. "Guilty," declared the judge. Then everything moved quickly, and then just as quickly stopped. Handcuffs. Down and away. I get a last glimpse of Patti and the others.

Guards Cal and Gil seem sorry to do this. They can barely look at me. My organic blueberries go into the garbage. My wedding ring, so recently acquired, goes into a little baggie. My jacket goes—it has an attached strap that could be used in harmful ways. Then the waiting begins. The holding cell is in the bottom floor of the beautiful Arthur Erickson courthouse.

I rest on the hard plastic bench; a sideways toilet roll is my pillow. I shake with cold. Gil checks on me, brings me an old red sweatshirt. It smells foul, but I take it with thanks. The yellow shining cement bricks become rosary markers and I pray: Lord Jesus Christ, Son of God, have mercy on me. Holy Mary, mother of God, Our Father: Save me from the time of trial. This is no trial: uncomfortable, inconvenient, but not that hard. Cold, clear, everything taken away, nothing to do. Pray, sing, sleep. My mind moves, slips into the border between dream and vision. A Holy Place of the great invisible. An Anarchic Vacation from the Law.

There is no clock or time, but the men come and go and peer into the window. I am cold even with the sweatshirt, so I get up and pace. That seems to be what one should do in jail. I try some of the salsa moves that Michael taught us before the wedding, but no. I can't remember a single thing . . . but then joy! I remember Swedish dancing from last winter! Step, lift, step, step. Step, turn step. I figure out how to time the twirl so it misses the semi-wall that shields the smelly toilet. The hours slide down into one another. Muffled, unrecognizable voices, distress, keys shaking. Time is measured by Gil's fifteen-minute footsteps, peering into the porthole, smiling, thumbs up, disappearing. He brings me lunch—a McDonald's chicken salad—and he's gone.

I dance and sing, I pace, I lie down again, I adjust my arms inside the sweater, leaving the sleeves dangling. Desperation begins to settle, boredom, apprehension, loneliness, fear—but not really.

Maria Choc is on trial this day in Guatemala. Edwin Espinal is in jail in Honduras. How many thousands of Guatemalans were kidnapped, tortured, disappeared? Was Beatriz even ever held in a jail before she was murdered?[3] I sing a lament.

The expected graffiti is scratched into the door. True love and R.I.P. and a few foul declarations: Fuck the cops. There all goofs. East Van Rules. Tracy and Joseph . . . Best Friends Alwayz. These markings say: Here I am, I loved, I lost, I mattered. Into the days and years to come, forgotten, dead maybe, in jail, slivers of staying, remnants of saying I am. I pray for Tracey and Joseph, for Shorty, for Bubs. At last Gil comes. He takes away the sweatshirt. We're moving. Handcuffs and this time shackles, which cut and hurt my sockless feet. Into a van. All in our own hot boxes. Gleeful men a few slots down yell, "Are you really a pastor? Is that a costume?" I forgot I was wearing my black shirt with a collar. "Ha! Ha! Hallelujah!" one man yells. My ankles ache. And then we're off in a van through the downtown streets to the Main Street courthouse.

I shuffle awkwardly into the building, off come the cuffs. I stand hands against a wall, lift one foot, and another, off come the shackles, and into another cold holding cell where I meet D., the first fellow prisoner I meet. I am about to hear the first of many stories.

These are not my stories to retell, but what I can say is that with everyone who shares—there is a common thread. Violence, sexual violence particularly, substance use, addictions, layer upon layer, from the very beginning of life. Beautiful girls, lovely women, every one.

D. paces a true jail pace, pounds on the door, anxious to leave. She got bail today and wants to get back to Alouette; maybe the people from the recovery house will wait for her—but she has to get there before seven. Chains and shackles again and out to the van. D. and I share a tight bench in a cage. There's a woman with black hair sitting on the narrow slit of floor in the next cage over. "What's your name?" yells D. The other woman looks up, shakes her head and looks down quickly. Its after 6 p.m. now; we head out along Cordova Street. Hi St. James, hello Commercial Drive, hello my darling new wife, my Patti. Hello and goodbye all: Fritz, garden, bread, cheese, coffee, chocolate, figs and tomatoes, blackberries, the last raspberries. Goodbye pillows, stuffies, books, photos of my boys and Oscar, flowers, birds, and spiderwebs strung across everything.

It is stinking hot and the woman in the cage beside us bangs the walls. She gets up, crouching, no one could stand. Highway 1 inches along. At last we stop in a parking lot, baking, waiting for another van, collecting prisoners to take home for the night. Our neighbour is ever more agitated until she is pounding and kicking at the door and walls. "I am dying! Help! I can't breathe!" D. tells her to shut up. Then somehow, I am helping D. take off her green sweatshirt, separating it from her green tee, so that it hangs over her cuffed hands. Our neighbour takes off her sweatshirt too, but she can't unattach the T-shirt, so it comes off too and tangles over her cuffs. She kicks again at the door, slumps, and is quiet.

I lean my head against the caged window between the two of us and shut my eyes. After a while I open them and look over. She's done the same thing at the same time and suddenly we see each other's eyes, both frozen, about four inches apart. We both jump, surprised at such strange closeness, almost nakedness, human and woman and sad. Who knows her great sadness? And mine? Why I am here? Global warming and pipelines and bitumen. And me.

Suddenly the van jerks, finally moving. D. cheers. I am relieved too, longing for the unknowns to end, and to rest somewhere. But there is yet another stop. We are moved to another van and getting in beside us—in a separate cage—come four young women, recently convicted, exhausted, still high, dirty, worn, and done. They stare at me.

One young woman is fierce-eyed, shorn head, tattoos on her face, and barefoot. D. says to me, "She's cursing us. Don't look at her." Obedient, I look down, but then as we're driving back up through Surrey, she throws herself at the window between our cages, head up to a small filtered screen. "My grandpa would want me to do this," she yells. "Are you a priest? Will you hear my confession?"

I'm too astonished to reply, and she starts to list things. I can't really hear her, the screen is too small, and the traffic too loud, but I hear some. Dear Lord, what to say, what to do? I know nothing about this young woman, not even her name, but I know she is reaching for that truth-star. I say what I've said many times before, though never in these circumstances: "I don't know you. I know nothing about you, but this I know: No matter what you have done, no matter what has been done to you, you are a beloved daughter of God. You are loved. God holds you in the palm of his hand, and God treasures your heart." I yell that through the grate. Then we sit in silence. Silence all around, or rather the steady roar of the van. It is less hot. The sun is setting and we are arriving home: The Alouette Correctional Centre for Women (ACCW). It is after seven. D. has missed her chance to leave tonight.

The shackles are rubbing a small sore on my shin, and the handcuffs are heavy. We shuffle into yet another bright room to be processed yet again. The young women are spent and throw themselves on the hard bench as we are called one by one. I go through the final process, am stripped of my own clothes and get green prison sweats.

I am going to Alpha: the special secure unit. I stumble down the long, nightmare hall with heavy locked doors on either side, into the tiered unit. I am inside now. Alpha in the secure zone is maximum but for the least troublesome—the immigration cases are here, they say. My ears perk up.

I'm too tired to notice much—an open area and clanging stairs. I'm up to the second floor, a small cell, a bag of sheets and a towel, the door closes and locks. I sit and plan the night. I don't have a toothbrush or soap, so I make my bed and arrange a shirt over my face. The lights never turn out here. And the day is done. Two thin slits show the outside, a patch of yellow grass under the glare of blazing light, and the dark forest beyond.

The days stretch out down the way, but first there's the first night. Industrial silence. I turn in and examine myself.

My heart is pierced through with love, none of it earned by my goodness. It just is: Patti, my beloved boys, their girls, Oscar, the new little one coming, my family and my family-in-law, my church, my brothers and sisters in Christ, my co-land defenders everywhere, especially in Latin America, and especially Guatemala, my doggie, the forest, the great sea, the looming mountains, and the wee sparrows. All these are my nest of prayer. I weave them all around me. Sleep comes gently and carries me into the heart of God, where I spend the night free.

August 9, 2018

I wake up stiff on the board-hard mattress, and I stretch before opening my eyes. Outside that thin light waits as dawn approaches over the trees. I no longer decide most things, so the things I do—I cherish. Mostly what I have is me, and how I can be with everyone I meet.

I am so absolutely conscious of my privilege. I will be here for a few days, loved and carried by all that I have. I have no life to reconstruct from scratch when I leave, my traumas are not deep and lasting. How can I mirror compassion without curiosity? Can I be open and vulnerable, reaching out with a measure of concern and confidence, in the flash moment of time that I will have here? I wait.

At seven the doors click unlocked. A guard, H., comes by and turns a key. I step out to the balcony, seeing for the first time others in green. Two women are busy in the common area below, setting up plastic trays. Breakfast is served: raisin bran with watery milk, a muffin, and two pieces of Wonder Bread. Coffee, powdered creamer, four packs of sugar, a portion each of margarine, jam, and peanut butter, and an apple. I'm eating quietly, politely. Slowly I say a few words. T.L. and J. start talking; I have delivered to me a story, and another. T.L. tells me some things, and her eyes narrow and she asks me to pray with her, not quite believing I will. "Of course," I say. "We'll find a place and a time. I'm not going anywhere, at least for a few days."

J., in the meantime, is telling me how things work. Fill in this form for this, that form for that.

I'm looking at the soggy bread on my tray, and over by the phones I spy a toaster. Toasted is so much better. "Can I just go over and toast this?" I ask J. "Oh no," she says. "You have to fill in a form first!" I look horrified, then she grins at me. We laugh. My first jail joke!

I give T.L. my muffin. "Really?" she asks. "You don't want it later?" "I'm good," I say.

E. comes by. I give her my sugar and whitener. "Jail candy!" she says. "Mix sugar, whitener, jam and p.b. Microwave for thirty seconds. Let harden. Eat."

Before we're shooed back to our cells, I find the book cart. I grab a Bible. And then *Atonement* by Ian McEwan. Back to my cell. Then I hear a call—yoga! And we're clattering down the steps and through the door to the only outdoor space, a weird, stuffy courtyard with a screen ceiling two floors above. But I can see that the sky is blue, and incongruously I'm lying on my back looking up, and then doing downward dog.

We have a jail meeting. I nod to everyone. There's some drama, some quiet, some promises, some pain.

The drama of me-not-being-able-to-phone begins. Deposit money in jail account. Done on arrival. Set up special phone voice recognition ID. Done. Try and call, no go. Oh. Must fill in form to transfer money from jail account to phone money. Do this. Must wait now until later. Notice while riffling bored through the request forms that we have to ask specially for a visitor. Fill in a request for a visitor. Wait. Get a small plastic toothbrush and a cheap slip of hotel soap. Celebrate.

The regular rhythm of the day plods along. Now it is lunch,

and then we are locked in for the afternoon. *Atonement* is seamless and transporting. So desperately quiet and alone.

Then the guard, S., comes in—we're moving you. Right now. Hurry! Pack, sort, clothes/bedclothes. Wait, I'm leaving T.L. and we never got to pray. Can I say goodbye, guards? No. Okay. Out. Long hall, nightmare doors. Strip off the green clothes, switching to grey. I've been moved from secure Alpha to medium Cedar B.

Cedar B—twenty-three women. The "girls" have finished their workday and they're lounging about. It is *loud*—jarring after the quiet of Alpha. Booming voices and roaring laughter.

The small bungalow shakes. It is three in the afternoon. Still hot and sunny. August air—for the first time in almost two days, I breathe. There are birdies, ants, dragonflies. And trees for 360 degrees, beautiful cedars and firs. There are gardens, a memory area, with painted stones for the dead, and a labyrinth—no, actually, a spiral. I come back after dinner and hop its painted tiles. I stay out until almost ten.

Some of the girls call this Camp Cupcake, but it is a prison, of course. We can see the forest, but not go into its cool shade. This day, the next, and the next, stories spill out. I hear them and I brace: mothers have died, and brothers; boyfriends are in jail too, and children have been taken away, who knows where they are; and worst of all, a child, a daughter who died. Drugs stab in and out of most stories. There is talk of lawyers and trials to come, and days and months and years to wait. And there is drama, exhaustion, frustration, and lots of swearing. I am uncomfortable with some women—the don't-give-a-shit types, loud and sarcastic.

Pretty soon they all know why I'm here—there's some amazement that someone would more or less do this voluntarily, but then some nods of interest, and good job, and that A-hole of a judge, and I look for a way to be still, show interest, compassion, welcome, with no prying, that I balance with trips out to the relative quiet and green.

Phone drama—I filled the request form, but it was done incorrectly in pencil and that doesn't count. Damn it. I borrow a pen and fill in the form again. It should work tomorrow. Okay, I say.

In the meantime, a guard, A., takes me to the library—looking for a replacement for *Atonement*, which they wouldn't let me take from one side to another. While we're there she whispers, "You did fill in the visitor request form? You have to fill it out before they can schedule a visit." "I have indeed," I reply. A. says under her breath, "I talked with *her, your wife*." A flash of sympathy, and then a sliver of her own story. She talks, and I nod and we smile furtively. Then she goes out. I follow. The flowers are singing: Patti is coming! But when? Tomorrow is Friday.

I take my new book outside. The sun has set into the trees to the west. The raucous girls laugh on the steps. One women ignores everything and waters the lawns and the flowers and the flower-pots with a rough determination. I write with my new glorious pen at a table, now shaded for the night. On the tops of the eastern trees, the sun still lights up the branches. A hawk, a fat one, flies straight over, from east to west.

There was morning, and there was evening. The first day.

August 10, 2018
Friday morning, a work day. I'm on Hort. After breakfast I get new clothes and workboots. I follow my new roomie, B., out to the spiral. Together with two other women, we weed, for hours, in an ever-tightening path towards the centre. On my knees I pull weeds from the stepping tiles, leaving the hens and chicks, which bubble up, thick, prickle-less succulents that spread and grow everywhere.

The two women I don't know are talking, loudly, well, one woman is talking, the other is listening, nodding, saying uh-hum, and a few words of comfort and solace. Pluck, pluck, dig, and I can't help but hear another tale of horror. My heart contracts. It actually aches. The speaker leaves, and I say to the woman left, "Your voice sounds so nice as you listen." She nods, and ping! We see each other.

After break we move to the lavender patch. I sit harvesting in the shade, surrounded by purple, breathing in calm, peace. The bees and I take turns reaching for the flowers. I watch one take its time and I wait for it to finish. Lavender saturates everything, my lap, my hands, my clothes, my hair, the scent stays for a while. We stack them, tray by tray in the greenhouse. B. warns me: "Don't even take one flower. You could get punished." Oh dear. I've already taken one small sprig and tucked it into my rib-squashing, chest-flattening bra. The contraband lavender pricks my skin guiltily. I don't plan to follow this rule.

After lunch it's too hot to be outside, so I'm allowed into the empty library. I sort and stack and arrange in cool silence—the Dog books and the God books are all jumbled up on two long, low shelves—until it's time to rush back to Cedar and stand with B. outside our door. We are counted at 7 a.m., 11 a.m., 1 p.m., 4 p.m., 7 p.m., and 10 p.m., standing like sentinels guarding our own cells.

I don't feel like going back to the library now, so I lie down for a while. But now there's nothing to do. I let a little bit of Patti-sad into my heart, just a small sliver of longing. I remember her singing—of course I do—and holding me, her wondering why I do what I do, and loving me right through it. My boys too, Abel at the demo with his sign. Oscar. His wispy red curls more precious than a million mountains of gold, die-for-him precious, give-the-whole-world-for-him precious. And the women here, their children, their love, their longing. It makes me furious. I cry two tears, that's all for now, in frustration. Maybe Patti's coming today, this afternoon. Two extra tears for hope.

After a while I spring up and go to the pay phone—maybe it will work at last. I follow the commands, punch in several series of numbers, say my name three times. The voice recognition ID fails. I go to a guard, can you check this out? "Oh, your voice ID has become invalid. Fill out a form (in pen) to request a reset. It should work by 3 p.m. tomorrow."

The afternoon is hot and maybe will never end. I go outside and sit by the roses for a while. The roses surround the closed-up Eagle Hut. The women tell me that the Elders used to come and smudge and drum, and mysteriously they no longer have these Healing Circles. But why? It's impossible to get any clear news of any sort here, but surely Indigenous spiritual care should be a priority. S. finds me on the bench by the hut. "I always come here to pray," she says. "I wish the Elders would still come. It used to help so much, you can feel it healing." There is a sad carved eagle outside guarding the way into the round building.

I head back inside, and coming around the corner of the bungalow I find a large group of women including A., the loudest-laughiest of them all. "Hey," she says. "Tell us more about why you are here." Deep breath.

"Well," I start, "the pipeline would bring really dirty oil from Alberta to a place in Burnaby where they plan to ship it over the ocean. There would be seven times as many oil tankers going through the water out to the sea. There could be an oil spill—and that would be the end of the orcas and the sea animals and fish and life along the coast. And the First Nations people there, the Tsleil-Waututh—they never gave their land away in the first place. There was no treaty or anything for their land, and they don't want the pipeline at all."

We enter into a robust talk about climate change and Indigenous rights and reconciliation—many of the women I've met along this jail journey are First Nations. There are lots of nods and more right-ons, until one woman stands up and says, "I'm all for the pipeline."

"Hmm," I say. "Tell me more."

"I'm from Alberta, and we need jobs," she says, looking defiant, if a bit nervous.

"I totally agree with you," I say. "About the jobs. Of course people need jobs." Her eyes are interested.

"My son's a carpenter," I go on. "He's been to the protests with a sign that says Carpenter for Sustainable Energy Projects. There's lots of jobs in making clean energy. More jobs for a long period of time. This pipeline will make some jobs, but mostly it is about a small group of people making a pile of money, and wrecking the earth."

The vigorous discussion continues until A. says, "Teach us to protest!" Uh-oh.

"Hmm," I say again. "Well, what would you like to protest?"

"The awful food and the expensive extras we have to buy from the canteen."

"What do you think you could do?"

"Write letters."

"Protest at the admin building."

"Blockade the kitchen."

"Go on a hunger strike!"

I smile and leave them to it, retiring again to read for a while before dinner. After about ten minutes I look out the window, and I see a huge crowd, shouting and gesticulating in front of the main building. I sink down behind my book again.

D. comes into our room.

"What's happening out there?" I ask timidly.

"Oh, nothing," she says. "We're just getting our meds."

"Oh," I say, slightly disappointed.

Dinnertime comes and is gone in ten minutes. My roomie is watching crime shows on TV, so I go outside and read, and then wander and wander. I'm tamping down a circle in the grass. Up to ten feet from the fence allowed, and then around and back. I remember the circling polar bear, disgracefully held in a cramped and crumbling enclosure at the Stanley Park zoo. Thank heavens it's gone. Poor bear. Pace, pace, turn around, pace, pace went the creature, twenty-five feet where a thousand miles were required.

In the north, the sea ice is melting; further south, the forests are burning. Over the thick green trees here to the west of the prison, Venus pops out shining.

August 11, 2018

Saturday morning. There is a thin haze over the pale sky. No work today, no lavender, no weeding, no hours in the cool library. And no breakfast! "Brunch" is at ten. One hard-boiled egg, one slice of bacon, Wonder Bread. The gals invite me to coffee—real coffee, strong, made from their canteen stash. The morning is long and drawn out. D. and I go to the gym for a bit. Huff, puff, step, pull.

The minutes go slow.

And then I hear there's a Catholic Mass. G. and I head over. G. is older, like me, and from a community up the Fraser River. She's hoping her brothers will put up some salmon for her for the winter. Some others hear we're going to Mass and come along. Father M. and the three volunteers who come with him look up in surprise. So many people. The small circle is full. And so we pray.

How could I, how could anyone come as a Christian to prison but as a penitent? Any wrongs by the women in grey were first wrongs done to them. In what way did the state, the church, fuck up first? Grabbing the land, outlawing the Potlatch, Indian Residential Schools, smallpox by intent or by accident, poisoning the waters, ripping down the trees, killing the buffalo, the caribou, the salmon, alcohol, poverty, derision, soul-crushing, body-crushing violence of every kind. And then to try to reform these women? These lovely, precious, fierce women—once girls, born perfect. T.L. back in Alpha said, "I'm so angry, so fucking angry at everyone."

Father M. is kind and encouraging, and we sing loudly, though I'm not sure that much we say and sing really makes sense here. But the beauty of the Christian Mass is that the words themselves carry our faith. Love embodied for you. Father M. tugs a bit at his collar, the earnest women with him smile helpfully. The vessels of his communion set shine brilliantly and clean. And somehow we take and taste and see that the Lord is good.

G. and I and the others trip out again into the blasting sunshine. It's lunchtime and then wait time. Will Patti come, did she even get the message?

I go to the phone one last time to see if I can make the damn thing work. Nope. I check with the guard yet again. She looks on the computer. "Oh, no. You are getting out tomorrow. Your phone money has been transferred back into your trust fund." Sigh.

Then the guard whispers to me, "Don't go far. She's coming at 2:45."

One hour from now! The longest hour of my life begins. Sixty seconds times sixty minutes. That's 3,600 seconds. I count slowly. I lie on my bed and feel guilty. Not many visits happen for these women, and I've been here for just a flash of time. I'm going home tomorrow. At last the guard comes for me. We walk over to the main building, down the nightmare hall of doors.

I wait outside the door of visiting room number one. Will I be able to hug her at least, a small kiss? Will we sit at a table, in a lounge? I go up the narrow stairs, open the door . . . shock. We are in real prison mode. A chair in a small, enclosed glass box, with a desk, facing an identical box with the same. A small circle-screen between us.

But never mind—there she is. My love. And I can't believe my eyes: she's wearing her wedding jacket. Nothing could have been better. Patti in that jacket, with her ring still on, and everything is restored in me. Jail is meant to kill the spirit, and in a small way mine had been suffering, until now.

We have the strangest conversation of our lives. Small talk, a few stories. How is the dog?

"I'm getting out tomorrow, 8:30 a.m.!" I say.

"Tomorrow! Damn, I'm working. I'll figure it out."

She brought chocolate (I can't have it) and a printout of all the messages she'd been receiving. Can't have that either.

"Should I read them?"

"No, I can't stand it."

"Well, I'm bringing a U-Haul of love, support, and prayers."

"I know you are." All I can think of is T.L. and S. and D. and G. and everyone.

And before we can end the awful, precious visit, the guard comes. Patti goes first. I'm left standing in the echo chamber of the stairwell. And what else could I do, but sing?

Back in the yard, I wander again. Everything is weird. I walk around the side to look at the lavender that's left to be clipped on Monday. Not by me.

My last ten-minute supper.

What to do now? I feel like there's nothing I can say that will heal or help anything at this point. I hang around and admire beautiful beading and lovely crochet blankets. If I were only here longer. "I like the rainbow unicorn one," I say, to the woman beading Snoopy. We talk a bit more about the people making a stand up on Burnaby Mountain.

"There will be more women coming," I tell them. "I'll tell them how nice you all are."

I decide to make the rounds of the grounds one last time, and say goodbye to the plants and the dragonflies. I stop to smell the smallest rose outside the boarded-up Eagle Hut. I sit on the grass.

S. finds me here, and I don't really want to talk much more, but I can listen. "I used to cry right here a whole lot," she says. "After my son was murdered. He was four years old." I sit and hold that pain in my lap for a while. She's so used to telling the story. I know it must still hurt, but she smiles at me. Generous and gracious and beautiful.

Others come around the Hut. One woman cuts the tiny rose and hands it to S., who puts it in her golden hair. I'm sure that's against the rules, but I'm sure they know that too. Later on, as we walk together, all of us, back to the bungalow, the rose is invisible.

In bed by 9:30, I say goodnight to sweet D. I sleep like a log until six the next morning. No one is up, and we are not allowed out to the common area until after seven—except to go to the bathroom. I quickly search for some coloured pencil crayons and

markers I saw yesterday. All put away, except a green highlighter. I
go back into the room and, in the penumbra of the early morning
in cell 25, Cedar B, I write out a prayer in blue ink and green highlighter to the women:

> To My New Friends on Cedar:
> May the Lord bless you and keep you.
> May the Lord make His face to shine upon you.
> May the Lord be gracious to you, and grant you peace.
> Love,
> Emilie

At 8:30 on the dot, after a pile of paperwork, I get my phone money
back plus $2 for working one day. I dig through my own clothes
and belongings until I find it—the little plastic bag with my wedding ring. Deep breath. I put it back on. The guard shouts: "Smith
for release!"

*This piece was edited from its original form published under the
same title in the journal* Reckoning, *July 4, 2019, reckoning.press.*

Part 3
Resistance from a place of privilege

Barbara and Robert Stowe with Greenpeace founder Rex Weyler (middle) and Nancy McLean (far left) at the TMX tank farm on Burnaby Mountain. ©Rogue Collective/Greenpeace

ELIZABETH MAY,
Leader of the Green Party of Canada

Biography

Elizabeth May's life is defined by one word: service. Service to community, country, and planet. One of Canada's best-known parliamentarians, she is a lifelong environmentalist. From 2006 to 2019, she led the Green Party of Canada through four federal elections, including the breakthrough 2011 election in which she became Canada's first elected Green. In November 2022, she was again elected leader in a co-leader proposal with Jonathan Pedneault.

From her early years as an environmental activist, struggling financially while waiting tables at the family restaurant in Cape Breton, to her work as a single mom, Elizabeth has been bringing the voices of underprivileged communities to the halls of power. She has been a trailblazer for generations of Canadian women and activists.

Elizabeth was the first Canadian environmentalist to point out how environmental racism caused marginalized people to be exposed to unacceptable threats to their health. She has used her legal training and resources to assist Indigenous Peoples in Canada and around the world.

When legal and political avenues failed to yield results, Elizabeth put her body, safety, and well-being on the line. In May 2001, she went on a seventeen-day hunger strike in front of Parliament Hill protesting toxic conditions for the only predominantly Black community on Cape Breton Island, near the infamous Sydney Tar Ponds. That work led directly to her private member's bill (PMB) on Environmental Racism (C-226). Two other of her PMBs have been adopted as law—one on Lyme disease and one that bans keeping cetaceans in captivity.

She stands on principle and resigned when her environment

minister boss broke the law in 1988, despite having had many successes in her role as senior policy advisor. One of those successes was contributing to the 1987 Montreal Protocol that saved the ozone layer. She was the only MP to intervene at the National Energy Board (NEB) against the Kinder Morgan pipeline.

———————

Elizabeth was arrested on March 23, 2018, and was sentenced in June 2018 with a fine of $1,500.

Narrative: My Resistance to TMX, or How the Canadian Taxpayers Got Shafted for $34 Billion

On March 23, 2018, I was arrested for violating the injunction granted by the British Columbia courts to Texas-based Kinder Morgan. As a former practising lawyer, admitted to the bars of Nova Scotia and Ontario, and as a sitting member of Parliament, what would possess me to break the law? That story begins years before my act of conscious, intentional, nonviolent civil disobedience.

I put in years of effort to stop the pipeline. Based on existing laws, I concluded that the pipeline was illegal and presented those arguments to the National Energy Board review panel. When we got to the moment on Burnaby Mountain when the RCMP advanced to read out the injunction to us, I was still acting in the public interest. The true lawbreakers were elsewhere.

The lies surrounding the former Kinder Morgan pipeline, now the Canadian government's Trans Mountain Pipeline Expansion (TMX for short), continue to be told, and the truth is rapidly being forgotten. Even memory of the lies themselves becomes lost in the collective amnesia. I would like to refresh our memory.

Stephen Harper's 2011 election platform specifically stated the Conservatives would not support the export of bitumen or other Canadian crude to any country with environmental regulations over refineries less onerous than Canada's. Then, not even Harper was pushing for "getting our product to tidewater." Rather, Harper was banking on the Keystone project, which expanded the usual route for Canadian oil—due south. It was only after the 2011 election, as Keystone faced increasing political opposition in the US, that projects to get Canadian bitumen to Asia were proposed. Enbridge's Northern Gateway project had been promoted informally for years, but its application was finally submitted to the National Energy Board in May 2010. It was approved by the Harper administration in 2014. Meanwhile, Kinder Morgan was also picking up steam.

Kinder Morgan had interesting roots. It was a fairly recent entrant in the world of multinational pipeline conglomerates. It sprang from the ashes of one of the most corrupt and fraudulent outfits in business history—Enron.

Some Enron executives ended up in jail. Others, including Richard Kinder, became billionaires. Kinder ended up owning a small subsidiary, Enron Pipelines Ltd., then joined with other Enron survivors to form Kinder Morgan Pipelines.

In 2005 Kinder Morgan purchased Trans Mountain, originally a public enterprise of the government of Canada. In the 1950s, the Trans Mountain Pipeline was built to ship Alberta crude oil to four refineries on the lower mainland of British Columbia. By the time Kinder Morgan bought it, Alberta was shipping a less valuable but more costly product—bitumen. This is a tarry substance extracted from Northern Alberta's tar sands at huge environmental cost, wreaking havoc on the local environment. Bitumen is a solid—like a lump of tar. It cannot be refined until upgraded into synthetic crude—or "syncrude." Diluting it in other petrochemical by-products like naphtha and other natural gas condensates allows the diluted mixture ("dilbit") to flow through a pipeline. This is cheaper than moving solid bitumen by rail.

Kinder Morgan's December 2013 application to the NEB described a very different economic prospect. Its "expansion" was actually an entirely new pipeline. Refining the product for domestic use in British Columbia gas stations was not contemplated. The goal of this pipeline was to move dilbit to the coast to be pumped into tankers and shipped elsewhere—supposedly to Asian markets. Kinder Morgan was never able to verify that those markets wanted this product, but they did have customers along the US Gulf Coast.

Kinder Morgan pitched its story, and as with its Enron predecessor, those pushing it did not care if the story was true. The story was that at "tidewater," dilbit would sell at a higher price (in business jargon, "discounted for less").

This is nonsense. Diluting bitumen to make dilbit is not a step in upgrading to syncrude. It merely dilutes a solid. Once at its destination outside Canada, the diluent is removed. The solid bitumen must then be upgraded, an expensive process. Thus, bitumen is inherently of lower value than crude oil. I repeat: high cost; low value. It is highly unlikely that the buyers of dilbit would pay a premium for a product that would cost them more to upgrade.

When the NEB started its public hearing process, I signed up as an intervenor. From the beginning, I pointed out that the NEB was absolutely the wrong body to conduct an environmental review. From Canada's very first environmental assessment—back in 1975 reviewing the Wreck Cove hydro project in the Cape Breton Highlands (yes, I was there)—no such review had ever been done by the NEB. Environmental assessments have always been conducted by the government's Environmental Assessment Boards. Since the early 1990s, the Canadian Environmental Assessment Act (CEAA) has governed thousands of reviews every year. No pipeline project had ever been rejected. But Stephen Harper thought CEAA was an obstacle to fossil fuel development. In spring 2012, omnibus budget bill C-38 repealed or rewrote seventy different laws, and killed proper environmental assessment, putting the NEB in charge of the environmental assessment for TMX.

The NEB was forced by time limits imposed by bill C-38 to alter its usual quasi-judicial process. Intervenors were denied procedural fairness—not allowed to cross-examine industry experts, or even allowed in the room during their testimony. I was granted intervenor status in April 2014. My final argument on January 24, 2016, was the first time I was permitted to enter the room, where I attempted in thirty minutes to cross-examine the 23,000-page Kinder Morgan submission. The abuse of normal procedural-fairness rules was breathtaking.

Another notable moment in this history of my road to arrest was the 2015 election that removed the Harper Conservatives from power. In the course of the campaign, while campaigning on Vancouver Island, Liberal leader Justin Trudeau said that the NEB process was so flawed that no project could be approved under it. After Trudeau and the Liberals' remarkable electoral success in October 2015, moving from third party in the House to majority government, a series of promises were broken. Kinder Morgan's approval was one of many.

On January 24, 2016, I made my way to the NEB hearings held in the Burnaby Delta Hotel. I had not stayed there; as is Green practice, I billeted. I had the honour of staying with an amazing scientist, Dr. Lynne Quarmby, who was then chair of the Simon Fraser University Department of Molecular Biology and Biochemistry. Her first anti-pipeline action was to write an opinion piece against the pipeline. This act of free speech provoked Kinder Morgan to file a $5.6 million lawsuit against her and four others. Such lawsuits are commonly called SLAPP suits, standing for "strategic litigation against public participation." In Lynne's case, the intimidation did not work. Faced with a crushing overreaction from Kinder Morgan, Lynne did not waver. Instead, she walked up Burnaby Mountain, where she was arrested on November 21, 2014.

As we drove up to the hotel and conference centre, it seemed only too appropriate that the NEB hearing was held in a complex that included a massive gambling destination—the Grand Villa Casino. Anything to do with the dilbit pipeline and tanker project was a gamble. The result of Harper having gutted environmental assessment was a hearing that left the NEB without actual evidence, only unsupported (and thus worthless) assertions.

For example, the only evidence from Kinder Morgan about whether bitumen and diluent could be cleaned up in the marine environment came from a one-time-only, nonpublished, non-peer-reviewed experiment over a ten-day period in Gainford, Alberta.[1]

The tests were done in tanks of various sizes using fresh water with salt stirred in. According to Kinder Morgan's evidence, the five-gallon pail and fish tank research went awry: "Errors occurred in the fish tank, because the spill was installed in a manner that resulted in a large amount of dispersion at the outset, due to air ingestion, and the resulting slick was larger than the ruler and developed an asymmetric form." (Larger than the ruler?!)

They concluded: "A better-equipped test is certainly recommended for future consideration." This Keystone Kops version of science was the entirety of Kinder Morgan's evidence for their assertion that bitumen mixed with diluent can be cleaned up. Published studies, peer-reviewed and conducted in conditions that replicate the marine environment, demonstrate that the dilbit mixture separates and that small "oil balls" of bitumen result, which then sink.[2] It is challenging enough to clean up surface oil; it's impossible to remove tar-balls scattered on the ocean floor.

Canada's premiere scientific academy, the Royal Society of Canada, sponsored a comprehensive review of the environmental and health impacts of tar sands operation in 2010,[3] where it was concluded that government regulatory capacity was inadequate for the pace of oil-sands development. And a joint report from the Departments of Environment, Fisheries and Oceans, and Natural Resources in 2013 concluded that the science on dilbit cleanup potential was lacking.[4] Yet the NEB ruled that accepting these conclusions would be unfair to Kinder Morgan.

The NEB was also unperturbed when a Kinder Morgan expert whited out the word "DRAFT" from a US EPA spill dispersion model, and introduced it to the NEB, claiming it was the approach used in the US. Another intervenor, economist Robyn Allan, contacted the EPA only to discover that they did not in fact use this model. EPA staff was shocked to learn that it was being referenced as their practice, as it had clearly been labelled draft until Kinder Morgan "fixed" it.

Even as I write, after all the scandalous distortions of normal practice, there has never been an independent review making the case that Kinder Morgan's pipeline is in the national interest. The NEB's review did not remotely meet the average citizen's understanding of what is in the public interest. For example, the largest union in the oil sands, UNIFOR, intervened before the NEB, offering evidence that building Kinder Morgan would cost jobs. Shipping out unprocessed solid bitumen to refineries in other countries ships out Canadian jobs and increases the carbon footprint of the product. Shipping solid bitumen diluted with toxic fossil fuel condensate for export bypasses the last remaining refinery in Burnaby, which cannot process bitumen. UNIFOR argued that if the Kinder Morgan pipeline were allowed to proceed, that refinery would likely close.

The NEB refused to allow this information to be filed as evidence. It ruled that its mandate did not include jobs—or climate, or upstream or downstream impacts. So Canada's "national interest," according to the NEB, did not include energy security, net employment benefits, environment, climate, GDP, or really anything other than getting the pipeline approved.

After a surge of citizen activism and the raising of many civic voices in protest, it became clear that the pipeline was not an economically viable proposition. Kinder Morgan wanted out. Richard Kinder used the skills he'd acquired at Enron in what seemed to me an epic fleecing of the Canadian public purse.

The financial machinations were extreme. Kinder Morgan had sworn, in the 2014 hearings before the NEB, that its financial capacity to deliver the mega-project was established by the financial health of the corporation as a whole, that Kinder Morgan of Texas was 100 percent responsible for delivering the project.

What happened next was that Richard Kinder subdivided the company, hiving off its Canadian assets. Kinder Morgan did so after getting the permit to proceed, but before it had the capital or the contracts to do so. This was step one in the exit strategy.

After carving off KM-Canada, Richard Kinder used all the funds the company raised to meet the equity stake demanded by Canadian banks to pay down the parent company's debt. It was clear that headquarters in Texas had no intention of investing in the pipeline. Somehow this evaded the notice of the federal finance minister and Canadian regulators.

But Kinder Morgan had a problem. As economist Robyn Allan discovered in looking at the long-term shipping contracts KM had secured, cancelling the contracts would have triggered penalties. These could be avoided if abandonment of the project was due to "third parties" or events outside the control of the company. So they used political obstruction as an excuse, although every permit requested by KM from the BC government had been granted without undue delay. There were over 1,000 needed permits remaining to be granted—but for which KM had not yet applied. In April 2018 they kidnapped their own project with a letter to the federal government that demanded a guarantee by the end of May 2018 that it could proceed. Without the federal government's guarantee, the company would withdraw its proposal and abandon the project.

In this situation, you'd expect politicians to provide the usual boilerplate answer: "The matter is before the courts . . . ministers cannot guarantee what courts will do or say, but you have our full support . . . blah blah blah . . ." Instead, Finance Minister Morneau and Prime Minister Trudeau decided they had to pay the ransom. No price was too high to avoid headlines saying they'd failed to deliver on their "the pipeline will be built" bravado.

I cannot begin to imagine the stories that were told in Houston about this gambit as Kinder Morgan deposited Canada's cheque for $4.4 billion—issued, by the way, after the value of the asset had fallen due to an August 2018 court ruling in favour of the First Nations plaintiff, which voided the permits. I wish that more journalists had held the federal government to account, because Morneau cut that cheque when there was no closing date in the contract and no reason to deliver the cheque the day after the Federal Court ruling.

In 2022, expected costs were $21 billion, and Canada's Parliamentary Budget Officer (PBO) warned that the costs and delays were very likely to increase.[5] As the PBO detailed at that time, we are in a project that offers us little chance of emerging with our shirts.

On March 23, 2018, as I stood at Kinder Morgan's gates wondering if the police would show up to arrest us, I never imagined that our government would bring us to this lunacy. As I stood there, I did know that the climate emergency was galloping. I have been working on the climate issue since long before it became an emergency. I learned my climate science back in the 1980s when I served as the minister of environment's senior policy advisor, before the myth of doubt was invented. I started working to avert a climate disaster when it was still a future threat. Now it is our everyday reality.

I decided to risk arrest because it was one possible way to stop the pipeline. I will never stop trying to get this climate-killing nightmare cancelled.

Studying the Intergovernmental Panel on Climate Change (IPCC) advice is hard going. What it tells me is that we are standing on the very edge of a precipice, but that a pathway to a livable world is still feasible. It is late but not yet too late. To preserve the possibility of a livable world, no new fossil fuel infrastructure can be added anywhere on the planet—according to the IPCC. Not one more inch of it.

Unlike other arrestees, fellow MP Kennedy Stewart and I chose not to make a statement in court. A special prosecutor had been appointed for us. My lawyer agreed to a shared statement of facts, a guilty plea from me, and a recommended sentence. Judge Affleck accepted the request for Stewart. But in my case, he rejected the shared recommendation from my lawyer and the prosecutor. He gave me a rather severe lecture about what a bad person I was. In contrast to Stewart, he pointed out I was a person of greater influence. I thought, "Kennedy . . . running for Mayor of Vancouver, and less significant?"

Judge Affleck doubled the fine that my lawyer and the prosecutor had agreed upon. If I had made a statement, this is what I would have said:

Sometimes the courts are wrong. Often our governments are wrong. The legal system should not be handed to private corporate interests like Kinder Morgan, converting our law enforcement agencies into private cops for the fossil fuel industry.

The courts, the government, and the respectable institutions that serve democracies must not be converted into the instruments of ecocide. If we have a future, if we succeed in averting the worst, future courts will find this judge, this court, and this government guilty of crimes against the biosphere.

Nonviolent civil disobedience is essential in solidarity with Indigenous land defenders. Nonviolent civil disobedience is essential in solidarity with our children and grandchildren.

We stand in solidarity with Mother Earth—even as we weep, still we stand.

ROMILLY CAVANAUGH,
Professional Engineer

Biography

Romilly Cavanaugh stands in solidarity with Indigenous Peoples, and gives thanks for being able to live and work on the unceded, unsurrendered, and traditional territories of the Tsleil-Waututh, Squamish, and Musqueam Peoples in so-called Vancouver, BC.

Romilly has had an environmental consulting company for over twenty-five years, and currently focuses on assisting organizations to understand and decrease their impacts on the climate. She was an environmental engineer with Trans Mountain from 1991 to 1996, where her responsibilities included conducting environmental impact assessments for construction projects, environmental monitoring and reporting, and obtaining government permits.

Eventually, she could no longer reconcile her love for the natural world with the damage caused by the oil and gas sector that employed her. At the time, Romilly was not aware of the extreme harm that the fossil fuel industry was having on the climate, but she knew of the *Exxon Valdez* tanker spill disaster and how it had resulted in widespread ecological damage in Alaska. So she decided to quit her job.

Romilly earned an undergraduate degree from UBC in 1988, and a master's in sustainability and environmental management from Harvard in 2015. She is a recipient of the Fellow of Engineers Canada award for outstanding contributions to the practice of engineering.

When she isn't working or participating in peaceful protests, Romilly loves to kitesurf, ski, and walk in the forest.

Romilly was arrested on October 15, 2020, and sentenced on February 23, 2023, to twenty-eight days' incarceration. Her sentence is being appealed.

Narrative: Protecting Sqeq'petsin

In October 2020, I travelled to Tk'emlúps (Kamloops) with a friend after I was invited by an Indigenous leader to stand in solidarity with the Secwépemc people, who opposed the Trans Mountain Pipeline Expansion project (TMX) through their unceded, unsurrendered, and traditional territories. Drilling was about to occur at Sqeq'petsin under the so-called North Thompson River, and the leaders were concerned about damage that would be caused by construction, as well as the threat of oil spills from the pipeline. They had heard I'd been arrested at a peaceful protest near the gates of the Trans Mountain tank farm on Burnaby Mountain in March 2018, and thought I might be able to help. After I received the call, I packed up my things and headed there without hesitation to support the land and water protectors.

Once we arrived in Tk'emlúps, we went to the solidarity camp at Sqeq'petsin, where several tents and a kitchen were set up in a grassy field and people were gathered around the Sacred Fire. There I met for the first time several Secwépemc Matriarchs, a Nlaka'pamux Matriarch, and Secwépemc Hereditary Chief Saw-Sês, who spoke with a gentle voice and began to teach me about the river. We warmed ourselves by the fire and got to know one another, then had a friendly and informal conversation about what actions we might take to protect the lands and waters.

Since I had worked as an engineer for Trans Mountain in the past, I knew that directional drilling could result in an accidental blowout, where mud and chemicals spill into the river, which can kill fish directly or smother their eggs with silt. I told the group about that, and affirmed that they were right to be concerned, since these construction techniques are difficult and don't always go as planned.

The next day, we returned to the solidarity camp, and in the late morning, a few members of the group quickly walked along the road towards the gates of the TMX drill site, which was about six hundred metres away. I felt nervous. I was taught as a little girl to follow the rules, and not "cause trouble." In the past, I have found the police intimidating because of the power they wield and the fact that they are permitted to use violence to achieve their goals. But the songs and prayers of the Indigenous land and water protectors helped to alleviate my fears and filled my heart with courage.

When we reached the drill site, I sat against the fence and attached myself to the chain link with a zip tie. Trans Mountain security appeared quickly and began filming and taking photos of us. Saw-Sês stayed with me, since he wanted to protect me. I hoped he would not get arrested, because Indigenous people are often treated much worse by the police than white people. Having seen how police brutalized Indigenous activists and other racialized people at the Ada'itsx (Fairy Creek) peaceful protests against old-growth logging, I was worried for him. But no matter how many times I assured him I would be safe and asked him to leave, Saw-Sês courageously stayed by my side. He whispered to me that I should ask for a blanket when I get to jail, because it's cold in there, which was a helpful tip since I'd never been in prison before. He wanted to protect me, both before and after the arrests.

Several supporters were live-streaming the action and filming our interactions with the police. At one point, some of the supporters left the area. Another action had spontaneously sprung up at a different location, so they were going to see what was happening there. I didn't know until later that three Indigenous leaders, Gwa, April, and Billie, were arrested on the opposite side of the road, near another Trans Mountain work site.

Meanwhile at the drill site, a large number of RCMP officers had arrived. Saw-Sês and I were read our rights and arrested. To make it more challenging for them, I did not walk, requiring that they carry me to the police SUV. This proved to be difficult, because I had on a big winter jacket and was sliding out of it as they lifted me. Eventually one officer grabbed me hard by the arm and twisted it around in an effort to get me to submit. The next day, I had bruises in the shape of fingers where he had painfully squeezed my upper arm. As I had feared, when they arrested Saw-Sês, they used excessive force, shoving him into the police vehicle and injuring his back.

I was taken to the police station, where I was told to take off my clothes except the last layer, which was long underwear—pants and top. A female police officer patted me down searching for weapons or contraband as another observed; then she escorted me through the police station, while I was still just in my underwear and socks. As I entered the hallway lined with holding cells, I could hear Indigenous women singing. I was surprised that it sounded so ethereal in that bleak and oppressive place, but the concrete walls created amazing acoustics. I assumed it was the land and water defenders who had been arrested on the other side of the road.

The holding cell consisted of cinder block walls enclosing a room approximately eight by six feet with a concrete bed covered by a thin cot, and a metal sink and toilet combination. The door was solid and had a small window, maybe six by four inches, that allowed me to see a small slice of hallway just in front of the door. Occasionally an officer would come by to check on me, and at one point offered me a sandwich, which I declined, and some juice. I sang along to any of the songs that I knew, and felt that we were connected by a powerful force that lifted our spirits and bonded us together through our common goal of protecting Mother Earth and our shared sacrifices.

Although it was hard to ascertain how much time was passing, it seemed that the singing went on for at least an hour, then it was quiet. I assumed that the other women had fallen asleep, and I tried to do the same but couldn't. I was given an opportunity to speak to a lawyer, who said that if I didn't sign the paperwork they gave me, I'd be held overnight until I could be brought before a judge.

I found out afterwards that supporters had posted the phone number of the police station on social media, and people had been calling over and over again demanding we be released; it was heartwarming to know that. After approximately seven hours in the cell, I was given paperwork to sign and was released.

It was about 10 p.m., cold and dark outside. The streets around the police station were deserted. As each person was released one by one, friends came to pick us up. Some of us went back to the Sacred Fire, which was about a fifteen-minute drive away, to be warmed by it in body and spirit, to talk about our experiences, and to thank our supporters.

I've been asked why I do this work, and if I believe that it will make a difference. I see it as my moral duty to protect Mother Earth and to encourage others to believe that they too can stand up to injustice, as well as an act of restitution for the atrocities inflicted on Indigenous Peoples in so-called Canada.

I also do this as a huge and heartfelt thank you to the Indigenous children who saved my grandmother from starvation at the St. Paul's Indian Residential School in so-called North Vancouver by showing her what was edible and nutritious in the nearby forest. Although she was of European descent, she was sent to St. Paul's after her father died and her mother was left penniless. Nana was there from age seven to sixteen, and was able to live a full life thanks to the kindness and generosity of the Indigenous children who looked out for her, in spite of the suffering that the Catholic Church was inflicting on them.

There is a beautiful lesson in their example of what it is to be a loving person.

Statement to BC Supreme Court Justice Shelley Fitzpatrick, February 23, 2023

Our arrests occurred on the unceded, unsurrendered, and traditional territories of the Secwépemc people in so-called Kamloops. As such, this court does not have jurisdiction over the land and waters that we were protecting at the time of our arrests; however, the colonial court has refused to acknowledge this reality, and has forced us to appear numerous times under duress with the threat of arrest and additional charges if we were to refuse to do so.

Having witnessed several trials in the past regarding the Trans Mountain Pipeline injunction, I understand that the court wishes to have information about those who stand accused. As such, I have prepared a statement about who I am and what motivated me to participate in this peaceful action.

I strongly believe that all people are of equal value and should be treated the same under the law, regardless of their socio-economic situation, level of education, race, gender, or other characteristics that our society typically uses to judge people. Having been lucky enough to attend university, I have lived a financially comfortable life, while others are not so fortunate, especially Indigenous people, who often live in extreme poverty in what we know as Canada.

I'm fifty-nine-years old, have been a law-abiding citizen my whole life, and have no criminal record. Given my age, I cannot claim youthful exuberance at the time of my arrest, but perhaps I can claim an elder's exasperation from witnessing injustice persist for so long.

I've worked as an environmental engineer for close to thirty-five years and currently focus on projects that address the climate crisis. Imagine working for more than three decades to improve a situation and having so little to show for it, as global emissions continue to increase.

My clients have included First Nations, Fortune 500 companies, small businesses, universities, and all levels of government. I spend most of my workday calculating the greenhouse gas emissions from organizations and helping them to set targets and create reduction plans. Despite my efforts and those of countless others, the climate crisis continues to worsen. I have watched this with a sense of ever-increasing dread about what the future holds for our planet.

Buddhist teachings use the term "right livelihood," which I understand to mean work that does not result in the suffering of sentient beings by harming or killing them. I have endeavoured to follow that principle. I worked for Trans Mountain Pipeline in the 1990s, but found it a disheartening job, since no amount of careful planning or skilful effort could prevent the oil and gas industry from causing harm to people and the planet. There came a time when I could no longer live with myself for benefiting financially from the fossil fuel industry. Having only graduated from university three years prior to starting work there, I was still a young person just starting out, but I decided I needed to quit.

At that time, I naively thought that the government of Canada would take action to protect people and the environment. Instead, it is complicit in crimes against humanity—the climate crisis is a moral and ethical failure that imperils billions of human lives and the survival of countless other species, calling into question our ability to survive on an overheated planet. The government has not only dragged its feet regarding climate change, but also actively funds and endorses the increase in production and use of fossil fuels, all the while criminalizing Indigenous leaders and other climate activists. After waiting decades for the government to address the climate catastrophe, I felt compelled to engage in civil disobedience. I, and many others, have tried various ways to bring about positive changes, all to no avail, including:

- signing petitions
- writing letters to and meeting with government representatives
- giving presentations to individuals, businesses, and universities
- participating in peaceful rallies and marches
- handing out pamphlets and painting signs
- making donations to numerous Indigenous, environmental, and social justice charities.

And yet we are all still on the path to an unlivable planet, and most people are either unaware of that fact, or, sadly, think they have no power to change our trajectory. Individual choices do matter, for example whether one drives a conventional vehicle, travels by air, heats their home with natural gas, or eats meat. However, these choices need to be magnified by the actions of our government, which is currently acting against the best interests of people and the planet. I believed that by getting arrested, I could in some small way change the dialogue and give others hope that we can still prevent the deaths of billions of people from climate change–induced disasters like floods, fires, and famines.

With increasing frequency, we see news of the climate crisis around the world. In April 2022, the United Nations Secretary-General stated: "We are on a pathway to global warming of more than double the 1.5°C limit agreed in Paris. Some Government and business leaders are saying one thing, but doing another. Simply put, they are lying. And the results will be catastrophic."[6]

In September 2022, one-third of Pakistan was under water due to extreme flooding, which displaced almost eight million people, leaving them without food, clean drinking water, shelter, or health care. Thousands have already died.

At the same time, forest fires burning in BC and across the border resulted in the Lower Mainland having the worst air quality in the world, worse than Beijing and Delhi, two cities with notoriously polluted skies. By October, the air quality in Chilliwack was classified as hazardous, meaning that adverse health effects could result, including respiratory and cardiovascular distress or failure.

In November 2021, the Fraser Valley was hit with severe flooding. More than 600,000 farm animals died, all highways east of Vancouver were impassable including Highways 1, 3, 5, and 7—people lost their homes and their livelihoods. Tragically, a few even lost their lives. Some media outlets have described this as a one-in-one-thousand-year event, meaning that, in all likelihood, this wouldn't happen again for another thousand years, but that was before climate change. Those estimates are based on historical data. That world doesn't exist anymore. Engineers cannot say at this point how frequent these events will be because the climate has changed so dramatically, but we could see another flood like that in the next one hundred years, or fifty, or ten.

In addition to the deleterious climate impacts that the Trans Mountain Pipeline Expansion would have, the project also significantly increases the risks of oil spills into the marine environment, because the company intends to load over four hundred tanker vessels per year at their Burnaby facility.

After an ecosystem has been damaged by an oil spill, it can take decades to recover, and some species never will. This was observed with the 1989 *Exxon Valdez* tanker spill in Alaska. To this day, you can turn over rocks on the beach and still see and smell oil. Scientists estimate the accident killed 250,000 seabirds, 3,100 marine mammals, and billions of salmon and herring eggs. The orca whale pod that was affected has not produced a single calf since the spill, and the last members are dying out. The Southern Resident orcas that live off the south coast of BC are already endangered, and the Trans Mountain expansion project would put them at even greater risk.

When I worked for Trans Mountain, the industry considered recovering 10 to 15 percent of a marine spill to be a successful outcome. Industry proponents will say that oil spill equipment has improved since then, but the reality is that very little has changed, as we've seen with more recent spills.

One of the saddest things I've ever heard in the workplace was at an oil spill conference I attended in the US, where the operator of a large vessel designed to recover oil spilled into the ocean described how he located the oil slick at night. He listened for the cries of birds and animals who were trapped in the poisonous layer floating on the water's surface, and would steer the ship in that direction so that the skimming equipment could pull the oil into a holding tank. It was clear that the wildlife would be smothered in the tank, then he laughed, which shows how desensitized people can become to the suffering of nature when working in harmful industries.

The impacts of the *Deepwater Horizon* drill rig explosion in 2010 illustrate that oil spill technology is grossly inadequate at containing major marine spills. That incident resulted in extensive damage to the Gulf of Mexico's environment, as well as US$5.9 billion in economic losses. What right does the oil and gas industry have to destroy nature and deprive those working in other sectors from earning a living?

Considering all that is at stake, and the fact that Indigenous Peoples did not give free, prior, and informed content for the pipeline expansion, this project should never have been approved by the federal government, which has shirked its regulatory duties and taken an immoral stance that will be harshly viewed by future generations. The co-accused and I stood up to protect Mother Earth, and are prepared to face the consequences meted out by the colonial court system.

On September 15, 2022, hundreds of legal professionals in the UK signed an open letter calling on their profession to actively support meaningful action on climate change.[7] Madame Justice, as a legal professional yourself, and a person who holds a great deal of power, you too could take a principled stance and make decisions that safeguard future generations, while still fulfilling your responsibilities as a judge. Their open letter states:

> In prosecutions concerning climate protest, both prosecutors and defence lawyers should ensure the court is aware that a) breach of the 1.5°C limit risks mass loss of life and the end of the rule of law and that b) there is substantial evidence that governments and businesses, individually and collectively, continue to pursue courses of action which they know to be inconsistent

with that limit. The courts must apply the law to such cases, but lawyers must ensure that they do so on the basis of the relevant facts.

Thank you for listening to my statement, and I ask that you have an open mind and an open heart when making your decision.

TIM BRAY,
Software Engineer and Writer

Biography

Tim Bray was born in Edmonton and brought up in Beirut, Lebanon, son of a farm boy turned professor of agriculture and a chemist turned librarian. He has lived in Vancouver between 1983 and 1987 and then again since 1992. He has been extremely lucky, stumbling into a talent for computer programming and online writing at just the right moment in history to yield (modest) fame and (adequate) fortune. He has a BSc and an honorary DSc from the University of Guelph. He is probably best known for helping develop Internet Standards and engaging in the big online technology debates, most recently as a fervent cryptocurrency skeptic and decentralized social media advocate.

In 2019, as a VP at Amazon's cloud-computing division, his activism surfaced in a surge of employee evangelism urging Amazon to become part of the climate-emergency solution. Subsequent activism led to his leaving the company in May 2020 in protest of the company's firing of activists who spoke out against the treatment of warehouse workers in the early days of the COVID-19 pandemic.

Tim keeps busy with parenting, open-source software, photography, Wikipedia editing, and miscellaneous activism. He blogs at tbray.org and is on Mastodon at @timbray@cosocial.ca. He is a hyper-overentitled well-off straight cis white man, playing the game of life at the lowest difficulty level, and tries to remain conscious of that fact.

Tim was arrested in front of the gates of Kinder Morgan on March 17, 2018. Since it was the first day of protest, he received lenient punishment in the form of a $500 fine.

Narrative: A Soft Brush with the Law

I was arrested on St. Patrick's Day 2018, a fine sunny West Coast spring afternoon. The first thing I want to say is a loud thank you to our gracious hosts on Burnaby Mountain, the good people of the Coast Salish Nations, whose unceded territory we were on. They were friendly, inspirational, supportive, eloquent, and politically savvy. This activism would have been inconceivable without their leadership and support, and they deserve the largest share of credit for any good we might end up accomplishing.

It was the first day of protests, so the media were there in force. The online support was widespread and warm, which was nice, except they repeatedly lauded our "courage." Which struck me as a bit silly; if this was a "brush with the law," it was a soft-bristled make-up brush. Now bear in mind that I am speaking from a position of maximum privilege as a grey-bearded, clean-cut, well-off white guy. The legal and financial consequences for me were mostly trivial, and there was an awesome support organization in place for those less privileged than me.

It was a pleasant day, all told. I took public transit to the protest, marched to Kinder Morgan's front gates, sat in the sun for a few hours singing songs, and was eventually courteously escorted away by affable officers. The only mildly scary bit was when a cop made a little speech claiming that getting arrested could damage one's ability to travel, get a job, volunteer, and so on. This was a pack of lies; I have since learned that it's standard police procedure.

It was a bit boring in places partly because I hadn't brought my phone, on advice that police like to confiscate them, then neglect to return them. In the event, nobody seemed to care what I had in my pockets.

I think I hardly need to argue why it's a toxic, stupid idea to spend billions in public funds to pump some of the world's dirtiest hydrocarbons away from the Northern Alberta tar sands, leaving a hellscape post-extraction, to send the diluted tar down to the Pacific, and then to load it every day onto tankers that will imperil Vancouver's harbour, wildlife, and people. In the process, this project adds fuel to the furnace that is driving climate catastrophe toward our children.

On the day of my arrest, we sang our songs and stood our ground, but the federal Liberal government, at the behest of its moneyed friends in the petroleum conspiracy, went ahead and built the pipeline. It's our profound hope that it'll be the last one ever, and my personal dream that it'll prove uneconomic and get shut down before it realizes its full potential for climate degradation. In any case, now is not the time to stop the activism.

Delay of fossil fuel infrastructure is the planet's friend. The economics of tar sands oil are still lousy, and every month the disastrous effects of global warming become more evident. Every month, renewable and battery technologies get better and cheaper. Which is to say, we don't really need to stop this pipeline, we just need to slow it down and make its awfulness visible; then go back and do it again and again. There's a not-bad chance that eventually the other side will, so to speak, run out of gas.

Let me break the fourth wall here and speak as a co-editor of the book you are now reading. As I work on the jail-time narratives from other arrestees, alternately graceful, funny, and terrifying, I am consumed with rage at the judicial system. It is apparently content to allow itself to be used as a hammer to beat down resistance to stupid and toxic rent-seeking behaviour, oblivious to issues of the greater good. At no point has anyone in the judiciary looked in the mirror as they jailed yet another group of self-sacrificing people trying to throw themselves between TMX's engine of destruction and the earth that sustains us, and asked themselves, Are we on the right side here?

Of necessity, the law is constructed of formalisms. But life is constructed on a basis of the oceans and the atmosphere and the mesh of interdependent ecosystems they sustain. At some point, the formalisms need to find the flexibility to favour life, not death. It seems little to ask.

My main disappointment is that in 2018, we tried to act as leaders but fell short. Suppose ten thousand people, instead of a few dozen, decided to do what we did, each requiring police intervention to process all those contempt charges. The day I was arrested they had thirty or so police officers at work, and it took them hours to arrest us and write us up. Suppose there were a hundred times more protesters? There just aren't enough police in the region to manage the job. Polls say that a vast majority of local people despise the pipeline project. We need to get them to stand up from their sofas and sit down in front of the things that need to be sat in front of.

Together as a people we can stop this noxious project, if we want to. And if we can't, we can at least ensure that it is the last foolish pipeline anyone will attempt to build.

Statement to BC Supreme Court Justice Kenneth Affleck, June 1, 2018

Good day, my lord. I am a businessman and an engineer, and consequently a numbers guy. I wanted to draw the court's attention to one number: 410. That is the amount of CO_2 in the atmosphere in parts per million. It is the highest number ever recorded, and it is climbing. The best climate science models, with this number as input, predict devastation for many nations and peoples; they are terrifying.[8]

It used to be the case that the biggest variables in the climate models were places where the data was weak, things like marine CO_2 absorption. These days, all the big variables are around policy and human behaviour, how much carbon we choose to emit. So our future is in our own hands.

My lord, you and I are of an age where we may not directly experience the devastation which is becoming increasingly likely. However, our children's generation, and their children's, will. This troubles me greatly.

When one confronts an impending disaster, extreme measures are sometimes called for. If you're a sixty-two-year-old businessman, sitting down in front of a gate on Burnaby Mountain feels like an extreme measure; who knows, possibly it will create back pressure against the oncoming disaster.

Finally, on the subject of the rule of law. I have a slightly unusual perspective in that I spent a large part of my youth in the Middle East, in a society where the rule of law obtained at best weakly. So my appreciation of its virtues is perhaps above average; the rule of law and a lot of luck have blessed me with a relatively untroubled life. But I think that the rule of law and civil disobedience, with an emphasis on "civil," can be good neighbours in a civilized society. That's why I'm here today doing what I'm doing.

When I was discussing my options in this proceeding with my lawyer, and there was some reasonable prospect of pursuing a not-guilty plea on the basis of lack of obstruction, she said, "On the other hand, Gandhi always pled guilty." Now, I'm not comparing myself to Gandhi. But it's good company to be in. That's all.

ROBERT A. HACKETT,

PhD, Professor Emeritus, SFU School of Communication

Biography

Although unaware of it as a child, Bob Hackett's journey on planet Earth began in the heartland of a former empire built on coal, colonization, and the slave trade—London, England. His parents, at that time a bank clerk and a schoolteacher, moved the family to Canada in 1958, settling in Richmond, BC.

Bob earned degrees in political science at Simon Fraser University and Queen's University, and taught in the School of Communication at SFU from 1984 until 2018. His focus there was on news media as political communication, media democratization as a social movement, peace journalism, and more recently, media and the climate crisis.

Wonderful colleagues and students helped to produce a number of often collaborative articles and eight books, including *Sustaining Democracy?: Journalism and the Politics of Objectivity* (1998); *The Missing News: Filters and Blind Spots in Canada's Press* (2002); *Remaking Media: The Struggle to Democratize Public Communication* (2006); and *Journalism and Climate Crisis: Public Engagement, Media Alternatives* (2017).

Bob co-founded several public-interfacing media activism and education projects: NewsWatch Canada with Donald Gutstein, researching biases in the news agenda; the annual Media Democracy Days, celebrating media reform and independent media; and the organization known as OpenMedia, advocating for an affordable and uncensored internet. He and his partner Angelika raised two daughters in Burnaby, Karina and Melanie, and now live in Powell River, a scenic coastal town on traditional Tla'amin lands and named after an architect of the Indian Act and residential schools. The Tla'amin have requested the city to find a more appropriate name as a small contribution towards reconciliation.

———————

Bob was arrested on March 23, 2018, and sentenced to pay a $500 fine on June 6, 2018.

Narrative: A Professor Gets an Education at the Front Lines

I'm standing at the end of a banner on a blustery March day, waiting my turn to be arrested. Next to me are several other climate and land defenders, including two parliamentarians—Kennedy Stewart (later, mayor of Vancouver), and national Green Party leader Elizabeth May. Behind me, other land defenders have fastened themselves to the gate leading into a modern Mordor—the Burnaby Terminal or tank farm, where Trans Mountain stores toxic bitumen.

What led me to this point? My journey started in high school. I became interested in political theory and action as a guide to a meaningful life and positive social change. This was, after all, the 1960s—years of protest. From the dragon lady who taught our French class to the Soviet occupation of Czechoslovakia and the American invasion of Vietnam, established power gave plenty of reason for cultural and political rebellion. At the same time, having been bullied for years in middle school, I developed an instinctive distrust of the crowd. I could never be a populist.

So if you believe in politics as an expression of ethics, but you resent authority and distrust the crowd, where do you go? To a kind of libertarianism—the celebration of the autonomous and reasoning individual. My favourite text was *On Liberty*, a classical rationale for liberal democracy by British philosopher John Stuart Mill. My political heroes were leaders who courageously fought nonviolently for social justice—Gandhi, Martin Luther King Jr., Salvador Allende, and Henry David Thoreau, a pioneer in the concept and practice of civil disobedience. That commitment to individual autonomy and reason still resonates in my statement to the court.

But I soon realized that the classical liberal celebration of the abstract individual is fundamentally inadequate, and even justifies profound inequality. People need not only the kind of negative freedom that libertarians celebrate (freedom from governments preventing what you want to do), but also positive freedom—access to the resources (housing, medical care, income, livable environment) required to meaningfully exercise their enshrined constitutional rights. Inequality looms when the latter form of freedom is denied.

In the 1970s, that line of thinking led me to democratic socialism, and to membership in its pale pink reflection, the New Democratic Party. But at that time, the Anglo-Canadian left was almost oblivious to colonialism's devastating impact on Indigenous Peoples and to the unfolding ecological crisis.

Like many Canadians across the political spectrum, I was barely aware of scientists' growing alarm about the dangers of global warming, starting with NASA scientist James Hansen's testimony to the US Congress in 1988. My own academic research continued to focus on media framing of other issues, like inequality, war and peace, and human rights. By the early 2000s, though, the weather was becoming visibly angrier. A high-water mark of public concern was Al Gore's 2006 slide-show-cum-film, *An Inconvenient Truth*. Briefly, it seemed that even establishment politicians and parties were taking the issue seriously. My research focus shifted towards media and climate change, including a project with the Canadian Centre for Policy Alternatives.

Academic publications are one thing. But what about engagement as a citizen? Canada is notionally a democracy whose health depends on public engagement. In 2014 I finally jumped into pro-climate activism, when my hometown of Burnaby was catapulted into the front line. In January of that year, my MP Kennedy Stewart called a town hall meeting. Scores of people jammed a community hall to hear his startling summary of the Kinder Morgan pipeline project and what threats it could pose. Homes along the proposed route could be expropriated. The expanded pipeline could rupture, as it already had in 2007, spewing toxic tar and other chemicals over a Burnaby neighbourhood. A massive increase in tanker traffic in the local waterways could spawn oil spills. It seemed that Burnaby was to become a "sacrifice zone," an area considered expendable if it stands in the way of expanding the fossil fuel juggernaut. These concerns did not even consider the global impact of unleashing billions more barrels of Athabasca bitumen for overseas export.

What a jolt! The next four years changed my political focus. There seemed to be well-travelled avenues to stop this madness. The National Energy Board, tasked to review fossil fuel projects in the public interest, allowed written interventions from people who were "directly affected." Kennedy offered help from his office. Driven by hope and alarm, folks in my townhouse complex near the proposed pipeline route got together and mustered dozens of objections to the NEB. We had more "directly affected" intervenors than any other neighbourhood in Burnaby.

That route got us nowhere. The process was maddeningly complex, doubtless intended to discourage genuine public input. The Harper government had cancelled the option of public hearings. Many intervenors soon dropped out of the process. Others turned to more public opposition.

On a frigid winter evening, I emceed a community protest meeting outside a local hotel where Kinder Morgan had set up an open house to display its proposal. Kennedy Stewart and Bob Chamberlin from the Union of BC Indian Chiefs were two of the speakers. Afterwards, we did an "intersaction," walking legally around the nearby intersection with signs—earning honks of appreciation from drivers, and an escort from an RCMP officer who insisted on video-recording us "for our own protection." Yeah, right.

Another avenue, for many, was electoral politics. I had quit the BC NDP in 2012 when, as the Official Opposition, it voted for Premier Christy Clark's liquefied natural gas (LNG) pipe dream, after months of criticizing it. Appreciative of Kennedy's work at the federal level, I rejoined when the new provincial leader John Horgan promised to use "every tool in the toolbox" to block the Kinder Morgan pipeline.

Another glimmer of hope was the promise from the federal Liberals' new leader, Justin Trudeau, to redo the process by which the NEB had rubber-stamped the Kinder Morgan proposal.

Memorably, one of his pre-election slogans was "Governments might grant permits, but only communities can grant permission."

After winning the 2015 election, rather than scrap the NEB process and start over, Trudeau launched a three-member federal review panel to hold public hearings along the proposed pipeline route. The closer the travelling road show got to Vancouver from Edmonton, the more vehement became the opposition, from residents, Indigenous groups, local councils, and environmental NGOs. The panel generated a surprisingly decent report, raising several fundamental questions that the feds should answer before approving the Kinder Morgan project. Then—nothing. No cabinet minister even read the document, a panel insider confided to me. The process let opponents express their concerns, which the panel summarized in the form of critical questions that the government should address before proceeding with the project; but the government ignored them. On November 29, 2016, Justin Trudeau marred my younger daughter's birthday—and her generation's future—by approving the pipeline. The community of activists was devastated.

The futility of the institutional avenues led me to recall Thoreau, Gandhi, and King. So when the Tsleil-Waututh Nation asked its settler allies to put their bodies on the line to help stop Kinder Morgan and bring the government to its senses, I was primed. After all, I was one of twenty thousand people who had signed a pledge to do whatever it takes to slay that beast.

If MP Stewart had supplied the informational nourishment, the courage and leadership of Indigenous people captured the heart. They were, after all, defending their ancestral homeland and waters, on unceded territory, and in line with the UN Declaration on the Rights of Indigenous Peoples (UNDRIP). The Tsleil-Waututh Nation commissioned a detailed study of the pipeline's potential impact. They erected the Kwekwecnewtxw Watch House near the Burnaby Mountain storage-tank facility. They organized events like a canoe blockade across Burrard Inlet to the Westridge terminal. Through the remarkable George family and others, they spoke frequently at public gatherings.

So when the two of my most admired parliamentarians said they would risk arrest at Tsleil-Waututh request, the time seemed ripe. But as the day approached, my mind churned. What were the potential repercussions of arrest? In particular, with governments increasingly pulling up the drawbridges, would it affect my international travel? What about my keynote address at an academic conference in Oregon and a month-long extended fellowship in New Zealand—both opportunities to acquaint international audiences with our resistance to Trans Mountain. At nonviolent civil disobedience training sessions near the Watch House, experienced activists suggested it might amount to little more than paying a parking ticket fine. But they took pains to emphasize uncertainty. What would we actually be charged with? What was the penalty?

Undecided even the night before, I struggled vainly to focus on a long-ago classmate's travel stories over a beer. He wrongly thought I was "bored." Hardly. I was wrestling with what seemed one of the most consequential decisions I'd ever make. As the day arrived, dozens of people gathered at the Watch House and walked through the woods to the gates of the flammable material storage facility, alongside Kennedy, his partner Jeanette Ashe, and my partner Angelika Hackett. Their support helped me decide to join the potential arrestees at the gates, where I was introduced to Elizabeth May and others. Even among a lot of white middle-class people outside their comfort zones, I was loud in expressing my anxiety about what the charge would be. The police officers there seemed to downplay it; one said they "just want to have everyone disperse."

When the local constabulary arrived to arrest us, one group at a time, the spectacle unfolded. First to be led off were the two MPs, a phalanx of police surrounding these terribly dangerous criminals, with TV newshounds thrusting mics towards them—and leaving once the MPs were processed in the specially erected tent. The officers' restraint and professionalism were appreciated, but also highlighted the double standard of policing in this country. We were a gathering of mostly white middle-class settlers, including many seniors, and accompanied by two high-profile parliamentarians. Compare our treatment to the violence inflicted upon Indigenous land defenders in Wet'suwet'en territory and elsewhere.

The pattern is not random, unfortunately.[9] I would understand if some think the acronym RCMP stands for racism, colonialism, militarism, and patriarchy.

There followed meetings with lawyers and six visits to the Robson Square law courts over the next eight weeks. The first session offered the most jarring moment. Justice Kenneth Affleck proclaimed that he was raising the charges from civil to criminal contempt. Yikes! Our violation of a court injunction, explained Judge Affleck, was a public action and brought into question the reputation of the court.

Reputation for what? Its jurisdictional claim over unceded Indigenous territories? Its apparent indifference to the climate emergency or the principles of UNDRIP?

On June 6, I followed my lawyer's advice and pleaded guilty, read my statement to the sparsely attended court, and paid a $500 fine. A bit anti-climactic (as well as anti-climate). Sadly, I missed a chance to supercharge my final appearance. After hearing my statement, the judge asked me an unexpected question, perhaps seeking some kind of absolution: Did I understand why he had no choice but to find me guilty? By that point, my stamina drained, I mumbled assent. Had I been prepared, or had I the on-the-run wit of a polished politician, I would have replied that there's always a choice. For example, British juries (though not judges) have recently been acquitting law-breaking but nonviolent climate activists.[10]

When will a Canadian judge have the courage and wisdom to recognize the right of citizens to take extraordinary action in the face of climate emergency? Or the jurisdiction of Indigenous law in their unceded ancestral lands? Or of international climate obligations over short-term domestic interests?

How did this episode affect my life? Overall, frankly, it was a blip, sometimes stressful, but always worthwhile. It wasn't a big topic of discussion with my mostly apolitical friends. Several other ex-friends have drifted so far rightward on climate or other issues that we are no longer in contact. Without bonds of kinship, friendships take effort to maintain, and to me, shared values are as important as shared memories. There were other inconveniences. I was able to attend the conference in Oregon without incident, but delayed my long-awaited fellowship to the University of Canterbury in New Zealand, given the uncertainties of court proceedings. I still wonder whether the thousands of dollars in legal fees could have been spent more strategically elsewhere, like donations to RAVEN and other land, water, and climate defenders.

The plus side of the ledger was vastly richer. My eight years of active involvement in eco-resistance has led to rewarding new friendships and collaborations, including with my fellow arrestees, as well as in my new hometown of Powell River, which had sent a contingent to Burnaby Mountain. As one of my Burnaby neighbours facetiously put it, "I'm very grateful to Kinder Morgan for bringing together such wonderful people."

For a few months, I and other arrestees were occasionally placed on public pedestals at meetings. I and some fellow convicts had our photos taken at a fundraiser with American eco-star Bill McKibben. We appreciated the recognition, tempered by awareness that others are making far greater sacrifices, including Indigenous land defenders far away from TV cameras and later arrestees knowingly facing prison time.

Still, I proudly placed my mug shot, which Angelika extracted from the massive files of police-gathered evidence, on our living room wall. It's next to my grandfather's plaques, signed by Churchill and the Queen, commending his service in the British army and the royal honour guard. I'd like to think pipeline resisters are also offering public service.

During a pretrial legal aid session on April 8, 2018, fellow arrestee Zack pointed urgently to his cell phone with some astonishing breaking news. Kinder Morgan was rethinking the pipeline and suspending all nonessential expenditures! While the company blamed jurisdictional disputes between BC and Alberta, we felt sure that our protest movement's unexpected strength played a role.

Jubilation erupted. Had we won? Would the Crown drop charges? Fat chance. Within two months, the Trudeau government rocked the political world by announcing it would buy the pipeline, in effect bailing out the company at taxpayers' expense—an expense that keeps climbing.

That's when it really dawned on me. My statement to the court was too deferential. I had framed it as a struggle between protesters and a foreign-owned company. But in fact, we were taking on the Canadian state: the courts, acting as a protective shield for extractivist capital; the police, with an iron fist behind a selectively genteel demeanour; the federal government, whose interlocking with fossil fuel industries extends to directly financing infrastructure; Canada's major banks, financial enablers; and major swaths of the corporate-owned Canadian media, especially the Postmedia newspaper chain. All these are components of what researchers have labelled the "petrobloc," or the anti-climate "regime of obstruction," or Oil's Deep State.[11] Was Canada itself becoming a petro-state? Is it one already?

My rethinking of Canada owed much to Indigenous teachings and leadership. The Tsleil-Waututh Nation admirably guided and motivated the local resistance. Indigenous people's resistance, and their legal standing, may be the best chance to halt the machinery of an economic system tending towards increased human inequality, misery and the death of millions. The concept of "exterminism," introduced by the late British historian E.P. Thompson vis-à-vis nuclear militarism, might also apply to global capitalism.[12] But it's a struggle for justice as well as survival. The death of thousands of children in residential schools is only the bayonet's edge of a colonial machine. The Canadian state rests upon a history of the appropriation of Indigenous lands and suppression of Indigenous Peoples.[13]

From these realities, some would reject Canada itself as a glorified colonial corporation. I prefer to regard Canada as an experiment in progress, based on a shared aspiration for a socially just, ecologically sustainable, and peaceable home. I hope this can be brought to fruition through individual acts of conscience in concert with mass movements employing a range of tactics, from legal challenges and electoral politics to nonviolent direct action, aiming not just for resistance, but for transformation.

Statement to BC Supreme Court Justice Kenneth Affleck, June 6, 2018

I am a professor of communication at Simon Fraser University on unceded Coast Salish territory, with a doctorate in political studies from Queen's University. I'd like to apologize to the court if my actions called into question the court's authority, when my concern is with the dangers of the Kinder Morgan pipeline. At the time of my arrest, I specifically asked the officer whether this was indeed

civil contempt—which I took to be a matter between the protectors and Kinder Morgan.

I have studied and engaged in Canadian politics for almost
fifty years, with no previous arrests. My recent academic research
concerns media, climate crisis, and the tactics of fossil fuel corporations like Kinder Morgan. The more I learned, the more I became
alarmed about their excessive influence in our democracy, as well as
the environmental risks, from global warming to the local threat of
a Burnaby Mountain tank farm expansion to the 30,000 members of
SFU's community, my second home since my undergrad days there.

Collectively, we are in a state of planetary emergency, yet political institutions are not responding with the urgency and integrity
required. I participated as a directly affected homeowner in the
National Energy Board's review process in 2014, and again in the
2016 Federal Ministerial Review panel. But my own experience as
well as recent revelations indicate that these were never intended
as good faith consultation exercises; the outcome was predetermined. There is growing reason to believe that the unaccountable
power of extractivist capital, and the unresponsiveness of governments to citizens, are major threats to public confidence in the
state's institutions.

My action on March 23 was one of personal conscience—a way
to open conversations with friends and family, and to stand alongside my city, my province, my MP Kennedy Stewart, and above
all, the Indigenous Peoples who have shown remarkable leadership on behalf of all of us living on their unceded lands. Having
visited countries struggling to emerge from dictatorship or civil
war, I understand the fundamental importance of a judicial system
with appropriate independence from the state. The actions of most
of the protectors who have been arrested are in a long tradition
of peaceful dissent—from the American civil rights movement
and elsewhere.

The intention is not to undermine or escape the rule of law,
but to call attention to injustice, and to encourage the evolution
of law to become more responsive to the desperate needs of our
time—including the rights of nature and future generations, and
international obligations like the Paris climate accord and the UN
Declaration on the Rights of Indigenous Peoples.

As former Alberta legislator Kevin Taft put it in his book *Oil's Deep State*: "The people fighting to block the expansion of pipelines . . . aren't just fighting to save the environment. Whether or not they realize it, they are fighting to save democracy. The biggest advances in addressing global warming will come from liberating our democratic institutions from their captors."

ROBERT STOWE,
MD, Neurologist

Biography

Dr. Robert Stowe, his sister Barbara, and Quaker parents Irving and Dorothy Stowe were founders of Greenpeace in the early 1970s. At that time, Bob was vice-chair of the Student Action Committee on Amchitka, which mobilized 10,000 high school students in a student strike and march to the US consulate in Vancouver to protest an impending underground nuclear test.

After studying political science at UBC, during which he served on the National Policy Council of the United Nations Association of Canada and on an advisory board for Canada World Youth, Bob completed his MD at Queen's, neurology residency at the University of Toronto, and behavioural neurology fellowship at Harvard Medical School. After ten years at the University of Pittsburgh, he moved to UBC, where he is currently Clinical Professor of Psychiatry and Neurology, practices clinical behavioural neurology and neuropsychiatry, and leads a research program into the genetics and biochemistry of schizophrenia.

Bob is a member of the UBC Clinical Research Ethics Board, and has served on neurotoxic exposure research grant review panels for the American Institute of the Biological Sciences.

Bob was arrested on March 19, 2018, was sentenced on June 8, 2018, and was fined $500.

Narrative: The Reawakening of an Activist

I have a confession to make. The day I was arrested on Burnaby Mountain (March 19, 2018), I was actually not planning on it at all.

I came mainly to support my sister Barbara, who was protesting despite my efforts to dissuade her.

Of course, I was opposed to the TMX (then Kinder Morgan) pipeline, being aware of the increase in tanker traffic it would occasion, and consequently, of the risk of a devastating spill in the Salish Sea. I had been horrified by aerial footage of the tar sands project, which reminded me of scenes of Mordor from the *Lord of the Rings* films, and was aware of the bloated carbon footprint of the whole enterprise. And I had gone to the mountain with Barbara and my partner Jose just nine days earlier, in a planned rendezvous with our old friend Bill Darnell. At that protest against the pipeline, organized by the Coast Salish First Nations (Protect the Inlet), and attended by over five thousand people, I was moved and energized by the crowds, and by the powerful speeches I heard by Union of BC Indian Chiefs Grand Chief Stewart Phillip, his wife Joan Phillip, Tsleil-Waututh Elders and Indigenous land protectors Swaysen (Will) George and Ta'ah (Amy) George,[14] Lubicon Cree Nation member and Greenpeace climate campaigner Melina Laboucan-Massimo, and other Indigenous land defenders. Finally, I was moved by the commitment and resolve that was evident among the protesters, particularly those from the Coast Salish First Nations, who in many respects stand to lose the most if this dinosaur project is ever completed.

However, on this next visit, I decided to join Barbara in attending an information session, conducted mainly by Kris Hermes of the Terminal City Legal Collective and Tsleil-Waututh land defenders, intended to provide potential arrestees with legal information and advice on how to conduct oneself if the police arrived, threatened charges, and/or "got physical." While I was mainly driven by concern over what Barbara was potentially getting herself into, once there, I started to wonder if I had the guts to join her.

There was never any question of "should" in my mind: my statement to the court amply illustrates all the reasons why nonviolent civil disobedience against the pipeline seemed the right thing to do. The main thing holding me back was concern about whether an arrest would jeopardize my medical licence, but it seemed that the potential consequences were not as dire as I had imagined. Typically, I was told, a first offence would incur a charge of civil contempt of court (which doesn't carry a criminal record), and a fine of $250. A conversation with Mike Hudema, Greenpeace Canada's lead Climate and Energy campaigner at the time, who was there on the mountain live-streaming the protests and arrests, was also helpful in putting things into perspective.

In the back of my mind, niggling away, was a remark made by a physician colleague who had presided over the influential US-led group Physicians for Social Responsibility. When I mentioned my history of student activism to her, which included co-organizing a student strike that saw over 10,000 high school students march to the US consulate in downtown Vancouver to protest an impending underground hydrogen bomb test at Amchitka Island in the Aleutians, and supporting my Quaker parents in co-founding Greenpeace back in the early 1970s, she asked somewhat pointedly, "Yes, and what have you done lately?"

That one remark started the wheels turning, and poked away insistently at my conscience. While I've supported Greenpeace and many other human rights, environmental, peace, and social and climate justice groups for many years, both financially and with advocacy work (letter writing, petitions, attending demonstrations, etc.), this paled in comparison to the commitment and engagement of my younger days, and especially to the daunting legacy of social justice, peace, and environmental activism left by my parents, which seems to loom larger and larger the older I get.

And I thought about the courage and commitment of the volunteers and staff I've met while visiting Greenpeace offices around the world, many of whom have engaged in nonviolent civil disobedience, sometimes literally risking life and liberty for the cause. And last but not least, I was impressed by the commitment of Indigenous protesters here in BC, many of whom cannot even afford legal representation, yet who put their liberty on the line time and time again, in the service of their beliefs and the protection of their ecosystems, communities, and traditional ways of life for current and future generations.

Finally, on the mountain, I ran into my friend Rex Weyler, an erudite and wise journalist and writer, and the elder statesman and historian of Greenpeace, who has also courageously put himself out there so many times over the years in the service of his beliefs. Rex told me he was planning on zip-tying himself to the gate at the Burnaby Mountain Kinder Morgan terminal, with the expectation that he would be arrested that day. This may have been the icing on the cake, when I decided, "I'm in!"

After our two-hour training workshop, a group of us marched resolutely to a gate at the tank farm, hoisting a banner proclaiming "PROTECT THE WATER, LAND, CLIMATE" and "STOP KINDER MORGAN," the text flanking Protect the Inlet's clenched-fist logo. As we marched, we chanted, "People gonna rise like the water, gotta calm this crisis down. Hear the voice of my great-granddaughter, sayin' climate justice now!"

I then marched to the gate, and Rex, who already had one arm tied down, helped zip-tie me to it. Barbara was already zipped in place, as was Nancy McLean, a children's bookseller and mother whose father had worked on the tar sands and had told her horror stories about the experience.

After the police arrived, Constable Nicolas Ste Croix read us the injunction and threatened us with arrest, then left us alone for a few minutes to see if we would leave voluntarily. Then one female and three male officers returned a few minutes later to arrest me, trailed by a CBC cameraman and other photojournalists, while nearby protesters chanted to drumbeats, "The people, united, will never be defeated!" Refusing to untie myself, I informed the officers that I would not resist arrest, nevertheless. One of them cut the zip tie, and I was marched off (albeit very civilly—no cuffs were used, and not even a hand was placed on me) to a nearby booking table in the woods. I was shaking visibly, and my teeth were chattering, but as I told the officers, it was not from fear but from the damp, bone-chilling cold that day on the mountain. I was told that by entering a five-metre radius stipulated by an injunction issued by Justice Kenneth Affleck of the BC Supreme Court, I had violated the injunction, and would be charged with civil contempt of court. Rex and Barbara were arrested next.

After the three of us were booked and released, as we walked down the mountain, we ran into David Suzuki and Ta'ah. As David approached, grinning, he yelled to us, "Troublemakers!" He gave Rex a handshake and a hug and said, "You know, I was telling people that you were the first guy I heard talking to me about Kinder Morgan, ten years ago!" Ta'ah said to Rex, "You got arrested . . . good for you!" and gave him a big hug.

Rex then introduced us to David and Ta'ah as the son and

daughter of Dorothy and Irving Stowe, "from the early Greenpeace days." I related that our family lived around the corner from David in Point Grey in those days, and that our cat, Haida (sleek black-furred, with a triangular Siamese face, a white bib, and white-tipped paws) completely ignored the television set, except when David Suzuki appeared on the screen. Whereupon Haida would go up to the TV and start meowing excitedly, then go around to the back of the set to try to find him! (We could never figure out whether she thought David was a cat because of his beard, or if he fed her catnip on his walks in the neighbourhood!) David and the rest of us got a good chuckle out of that anecdote: a little comic relief on an otherwise rather stressful day.

We were the first, but not the only, protesters arrested that day; at least eleven others followed us. And four days later, Elizabeth May, MP for Saanich–Gulf Islands and leader of the federal Green Party at the time, and Kennedy Stewart, NDP MP for Burnaby and future mayor of Vancouver, were among the dozens of others who joined the ranks of arrestees.

Three weeks later, a process server arrived on my front door-step with a two-and-a-half-inch stack of documents, including a Short Notice Application by Kinder Morgan requiring me to appear in BC Supreme Court only four days later, on April 11, 2018. Kinder Morgan was moving to add us (at this point, 168 protesters in all) to their lawsuit, claiming millions of dollars in damages. This lawsuit was later dropped, thanks to the NDP's enactment of anti-SLAPP legislation. The backstory on this was that Kinder Morgan wanted the Crown to take over the prosecutions, as it was costing them a fortune in legal fees and in costs for serving documents on the many arrestees living in the Gulf Islands. So the Crown offered to take over the prosecutions in exchange for Kinder Morgan dropping their lawsuits against protesters.

Justice Kenneth Affleck had already announced his intention to try defendants in groups of ten. On April 11, he informed dozens of us that he could "write the rules," and he was going to, warning that he considered any arguments about the legality, morality, or adverse climate impact of the pipeline to be irrelevant; if we had violated his injunction, we must pay the price. Furthermore, he had decided we should be charged with criminal, rather than civil, contempt of court. An "initial sentencing position" of a $500 fine or twenty-five hours of community service was then offered by the Crown to nonviolent defendants who did not resist arrest, had no history of contempt citations in the preceding five years, and had only been arrested once between March 17 and April 16 (when the plan to charge defendants with criminal contempt, going forward, was announced).

My court appearance for sentencing was pretty anticlimactic; I had agreed to plead guilty in exchange for a $500 fine, as part of a plea bargain with the Crown, while Barbara chose community service. I recall our lawyer, Neil Chantler, reading a biographical statement to Justice Affleck, emphasizing my professional contributions as a physician (which included expert testimony as a neurologist for the Crown), the fact that I had been a law-abiding citizen, and so on. I was then allowed to read my statement for the court explaining why I had chosen to be arrested. I recall Justice Affleck stating that the court understood that I was not a "common criminal" and acknowledging that there was a tradition of nonviolent civil disobedience. He remarked that criminal contempt of court was the only criminal offence not codified in the Criminal Code of Canada, and that if I was ever asked if I'd been convicted of a criminal offence, I should (and could honestly) deny it. He ordered that my conviction (and also Barbara's) be sealed in the registry.

However, some of my fellow arrestees (especially Indigenous land defenders) were treated more harshly, both during their arrest and/or their court appearance (sometimes handcuffs and shackles were used), and the penalties now for nonviolently violating the same injunction are also more severe. Elderly grandmothers have been sentenced to seven to fourteen days in jail. On May 10, 2022, Will George received a twenty-eight-day jail sentence for his role in helping to organize the protests, and on June 15, 2022, my physician colleague and fellow Quaker Dr. Tim Takaro (an emeritus professor of health sciences at SFU and the senior author on Health Canada's 2022 report *Health of Canadians in a Changing Climate*) was egregiously led away in handcuffs, after being sentenced to thirty days in jail for sitting in a tree at the TMX site.[15]

Overall, my arrest and subsequent legal proceedings have been a game changer, inspiring and motivating me to reconnect with my activist roots. In the course of preparing my statement to the court, I learned much more about the risks of pipeline rupture, a tanker disaster, and the flawed approval process that allowed construction on the project to proceed. This made me even more convinced of the urgency to stop this pipeline and related new fossil fuel infrastructure projects, such as the Coastal GasLink pipeline and terminal. As a result, I became more directly involved in climate justice and anti-pipeline activism, engaging with Canadian Association of Physicians for the Environment (CAPE), whose "unnatural gas" campaign enlightened me about the health and environmental hazards and negative impact on Indigenous communities of fracking (hydraulic fracturing) in northern BC, and the imperative to stop the CGL pipeline.[16]

I became particularly active with a local group, Doctors for Planetary Heath (D4PH)—West Coast,[17] speaking outside the BC Legislature at what we believe was the first demonstration of health professionals for climate justice in Canada, Code Red for Humanity—Doctors and Nurses Climate Rally, on November 6, 2021. With D4PH colleagues, I have attended countless meetings and demonstrations, and met with BC's then attorney-general David Eby and former minister of mental health and addictions Sheila Malcolmson.

I've learned a great deal from my CAPE and Doctors for Planetary Health colleagues, and continue to be inspired by their knowledge, wisdom, energy, and commitment to social justice, Indigenous rights, and climate change activism.

At the time, I had no idea how transformative, empowering, and validating this single act of civil disobedience would be for me. I can hold my head high now and a huge burden of guilt has been relieved. I feel whole again.

Statement to BC Supreme Court Justice Kenneth Affleck, June 8, 2018

M'lord, as Mr. Chantler has stated, I am a law-abiding citizen, and have never been arrested before or been charged or convicted of any criminal offence. I did not intend any disrespect for your Lordship or the court. I appreciate this opportunity to make a brief statement as to why I chose to risk arrest on March 19.

Forty-five years ago, as president of the Environmental Council of BC and a founder of an organization called SPOILS

(Stop Pollution from Oil Spills), my father organized a seven-mile march to demonstrate the stopping distance of a supertanker in the Strait of Juan de Fuca. That was instrumental in convincing Prime Minister Pierre Elliott Trudeau to bring in a moratorium on supertanker traffic in those waters.

The risks now are far higher than they were forty-five years ago. If this pipeline goes ahead, at full capacity it will result in an almost seven-fold increase in tanker traffic (from 60 to 408 tankers per year, more than one a day) in these waters (docking at the Westridge Marine Terminal). The tankers have gotten bigger, and now they are carrying diluted bitumen rather than crude oil. Bitumen does not flow naturally, and must be diluted with condensed natural gas (forming "dilbit") to allow it to be transported in a pipeline. Ten to thirty percent of dilbit is volatile, and contains significant concentrations of toxic compounds such as benzene (a known carcinogen) and n-hexane and toluene (which cause damage to the peripheral and central nervous systems).

Unlike crude oil, which floats, bitumen separates out, with volatile organics (polycyclic aromatic hydrocarbons) dissolving and contaminating ground water, rivers, and oceans that can result in chronic toxicity and malformations to developing fish at concentrations as low as 3 to 20 ppm.[18] Some of these compounds cause genetic damage in human reproductive organs in minute quantities. As a physician specializing in neuropsychiatric genetics who cares for patients with autism, intellectual disability, and schizophrenia that can result from mutations that arise in sperm and eggs prior to conception, this is very concerning.

Meanwhile, the heavier hydrocarbons (asphalt/tar) sink to the bottom in both fresh and salt water. This renders the usual strategies to contain and clean up the spill, such as skimmers and oil booms, grossly inadequate. An 843,000-gallon spill resulting from rupture of an Enbridge pipeline carrying Alberta tar sands bitumen resulted in contamination of the Kalamazoo River that required four years and almost US$1.5 billion to "clean up."[19] The bottom of the Kalamazoo River was still being dredged five years after this rupture.

If there is a large oil spill into Burrard Inlet, the effect on BC's tourist and fishing industries will be devastating. A 2012 study conducted by the director of the UBC Fisheries Centre (Dr. Rashid

Sumaila) and a UBC fisheries economist (Ngaio Hotte) estimated that the cost of cleaning up a major oil spill on the North Coast of BC could reach $9.6 billion. The resulting loss of tax revenues and enormous costs of cleanup (which history has shown usually falls mainly on taxpayers) will result in significant cutbacks in health-care spending that inevitably result from contractions of the BC economy, with a negative impact on health care.

Dilbit-handling equipment can accumulate iron sulphide, which (if dry) ignites on contact with air. Upon combustion, in addition to carbon dioxide (the main greenhouse gas), dilbit releases toxic carbon monoxide, hydrogen sulphide, and sulphur dioxide.

The bitumen is stored in huge tanks on the Burnaby Mountain tank farm, which will require at least twice the number of existing tanks when the new pipeline is operational. Tank farm fires are not rare events, and result in dense clouds of toxic smoke. An analysis by the deputy chief of the Burnaby Fire Department predicted that millions of barrels of crude oil could erupt in flames, and winds would carry burning oil beyond the boundaries of the tank farm.[20] The resulting forest fire would be almost impossible to extinguish, and would race up Burnaby Mountain toward Simon Fraser University, potentially isolating the campus by burning across access roads and creating toxic fumes that may require large-scale evacuations of areas of Burnaby.

An Imperial Oil material data safety sheet for dilbit warns: "High vapour concentrations are irritating to the eyes, nose, throat and lungs; may cause headaches and dizziness; may be anesthetic and may cause other central nervous system effects, including death. Hydrogen sulphide gas may be released. Hydrogen sulphide may cause irritation, breathing failure, coma and death, without necessarily any warning odour being sensed. Avoid breathing vapours or mists . . . extremely flammable; material will readily ignite at normal temperatures. Toxic gases will form on combustion."

Pipeline leaks and ruptures themselves can result in huge toxic waste spills that contaminate soil and ground water and flow into rivers and oceans. Kinder Morgan has had a significant spill every four years on average. In 2007, the existing Kinder Morgan pipeline ruptured in north Burnaby, leaking 224,000 litres of heavy synthetic crude. About 100,000 litres entered Burrard Inlet and Kask Creek. The cleanup cost $15 million. Over 5,000 litres were not recovered and entered the marine ecosystem.[21] The Kinder Morgan pipeline passes through an active earthquake region, with a 73 percent predicted likelihood of a major earthquake within the next fifty years. In the event of a major earthquake, emergency responders, including firefighters, will be overwhelmed trying to save lives in densely populated areas. Meanwhile, the toxic fumes from the resulting fires could have a very serious impact on human health in the region.

I was, and remain, concerned that construction on the pipeline was allowed to proceed based on a flawed National Energy Board review process that put the lie to the Liberal Party's promises for full consultation with First Nations and environmental organizations, and Prime Minister Justin Trudeau's statements prior to the last election that "governments grant permits, but communities grant permission." I believe that this process may have violated the UN Declaration of the Rights of Indigenous Peoples, and the international legal principle of free and prior informed consent from Indigenous Peoples. It is deeply concerning that construction has been allowed to proceed before rulings by the Federal Court of Appeal have been issued on legal challenges by the Coast Salish First Nations, the Cities of Vancouver and Burnaby, and the Province of BC.

I would like to state again that I meant no disrespect for this court with my action, and I wish to apologize for any offence that I might have given in this matter. I do not intend to violate the injunction again. I have chosen to plead guilty and accept the sentencing recommendation of the Crown to expedite this matter, rather than burdening the court with the additional time and expense of a trial.

BARBARA STOWE,
Writer

Biography

Barbara Stowe was two when her father lifted her onto his shoulders and joined a march against Polaris nuclear submarines. Activism was a core value for Barbara's parents, Irving and Dorothy Stowe, who embraced Quaker principles of pacifism, social justice, and speaking truth to power. Irving worked pro bono for the NAACP in the 1950s, and in later decades became an environmental activist. Dorothy, a union president, performed some of the first gay and lesbian marriages in BC as an elder of the Quaker meeting, and volunteered for Everywoman's Health Centre, the first freestanding abortion clinic in the province. The Stowe's Vancouver home headquartered the first Greenpeace campaign in the early 1970s, and Barbara and her brother Robert, teenagers at the time, participated in that and other Greenpeace campaigns over the years.

An artistic bent led to a career in ballet and modern dance, after which Barbara earned a master's degree at UBC in creative writing. Her short fiction, articles, and essays have been published in literary magazines and newspapers such as the *Globe and Mail* and the *Georgia Straight*.

Barbara was arrested March 19, 2018 (with her brother) and was sentenced to twenty-five hours of community service on June 8, 2018.

Narrative: To Serve and Protect

Near the end of November 2014, I received an email message from Bill Darnell, a long-time family friend. "I am planning to go to

Vancouver this week to support the people on Burnaby Mountain," he wrote. "Are you thinking about going?"

I'd known Bill since I was fourteen years old. We'd sat side-by-side on the floor in early Greenpeace meetings, and though he was only ten years older than me, I thought of him as an honorary uncle. A still-waters-run-deep kind of guy, he'd put "green" and "peace" together, and I'd always respected his quiet, thoughtful manner.

Bill's views on the TMX project echoed mine. Besides all the reasons elucidated earlier in this book, my husband and I live on S,DÁYES (Pender Island), and it was all too easy to envisage what the waters around our island might look like after a supertanker spill. Humpbacks and orcas swim off our shores, and the risk to marine life was also painfully clear. Not to mention the impact a spill could have on the food security of Coast Salish Peoples who live along the Fraser River. Before moving to S,DÁYES in 2013, Joe and I had rented a house on the Musqueam reserve and seen Indigenous fishermen feeding their community with fresh-caught salmon, taking it first to the homes of Elders. Polluting the Fraser River with diluted bitumen would be unconscionable.

On November 27, 2014, I walked up Burnaby Mountain with Bill and Greenpeace forests campaigner Eduardo Sousa, to join a crowd intent on protecting this territory. Tsleil-Waututh spiritual leaders spoke, and when one said that Kinder Morgan had marked certain trees to be cut down, and "the she-bear, she scratched those marks off," the passion in her voice resonated so deeply that for a moment I thought she was talking about a real bear. Or that she'd somehow conjured one. This pipeline project, forced upon people who'd never ceded this territory, never consented to this project, was nothing less than a home invasion.

Indigenous drummers and singers led us down a narrow trail into the woods. It had been raining, and the earth was so wet, we were ankle-deep in mud, slipping and sliding in brown sludge, but I was enjoying the cedar-scented air, the drum and the song, the deep green ferns and velvety moss. Bill noticed something else. "Where are the birds?" Drilling—loud, persistent, vibrating—began, and when it stopped, Bill said, "Look," pointing to the sky, and a bald eagle flew over our heads.

Deep in the forest, the line stopped. We stood in the mud: one hour, two hours, until time went away. A voice came through a bullhorn, then more voices. When the line moved forward, we saw those who'd been leading us were standing behind yellow crime scene tape. They'd stepped across a line dictated by a court injunction, and police were arresting them.

A thirteen-year-old girl in a pink hoodie crossed the line. A Canadian soldier. Bill Darnell, and more, until the RCMP had arrested twenty-two people, and long-time activist Tzeporah Berman raised the bullhorn and said enough people had been arrested today, would others come back tomorrow, and everyone started leaving. Eduardo shouldered Bill's knapsack and we headed down the mountain.

I knew I'd be back. Despite my activist upbringing, at heart I'm a reticent, risk-averse individual, and I was glad to return to an island far away from Burnaby Mountain, but my heart ached and when I got home, I felt split in two. Half of me was still with the people in the forest. The Tsleil-Waututh's powerful, rightful, spiritual presence, their oratory, drumming, silence, and spirit had done something to me I couldn't explain.

Bill and others arrested that day were given "catch and release" treatment. Lawyers proved the line demarcating the borders of the injunction was in the wrong place. But the project continued, and several years later, on the 18th of March 2018, I headed back to Vancouver, with the intention of joining those standing, not in the forest this time, but in front of the gates of the Kinder Morgan tank farm.

That night I stayed at my brother's house in Kitsilano.

"I'm coming with you tomorrow morning," he said. "For support. I'm sorry, I can't get arrested."

"Please don't get arrested, Bobby!" was my instant response. A busy behavioural neurologist with patients booked months in advance, he couldn't risk incarceration. When we got there, though, he said he'd changed his mind.

"Are you sure?" I knew it sounded patronizing but couldn't help myself. He nodded firmly.

About ten of us took a few hours of civil disobedience training, then we all hoisted a long banner and started walking through the woods towards the gates. Our trainers suggested a song to keep us calm: "Hear the voice of my great-granddaughter" we sang, over and over, and I felt our group's jittery, nervous energy settle. But when we emerged from the forest into the light, the tension rose sharply. Most of us, Bobby and I included, had never put our freedom on the line before.

Rex Weyler, a Greenpeace International co-founder, had. He went first, stepping out from behind the banner, modelling an admirable calm. "I'm seventy years old," he told the media as cameras swung his way. "I'm doing this for my grandchildren." Then he walked to the tall metal fence and zip-tied himself to the gates.

I thought my jaw might lock from tension as I stepped forward. Instead, I felt what I can only describe as an invisible, impenetrable blanket of protection surround not just my entire body, but a wide swath of space around it. In my most vulnerable moment, I'd never felt so safe. When I later told this to Romilly Cavanaugh, a former Trans Mountain employee who also stood for arrest, she nodded. "That's what happens when you're standing in the truth." The message was clear: a universal force for good partners with us when we go the distance for social justice.

A television reporter shoved a fuzzy mike in my face as I sat down beside Rex.

"How long are you going to be here?" His tone and body language was confrontational.

"I will be here as long as it takes," I replied. He continued to glare at me, and, when I wouldn't look away, turned to Rex.

"How long will you be here?"

"Oh," Rex sighed. "I'll be here forever."

By noon, the RCMP had arrested Rex, my brother, myself, and Nancy McLean, whose father had worked in the Alberta oil sands and said she knew firsthand "what that industry does to families." The police clipped off our zip ties and led us into a processing area in the woods, and four more took our places at the gates.

Twenty of us were arrested that day. We weren't the first, and we certainly wouldn't be the last. That week alone, the police would process 144 protectors, with many more to follow.

Four more people from my island got arrested. Our community forum on Facebook lit up with praise for "the Pender Five." But while those who swung green were vocal, many people from Alberta with ties to the oil industry live on our island, and their voices were silent.

I asked myself, how would I feel if I was them? Angry? Scared?

That we were threatening their livelihood, attacking their economic survival? I decided to post reports of the ongoing protest and court appearances on our forum in as neutral a tone as possible. When an angry young man took me to task for taking action, I responded with care instead of defensively, and he said he'd just been very upset, needed to be heard, and felt he had been heard. In a walking group, a woman in a Shell Oil ball cap called one of my Facebook posts—acknowledging the immense difficulty of our society's transition from fossil fuels to clean energy, and offering sincere respect for those trying to support their families—"beautiful." A mother from the local Bible camp, who I'd mentally stereotyped as disapproving of the Pender Five, stopped her pickup to say "good for you." These unexpected points of connection buoyed me through the tense weeks of waiting for court appearances and sentencing.

Our arrests also had a ripple effect. Just as Bill's outreach had brought me to the TMX protests, so, after my brother and I were arrested, several family members who'd never in their lives come to a demonstration joined marches up Burnaby Mountain. Two sisters-in-law were with me April 7, when First Nations Chiefs blocked the gates. That day, the police never came. The optics of multiple Chiefs in traditional regalia were crippling for Kinder Morgan, which announced it was selling the project.

We were all jubilant.

Until a few weeks later, when our federal government bought it.

Rage, disgust, and despair can take you down. Blocking those feelings doesn't help, and I vented with my friends in bitter conversations. Some activists do great things driven by anger, but my nervous system won't handle it for long, so then I started searching for inspiration, for what would lift me up. I remembered standing in my mother's kitchen in 2007, drinking Granville Island lager with Captain Peter Willcox—who in 2013 would be thrown into a Russian jail for sailing a Greenpeace boat to protest Russian drilling in the Arctic—and what he'd said about peaceful civil disobedience. "Barbara, actions have such a powerful effect on those who do them!"

He didn't mean, just on individuals who take direct action. He meant that committing peaceful civil disobedience is an act ignited by a sacred fire that spreads outward, connecting protectors with a powerful universal force for good. I'd experienced that force. Fighting TMX unified us all, everyone arrested on Burnaby Mountain, all pipeline protesters everywhere. We were all connected, all in this together.

And while our resistance had halted when Kinder Morgan stopped work on the TMX project, when our federal government started work up again, protests would resume.

The ripple effect that inspired some relatives to come to marches for the first time had a downside. I saw the tension in the bodies and faces of family members with differing opinions as they struggled to contain anger, bewilderment, and worry in passionate exchanges. My extended family is caring and courteous, and everyone remained civil, but conversations and relationships became strained. And while I had no regrets about my action, I felt bad about being the catalyst for this schism.

In spring 2019, as we waited for preliminary hearings, I opened the front door to find a 500+ page SLAPP suit from Kinder Morgan on the doormat (a clear intimidation tactic). It smelled nasty. Our cat had peed on the envelope. She'd never urinated on any of our belongings before, and when I told my brother, he said: "That cat obviously has an astute political consciousness. Piss on Kinder Morgan!"

We needed humour. My brother was calling me every night after his long workdays. We were both worried about sentencing and the SLAPP suit, and I feared my passion for this cause had inspired Bobby to action that in the long run might hurt his patients and the international research project on schizophrenia he was heading up. What if he got a jail sentence? Would the BC College of Physicians and Surgeons sanction him? Our anxieties kept us up at night, and while our partners were nothing but supportive, what toll would all this stress take on them, and on our relationships, as time wore on?

Legal equity and lawyers' bills were a further grave concern. Friends offered support, but many defendants didn't fit the narrow criteria for legal aid and couldn't afford counsel. Piggybacking on a local activist's film event, and assisted by Romilly, I organized a modest benefit for arrestees; others organized much bigger events and a legal defence fund, but we all knew legal costs would be steep, and many defendants would go unrepresented.

April 11, 2018, was our first mandated court appearance. Kat Roivas, a transgender Indigenous defendant, offered hugs to all. She limped over using a cane, slender in blue jeans and a black leather jacket hanging open over a black T-shirt, and I felt her warm heart as we embraced.

This comfort, freely offered by a complete stranger, was bolstered by the presence of Kris Hermes, hired by a coalition led by Coast Salish spiritual leaders, to provide some legal support. Anxious arrestees peppered Kris with questions as we waited for Justice Kenneth Affleck to arrive.

The courtroom was so full that when the black-robed judge swept in, the order to stand was superfluous for many of us. There was nowhere to sit. He lectured us sternly for about twenty minutes, warning he wouldn't hear any arguments about whether what Kinder Morgan was doing was immoral, illegal, or "environmentally unwise." The police had charged us with civil contempt; he changed that to criminal contempt.

What would the ramifications of that be? Bobby and I hadn't held hands since childhood, but instinctively reached out to support each other.

Before we could leave, we were all ordered to sign a Promise to Appear. My friend Peter Pare, a lung doctor, was outraged. "I'm thinking of not signing that piece of paper," he sputtered to me. "I already signed a Promise to Appear when the RCMP processed us in the woods!" We all had. This judge doesn't know who we are, I thought. He's scared of us.

And indeed, we were very dangerous people, though not in the way Judge Affleck believed. Concerned citizens who'd obeyed the summons to this hearing, we weren't about to skip out on him. But when resistance reaches a tipping point, when enough people are willing to sacrifice personal freedom for a cause, anarchy is afoot. Even highly visible politicians had been arrested for this cause. The ground was shaking under the powers that be.

Civil disobedience has helped change unjust laws. Even South African judges committed civil disobedience during the powerful movement to end apartheid. They, too, were a danger to the state, and by challenging grave injustice, helped bring an end to it.

Justice Affleck, however, seemed firmly planted on the side of the status quo.

At our second appearance, Kat Roivas limped to the mike and schooled His Lordship in colonialism. "You may be a lord, but you are not my lord," she said, and defendants started rising, hands held high in an Indigenous blessing. Judge Affleck warned he'd clear the court if we continued.

And yet, as further hearings followed, the judge's hard-line attitude seemed to waver at times. After warning us on day one about the narrow range of arguments he would allow, he let a defendant argue the necessity defence, a long shot, all morning. When a man who'd won the Queen's Jubilee Medal for public service came up for sentencing, the judge seemed shaken. "I am sure you are an exemplary citizen," he said. An opera singer belted out a few lines of his statement to the tune of "Old Man River"—"Kinder Morgan . . . just keeps rolling along"—and the judge responded with: "You have a beautiful voice, sir. Thank you."

He reduced, by two weeks, the sentence of a woman concerned that her probationary period would prohibit a visit to her daughter in PEI. Then an Indigenous teen came before the bench, a boy with a gentle manner who appeared overwhelmed and intimidated at being in court for the first time. Judge Affleck granted diversion to Youth Court (a decision he would later rescind), but instead of then dismissing the teen, appeared to focus on paperwork. The boy stood there waiting. And waiting. And waiting, until finally he spoke up softly, in an anxious, frightened tone: "Can I go now?"

It was infuriating, heartbreaking. The boy's "crime"? Standing on the road near the gates, prayerfully smudging protectors. The only thing I could see that was different about this defendant was his youth and that he was Indigenous, and all I could think was how blinkered I'd been about the profound racism inherent in our so-called justice system. In the end, this boy was called to court nine times, for reasons none of us can fathom.[22]

As I wrote a statement, preparing for sentencing, I was thinking of those defendants who would be sentenced after me. Those who'd preceded me had already laid out all the reasons this pipeline project was disastrous, and how would I feel if I was a judge sitting up there, hearing the same arguments repeatedly? So, while expressing outrage, I also wove in praise for the times I'd seen compassion in the court.

Of course, I also worried about my own sentencing. Our

lawyer, Neil Chantler, had warned Bobby and me there were three reasons we could be sentenced more harshly than some other defendants: we'd zip-tied ourselves to the gates; we'd made statements to the media (which Greenpeace had then circulated); and our family connection to Greenpeace increased our public profile, a danger to the powers that be from any resistance movement. On the day of sentencing, I shocked myself by grabbing Neil in a hug and not being able to let go.

My brother and I were each offered a choice of a $500 fine or twenty-five hours of community work service, an ironic term given the amount of support we'd both received from many people in our respective communities, who proclaimed our arrests service to the greater good. It was a relatively mild punishment compared to some other sentences, and our relief was tainted by the injustice. One arrestee got 150 hours. In the months that followed almost all of the defendants were sent to jail.[23] For my community service, I volunteered for the Pender Island Health Care Society community support program on two projects: hosting a walking group for seniors; and producing a multigenerational performance celebrating the artistic talents of my community. Titled *O Snail!* and performed on a labyrinth, this multidisciplinary work explored the beauty of connection and going slow.

A virtual media blackout on court proceedings and incarcerations meant the general public didn't know how many peaceful protectors were being jailed. Save for a handful of reliable sources such as APTN (Aboriginal Peoples Television Network), the *Tyee*, and the *National Observer*, the media has all but ignored the fact that nonviolent protesters are getting jail terms.

Friends voiced shock at hearing details of court proceedings only on social media. I, too, was shocked: by reports from peaceful protectors about being transported from court to jail handcuffed, sometimes shackled, in transport wagons without seatbelts, and therefore, no way to keep from being thrown about in transit. Placed in freezing cells with no blankets. Bring $20 (or even more!), or forget about making a phone call. How naive I was, to imagine that in the new millennium, our "justice system" was more humane than this.

The harsh sentencing of Indigenous activists protecting their own lawful rights and property is the most heinous crime of all.

On May 10, 2022, Will George, whose family spearheaded Protect the Inlet and the mass arrests that followed, was sentenced to twenty-eight days in jail. CBC, our national broadcaster, gave this news short shrift and has virtually ignored the court proceedings. What conclusion can be drawn, other than that we are living in a petro-state, an oiligarchy?

After sentencing, I reported to a probation office, and then my brother and I took our partners out to lunch.

"If you had it to do all over again, would you?" Bobby asked.

"Yes," I said, surprising myself. I hadn't even hesitated.

He didn't hesitate either. "So would I."

Statement to BC Supreme Court Justice Kenneth Affleck, June 8, 2018

Your Honour,

Other defendants have so eloquently outlined reasons that mirror my own for committing nonviolent civil disobedience against this pipeline project, that I can add little to their statements. So I am not planning to talk about Indigenous rights, climate change, the Salish Sea, the resident orcas, or the children in the twenty-two Burnaby elementary schools for whom there is no safe plan should this pipeline leak or the storage tanks catch fire.

Instead, I would like to extend my sincere gratitude to your Lordship, and to all the lawyers and my fellow defendants, for the wisdom imparted to me on this journey of conscience we have all been travelling together. And I would like to add just a few thoughts and observations on this journey.

I know it is the court's job to preserve law and order, and despite my horror at how the law in Canada has been used against Indigenous people and the disadvantaged, I recognize the protections the law offers when administered with compassion. I have seen this compassion manifest in this courtroom on many occasions during these hearings.

Coming to this court with no criminal record, never having been arrested before, I have been overwhelmed by this process and had much need for guidance. I recognize the privileged position I am in, having legal counsel. Many defendants have no legal counsel, and I appreciate that the court recognized how important duty counsel, an amicus curiae, or legal aid would be (if such were available) in some comments the other day.

I deliberately and soberly violated the injunction and accept my punishment. And yet, if such a plea were allowed in a Canadian court, I would plead *nolo contendere*, because while I am guilty, I acted solely to oppose a greater crime. When even those whom our society recognizes as figures of authority, such as doctors, professors, politicians, and faith leaders, start committing civil disobedience, it begs the question: Who and what is the real danger to our society, to all that we hold dear? Are people sitting in front of a fence, putting their freedom at risk, willing to pay fines and do community service or go to jail displaying a greater contempt for the law than those who ride roughshod over the rights and safety of tribes, communities, cities, this province, and the environment that sustains us all?

In closing, I would just like to add that if I owned property, I would hope that strangers never trespassed on my land to start drilling without my approval or consent. But if they did, I would hope that my neighbours would come and stand in front of them while I called the police. And when the police came, I'd hope they'd arrest the strangers with the drill and not my neighbours. I would hope justice would prevail.

Part 4

Resistance from high in the trees:
The Brunette River Six

Climber descending from tree fort in the Brunette watershed.
Photo: Mike Galliford

TIM K. TAKARO,
MD, Public
Health Researcher

Biography

Dr. Tim Takaro is a professor emeritus and physician-scientist in the Faculty of Health Sciences at Simon Fraser University, husband to Aggie Black, and father to Annie and Ben. He trained in occupational and environmental medicine, public health, and toxicology, at Yale, the University of North Carolina, and the University of Washington. Dr. Takaro's research is primarily about the links between human exposures and disease, and determining effective public-health-based preventive solutions to such risks.

Planetary change poses complex problems for public health, never more apparent than during the COVID-19 pandemic. These challenges demand an interdisciplinary approach both in research and action. To this end, Takaro is a member of the Planetary Health Research group at SFU and a lead author of the Health Canada 2022 report *Health of Canadians in a Changing Climate: Advancing Knowledge for Action*. His current research program explores the impacts of resource extraction on human health and the relationship to our land and waters. With immense gratitude to the First Peoples, he is beginning to use Indigenous knowledge to relearn environmental health as he tests different interventions in climate action and planet protection.

Dr. Takaro was arrested from his tree perch on November 26, 2021, in Burnaby and sentenced to thirty days' incarceration on June 13, 2022, serving twenty-one days.

Statement to BC Supreme Court Justice Shelley Fitzpatrick, June 13, 2022

Thank you for the opportunity to speak, Madame Justice.

As Mr. Chantler has outlined, I have had a privileged academic career while working for the public's health. I have been most privileged to live uninvited, on these beautiful Coast Salish lands and waters, for the past seventeen years. The lands, waters, and people of the inlet have nourished me and taught me much about the long arc of the moral universe, that Martin Luther King Jr. assured us bends towards justice.

My commitment to protecting the planet is indeed both a professional and a moral calling. Until this event, I had never been arrested. I have an unblemished criminal record. I frequently volunteer as a health expert for community groups who need assistance navigating complex public health problems. I am a Fraser River-keeper and member of many organizations and boards working to protect the planet. I am a board member of the International Physicians for the Prevention of Nuclear War (IPPNW) and was an active medical student member when IPPNW won the Nobel Peace prize in 1985. Through this work, I was involved in the International Campaign to Abolish Nuclear Weapons, which won the 2017 Nobel Peace Prize. After my internship in medicine and receiving my licence to practise, I spent two and a half years working as a doctor in a war zone in Nicaragua. I try to do what I can to make the world a safer place and bend that arc in the universe.

As part of my work as a public health physician, I have been engaged in the Trans Mountain Expansion project's impact assessment since 2014. This pipeline expansion project is a perfect example of an outdated infrastructure project that flies in the face of the promised energy transition, in a climate emergency and in a stunningly beautiful, yet fragile, place we call home. My skills as a physician, epidemiologist, and toxicologist are a perfect fit for assessing and challenging the project at multiple levels. As a result, I became an intervenor in the review process addressing the health impacts of the project.

I led two major reports on the health impacts of the pipeline and its associated hazards. Despite my expertise, my evidence of potential harms from this project has been ignored by the National Energy Board (NEB), now the Canada Energy Regulator. In April of 2019, fellow members of the Health Officers Council of BC recognized the inadequate review that the Trans Mountain Pipeline Expansion project had undergone in terms of impacts on health, and demanded an independent, cumulative health-impacts assessment. This is the same group of doctors that brought us the incredible provincial response to the COVID-19 pandemic. Their entreaties have also been ignored.

When the project was initially considered, Prime Minister Stephen Harper ensured that climate change could not be considered as a factor in the review. Because of this prohibition, I was not allowed to include in my two reports anything about the most profound health impacts of the project, namely the health impacts from climate change, with its devastating and inevitable chaos for future generations. We had a preview of these impacts last year, with over six hundred climate-related deaths in BC alone.

A lot has changed since the injunction was ordered by Judge Affleck in June of 2018. The cost of the project to taxpayers has ballooned from $4.2 billion to $21.4 billion.[1] Violations of conditions all along the route and the construction delays continue. Many economists and the government's own Parliamentary Budget Officer show how the project will likely lose money if ever made operational, as the world weans itself from fossil fuels and Canada strives to meet our international commitments to reduce emissions.

The most important wake-up call since the injunction was issued involved the hundreds of British Columbians who have died from global heating and the floods which also killed hundreds of thousands of farm animals in the Fraser Valley, approximately one billion sea creatures along the shores of the Salish Sea, and displaced thousands of residents. The devastation caused billions of dollars in losses last year alone. As Premier Horgan put it in his year-end speech in December 2021, "For many, this will be remembered as the year that climate change arrived at our doorsteps. Here in BC, we faced record-setting droughts, heat waves and forest fires, floods and mudslides. Even for an optimist like myself it has been an exceptionally challenging time."

We know that the Trans Mountain Pipeline Expansion project

will worsen global heating and kill more people. It is an existential threat. We also know from the government's own analysis that we cannot meet our greenhouse gas (GHG) emissions commitments if we complete and operationalize this pipeline expansion. We heard loud and clear earlier this year from the UN Secretary-General that we must stop building new fossil energy infrastructure to ensure a future for our children. On April 4 of this year, in announcing a new UN report on climate change, he said, "Investing in new fossil fuels infrastructure is moral and economic madness."

Health Canada's report that I referred to earlier states un-equivocally that health risks will increase as warming continues and that much of the mortality and morbidity is preventable. The UN's Intergovernmental Panel on Climate Change states with "high confidence" that "climate change is a threat to human well-being and the health of the planet." Any further delay in concerted anticipatory global action on adaptation and mitigation "will miss a brief and rapidly closing window to secure a liveable future."[2] Your Honour, what will we tell our grandchildren that we did to address this "code red for humanity"?

The climate impacts of this project are not the only threats to public health that it poses. In my intervenor reports, we outlined the toxic effects of a diluted bitumen spill, childhood leukemia risks, and toxic releases magnified by the hot summers of future climates and mental health effects, to name just a few. These health issues remain unaddressed. The NEB itself stated in its February 22, 2019, re-review (following the federal appeals court order quashing NEB's original decision) that, even without the much larger downstream emissions (85 percent of the total), "green-house gas emissions from Project-related marine vessels would likely be significant." And that, "while a credible worst-case spill from the Project or a Project-related marine vessel is not likely, if it were to occur the environmental effects would be significant." These admissions about the project happened after the injunction to keep away from the TMX worksite was issued and are critical to Canada's national interest.

Once I realized that the scientific evidence was not going to stop the project, I began to look to direct action as the next logical step in the efforts to stop the project. I found guidance and sup-port from the People of the Inlet, the Tsleil-Waututh, who along with the Squamish and Musqueam, have stewarded this land since time immemorial.

The modern Hippocratic oath requires that I protect the health of my patients *and* the public *and* to inform or warn about impending health threats. This is an essential expectation in my professional role. The American Medical Association states that "ethical responsibilities usually exceed legal duties ... When physicians believe a law violates ethical values or is unjust they should work to change the law. In exceptional circumstances of unjust laws, ethical responsibilities should supersede legal duties."

Your Honour, at the time of my arrest, I was in a difficult position in light of my professional knowledge of the grave danger we face from climate change. I have the utmost respect for the court, but here in Canada we are in deep trouble, trouble that the UN secretary-general calls moral trouble, because our fossil energy policies are exactly the opposite of what is required to reduce the numbers of people who will die from climate change. These environmental concerns are the concerns of everyone in a climate emergency. When faced with this choice, my professional responsibility and obligations led me to stay in the tree until November 26, when I was removed. I do feel remorseful for breaking the law. But I was stuck in this dilemma.

Quoting from the Crown's Book of Authorities regarding the political principle of civil disobedience:

> that political principle contemplates that a public and, as far as possible, passive act of resistance to a law that is perceived to be unjust, coupled with an embracing of the appropriate punishment for the offence, is consistent with the procedure for bringing about democratic change, and when properly understood, indicates the highest respect for the rule of law as a benign and necessary part of the structure of a just and democratic society.

Acting in accordance with the principle of civil disobedience is not a defence in law. But surely it must be a relevant factor in assessing moral culpability for the offences. Previous jurists in this province have also asked if the rule of law is truly at risk every time there is a public breach of a court order.[3] I ask that you assess the gravity of my nonviolent civil disobedience in this context, along with my expression of remorse for violating the law.

Your Honour, I am also asking you also to consider my health in your sentencing. I am sixty-five years old, have hypertension and three artificial stents in the arteries of my heart. In his letter, my cardiologist has outlined that the stress of sleep deprivation and sudden loud noise in prison is significant physiologic stress in my condition. Conditions that have been recently verified by former inmates at the facility in question. As Dr. Charania has stated, "His risk of suffering a heart attack would be minimized if he is able to avoid excessive and repetitive loud noises during the day and night and if he is able to avoid chronic sleep deprivation." I appreciate your need to deter future violations of the injunction. I am asking you to consider the significant potential danger of cardiac arrest in prison and that you find a proportionate sentence that serves the Crown's need for deterrence but does not put my life at risk.

Thank you for your consideration.

Narrative: How I Came to the End of My Rope and Engaged in Bold Climate Action

As a physician, I will start with a prescription: Action is the Antidote to Despair. Use it liberally!

I am humbled by the thousands of people around the globe who are standing up to show their love of the planet and to protect her from the human greed that is fuelling the climate emergency. I'm a proud member of the Brunette River Six, along with Janette McIntosh, Catherine Hembling, Ruth Walmsley, Bill Winder, and Zain Haq, who have gone to jail for choosing a lesser crime of violating industry's injunction to prevent the greater crime of building new fossil energy infrastructure that contributes to the climate emergency.

We stand on the shoulders of giants, like Ta'ah and Will George of the Tsleil-Waututh, Jim Leyden, Kanahus Manuel, and all their relations. It is all the planet protectors who have come before that enabled our group to be high in the treetops blocking TMX for sixteen months.

And it is these planet protectors that enable us now to follow the money to the Big Five Canadian banks who finance climate catastrophe. This fight against finance is a crucial part of the struggle by the broad and deep community who stand up for the planet. This is my story, one of many from Protect the Planet's tree-sits in Burnaby, which began in August 2020 and are still going in 2023.

I am grateful to reside on unceded Coast Salish lands. My parents are of European ancestry; my father was born in Budapest and my mother in Iowa. As a youth I roamed the stunning Blue Ridge Mountains stolen from the Cherokee Nation in 1838, when they were force-marched to Oklahoma and four thousand died along the way. Hundreds stayed in the mountains and now make up the Eastern Band of the Cherokee Nation. Thinking about their resilience gives me strength in my efforts to stand up to fossil-fuelled power. I dearly love my two children, Annie and Ben, and, along with my climate activist partner Aggie, want them to have a safe and secure planet on which to live.

After attending medical and public health school at the University of North Carolina, I moved west to Oregon, then Washington to continue training in occupational and environmental medicine. I spent three years in Nicaragua, facing a war brought on by my own country. The experience was life-changing. I lost my best friend to American bullets there, Benjamin Linder from Portland. I also met my future partner, Aggie. We learned tough lessons about social justice. We learned how to speak truth to power in Washington, DC, and state capitals. Upon returning to the University of Washington as a faculty member, I began to lecture on the emerging knowledge about the potential health impacts of climate change.

Our family resettled easily in Canada in 2005 where I helped to start a new Faculty of Health Sciences at SFU. I was also busy making new connections and learning of the incredible wisdom and strength of the Coast Salish, the Haida, and other Indigenous Peoples of the land and waters of the region. I gained a deep appreciation for the struggles of these First Peoples and how their rights and title were subjugated to the rapacious appetite of settler development over the history of Canada.

Through a lens of environmental health, I viewed the inextricably woven threads of life that make the beautiful tapestry of our common lands and waters. I brought this science into my teaching and research on the health impacts of climate change. I eventually learned that much of what I was teaching had been taught before, for thousands of years, in fact, by those First Peoples. I learned the two-eyed-seeing approach to public health and I am honoured to work with the First Nations Health Authority since it was established in these lands we call British Columbia.

I suppose it was inevitable that all this learning and training on the health impacts of climate change would eventually lead me into direct conflict with the fossil-fuelled energy policy of Canadian governments. It has been clear for some time that fossil-fuelled power in Canada, coupled with our own dependence on energy, has captured our leaders and threatens our future.

In 2014, the Trans Mountain Pipeline, which I sometimes refer to as the Trudeau™ pipeline, since he bought it and could stop it with a tweet, became a focus of my work. This pipeline expansion project is a perfect example of an outdated infrastructure project that flies in the face of the promised energy transition, in a climate emergency and in a stunningly beautiful yet fragile place we call home. My skills as a physician, epidemiologist, and toxicologist are a perfect fit for fighting the project at multiple levels. Soon I became an intervenor in the review process addressing the health impacts of the project.

Four years and two reports later, my science was ignored. After outlining the toxic effects of a diluted bitumen spill, childhood leukemia risks, toxic releases magnified by the hot summers of future climates, and mental health effects, to name a few, I knew that evidence would not stop the project. I began to look to direct action as the next logical step in the fight. I grew up in North Carolina at a time when the first Woolworth sit-ins provided a kick-start to the racial justice movement. Martin Luther King Jr., John Lewis, Rosa Parks, and many Black leaders from the South inspired me, eventually leading me to examine direct action as a last resort to protect the planet. As I told the judge, the modern Hippocratic oath requires that I protect the health of my patients *and* the public *and* to inform or warn about impending health threats.

The perfect moment to do so came in the summer of 2020 when Trans Mountain announced they must cut trees along the Holmes Creek riparian area during the so-called least-risk window for fish, or risk the viability of the project. I found my spot and my climbing buddy, and with support of many old and new friends set up the first tree-sit, along a lovely tributary to the Brunette at Holmes Creek. This was August 3, 2020. Protect the Planet: Stop TMX was born.

August and September went by in a flash. After the first ten days on the Holmes Creek portaledge, I was replaced by YouTuber and science teacher Kurtis Baute. We trained Maureen Curran and Christine Thuring to climb. The Holmes Creek support camp and network grew. We had an initial flurry of media attention spurred by articles in *Newsweek* and the *Seattle Times*. Getting traction in the mainstream Canadian press, though, continued to be a challenge.

When the six-week window for cutting closed on September 15, we held a great party outdoors at Hume Park, and others joined online. However, there was very little media coverage of this victory by citizens over this multibillion-dollar government boondoggle.

Pistachio and Cauliflower[4] joined Protect the Planet and the first treehouse began to take shape in the Raven cottonwood, right next to Eagle, the giant cottonwood that held the main line to the portaledge. The Prayer Circle that had been meeting on Burnaby Mountain began looking for opportunities for direct action along the pipeline route in Burnaby. With strong backing from the Tsleil-Waututh and other Coast Salish Nations, we reached out to support other struggles along the pipeline route. We gained strength from each other in the struggle to kill the black serpent of Trans Mountain.

In a pre-dawn raid in December 2020, Trans Mountain and their private police swept in, fenced off a perimeter with razor wire, and took the Holmes Creek camp along with the two majestic cottonwoods. They built a thirty-five-metre-high scaffold to dismantle the treehouse and stole our most valuable equipment. They trashed Holmes Creek and covered the destruction in plastic sheeting, leaving a trickle of stream running on top of the plastic. It was a dark day for Protect the Planet.

There were several arrests, but a week later we were back up in a new tree-sit after an all-night effort in the rain with a small and devoted team. The new sit, built largely by Pistachio and Cauliflower, was a few hundred metres upstream on the next Brunette River tributary, on another beautiful stream known as Lost Creek.

Pistachio set a new record for continuous time in the sit,

three weeks, a record that stands to this day. Our resolve stiffened throughout the winter as more and more people joined to support. The food, brought almost daily, was plentiful, healthy, and (mostly) delicious. We organized COVID-safe weekly tours to the trees to tell hundreds the story of the pipeline and our peaceful resistance. People brought other gifts besides food: art, poems, and song.

I will never forget when Cinara brought her and Marvio's children to play their violins for me on a chilly day in February. Mozart wafting through the branches up to my tent was magical and so uplifting. More climbers and supporters joined us and the Prayer Circle actions grew bolder. Gates were blocked, more arrests were made, and despite the hardships and a never-ending pandemic, we continued the fight.

The hummingbirds began visiting in early spring. This was a miracle in the making, though at first we didn't know it. But the Anna's hummingbird is a migratory species, protected by Canada's Migratory Birds Convention Act.

A nest-finding team was added to our construction surveillance work and after weeks of watching, they were able to get an Environment and Climate Change Canada officer onto the Trans Mountain work site at Lost Creek. The officer watched as workers felled a tree with a nest. He immediately stopped work in the Brunette River greenway for four months!

We learned from Kukpi7 Judy Wilson how symbolic it was that this action by that tiny hummingbird had stopped local construction of this massive pipeline. She told us, "Many stories honour the qualities of Hummingbird, and one that stands out, in particular, is Hummingbird's tenacious loyalty to the forest. When a massive fire began consuming everything, even as the forest burned and all the other animals fled, Hummingbird carried drops of water—in her tiny beak—from the river to the forest fire, back and forth for hours. When the other animals asked why she tried and pointed out the dangers, Hummingbird said: 'I'm doing what I can.'"[5] The Hummingbird as planet protector is a powerful image that continues to guide us in our work.

Though ordered not to continue their work in the forest, we did not trust the Crown corporation to adhere to the order, so we stayed in the trees consolidating our position, while exploring legal avenues to protect the trees and streams from future destruction.

The heat dome came and killed more than six hundred of our fellow British Columbians. We thought that would be enough to end this climate-killing project. It was not.

Immediately following Trudeau's re-election in late September, Trans Mountain, backed by a militarized unit of the RCMP known as the Community-Industry Response Group (CIRG), moved forcefully against us. We had established two additional skypods and a sleeping dragon on the defensive perimeter of the two remaining treehouses. Skypods are simply hammocks suspended from the trees, not nearly as comfortable as our treehouses. Sleeping dragons are devices used by resisters to hamper arrest, such as inserting an arm through a tube full of cement. These, along with strategic blockades and arrests by the courageous Protect the Planet Prayer Circle, slowed down the cutting machines for two weeks. Bill Winder, also known as Big Bird, sat in a skypod for nine days straight, then went back up after a two-day rest only to be arrested a few days later. I will never forget his last stand! Eventually the chainsaws, cherry picker on tank tracks, and militarized police were too much for us. Five were arrested and the treehouses fell.

Then on another dark night in November 2021, I and two friends walked behind the New Life Community Church in Burnaby to our third sit. A cushy two-person portaledge was quickly placed, and I shimmied up to spend four nights, sitting though one of the atmospheric rivers that flooded much of the southern part of the province, causing massive damage to critical infrastructure including, ironically, TMX.

I was perched in a tree at the bottom of the mountain where I had taught hundreds of bright young students about the health impacts of climate change for seventeen years. Nearby a dangerous dilbit storage facility threatens the safety of residents, students, and workers on the mountain. I was arrested on November 26 by armed men on a tank with a long-armed cherry picker. It was a fitting place for a last stand. I expected jail time for my actions, and I have very few regrets.

I will miss the serene and peaceful times I spent among the high branches with their fern, lichen, and moss gardens. The predictable changing seasons and rhythms in the trees are soothing and peaceful. The indefatigable support from people was so uplifting. Though I was immersed in front-line action on climate change, it was also a meditative space. I spent many hours alone in reflection on how I fit into the complex ecosystem of the trees and waters on Coast Salish lands, and how Protect the Planet could influence the unpredictable political system that attempts to control and, in these times, destroy the ecosystems that sustain us.

As described most recently by UN Secretary-General António Guterres, based upon the scientific findings of the IPCC, humanity is at a crossroads. We can either continue on a pathway that will fail to reduce emissions and will lead to, in his words, "an atlas of human suffering"[6] from climate catastrophe, or we can strive "to keep the 1.5°C limit agreed in Paris within reach" which will require that we "triple the speed of the shift to renewable energy. That means moving investments and subsidies from fossil fuels to renewables—now. . . . It means climate coalitions, made up of developed countries, multilateral development banks, private financial institutions and corporations, supporting major emerging economies in making this shift. It means protecting forests and ecosystems as powerful climate solutions. It means rapid progress in reducing methane emissions. And it means implementing the pledges made in Paris and Glasgow."[7]

We have only a few years left to make real reductions in our emissions.

There is, of course, a moral dimension to this fight. While continuing to construct this tar sands pipeline, Canada is wilfully endangering the lives of my fellow citizens. I am a public health physician. I took an oath to protect the health of people. With my training, I am required to block this dangerous project. The Crown is telling me, If you encourage other people to protect the planet, we will treat you more harshly. I accept the state's punishment. My professional and moral responsibilities tell me I must help humanity connect the dots between this pipeline, future emissions, climate death, and life for future generations on this beautiful planet. I had to do what government refuses to do, which is stop the construction of new fossil energy infrastructure.

Following a raucous protest on the steps of the BC Supreme Court, I began my punishment in mid-June and spent three weeks in jail. The experience was an important part of my activist's journey, giving more time for reflection, reading, and writing while experiencing the dehumanizing nature of our so-called corrections system. I was readily accepted and made new friends. I'm no longer afraid of prison. A universal response from my fellow convicts was, "You're in for that? That's crazy."

And of course, it is. Oil executives find ways to hide the truth about their companies' role in climate change. Who are the real criminals here?

While I was incarcerated, the Parliamentary Budget Officer reported that the project's value had dropped into negative territory, in fact, minus $600 million.[8] Losing money is something Canadian mainstream press will report on, and efforts to stop the "money pipeline" have gained new strength. As I write this summary, the Stop the Money Pipeline effort has gained new strength. Royal Bank of Canada is a favourite target because it is the country's largest fossil fuel financier. They are starting to feel the heat all across the country.

As I write this, the TMX pipeline remains unfinished and is years behind schedule with its cost rising every day. Resistance to the project remains strong because new fossil energy infrastructure in 2023 is morally wrong. TMX will not kill anyone if it is never used.

We can't just talk about how the fossil energy era is winding down, we must do it. And like Hummingbird, I will continue to do what I can.

WILLIAM WINDER,
PhD, Emeritus
Professor of
French Linguistics

Biography

Bill Winder is a dual American/Canadian citizen, originally from North Carolina and now retired after thirty-one years teaching at UBC's French, Hispanic and Italian Studies department. His childhood experience at a natural history museum in Winston-Salem led him to pursue a BSc in zoology at North Carolina State University and further postgraduate work at the University of Edinburgh in epigenetics. Europe, and particularly France, were for Bill the source of a culture shock that redirected his interests to the most abstract and ethereal level of living systems: language, culture, and literature. He was introduced to Peircean semiotics at the University of Perpignan, France, continued to study linguistics, semiotics, and literature in France, and then pursued a PhD at the University of Toronto studying Maupassant's short stories. His research at UBC included linguistic and literary database design, implementation and exploitation for computer-assisted translation, interpretation, and semantic analysis.

Though Bill has always had an interest in our natural world, he was a mind-your-own-research academic until 2014 when the Burnaby Mountain protests began. From that point on, he has been involved in many protests, to the point of graduating with a further "degree" from the North Fraser Pretrial Centre after protesting the Trans Mountain Expansion (TMX).

Bill was arrested on September 22, 2021, in Burnaby and sentenced to twenty-one days on February 15, 2022, serving 14.

Statement to BC Supreme Court Justice Shelley Fitzpatrick, February 15, 2022

Good morning, Madame Justice, Crown counsel, and clerk.

I would like to acknowledge that we are on the unceded territories of the Tsleil-Waututh, Musqueam, and Squamish Nations. They have lived here sustainably for thousands of years. Our western values have had the unintended consequence of bringing us to the brink of climate collapse. In response to the crisis, western institutions are drawing up new legislation, such as the recognition of ecocide, that reflect the principles of Indigenous respect for nature. I will come back to this point later.

The Crown's sentencing position of twenty-one days in jail is an extension of the Crown's 2018 Amended Guide to Sentencing. The world has changed in the four years since those guidelines were drawn up. The sentencing I am proposing accepts the precedent of a jail sentence but at the same time recognizes the impact of the extreme climate events since 2018 and new declarations of emergency. The justifications for my position fall into three areas.

First: Climate breakdown has arrived in BC in 2022. We have real-world proof of the emergency. Second: Since 2019 governments at all levels have declared a climate emergency. Third: The crime of ecocide has made its way into the general public's understanding.

I believe all these factors are mitigating circumstances that explain my motivation for risking arrest to stop the Trans Mountain Expansion and justify a sentence that includes community service. I will deal with each of these three areas in more detail, but first I would like to briefly describe how I came to be arrested.

I'm sixty-nine-years old. I retired two years ago from UBC after teaching French there for thirty-one years. I have one adult son. I am well aware of the challenges his and future generations face. This is the first charge I have ever faced.

Climate Protest
I have been advocating for a livable climate since 2014, when I

participated in the protests against Trans Mountain on Burnaby Mountain. I was drawn to that protest because of the clear danger the Trans Mountain oil storage facility poses for the people who live nearby. The Burnaby Fire Department chief has said his unit cannot extinguish a fire at that facility, especially after the tank farm expansion. If there is a fire, a quarter of a million people are at risk of sulphur dioxide poisoning. International experts on oil storage facilities around the world have assessed the location and have said it is a catastrophe waiting to happen. We wrote letters to the minister of public safety, who then referred us to the minister of the environment, who did not reply. The storage facility is on the side of a mountain, in an earthquake zone, with houses on one side and forest on the other that is tinder-dry during the summer. The single road off the mountain from Simon Fraser University goes next to the facility. The twenty-five thousand students and staff have been told to shelter in place in case of a fire.

When Trans Mountain's work on Burnaby Mountain stopped and the protests subsided, my advocacy for the climate turned to the usual marches, petitions, and organizing with friends. None of this had the slightest impact on the growth of fossil fuel infra-structure or the growth in atmospheric CO_2 levels, which have gone from 402 ppm in 2014 to 417 ppm today. The NASA climate scientist James Hansen has famously warned that life as we know it is incompatible with anything above 350 ppm.

I expressly avoided arrest in 2014. This past summer I reluc-tantly accepted it. The earlier protest on Burnaby Mountain was about what might happen. In 2014 we had not yet seen the disas-ters we saw this past summer and fall. My decision to obstruct the pipeline expansion was not just about what might happen, but rather what was already happening. Extreme wildfires in the Pacific Northwest have given Vancouver the worst air quality in the world for the past two summers. Six hundred people died during the heat dome in BC. A billion sea creatures were destroyed as well. Lytton burned down and two seniors burned to death there. Over a half-million farm animals died in the Sumas Prairie floods. None of these deaths were necessary. None were natural disasters. They were all manmade disasters hastened by the fossil fuel industry.

That same spring, 215 Indigenous children were found in unmarked graves around the Kamloops residential school, with thousands more found across Canada. Nothing could bring home more urgently the obligation for the public to intervene and oppose destructive government policies. The government neglected its duty of care towards Canada's Indigenous children. It has neglected its duty of care to Missing and Murdered Indigenous Women and Girls. Canada's rising emissions and investments in fossil fuels are clear indications that once again the government is shirking its duty of care to present and future children who are facing climate breakdown. I continue to believe the public cannot remain a bystander to unhealthy government policies and must work to bring the government in line with its climate commitments.

I'm truly sorry that we are at odds here, when in fact I sincerely believe we want the same thing, that is, to preserve the rule of law. The Crown must follow the letter of the law and therefore quite reasonably charged me with criminal contempt of court. Under normal circumstances, I would applaud the good work of the RCMP, the Crown, and the court. But we are in such unprecedented times that I am paradoxically at odds with the Crown even when I fundamentally agree with the Crown's goals. That is one dimension of the unprecedented nature of climate breakdown. It divides people who would otherwise be united. The fear that drives me is that climate breakdown has the potential to destroy organized society and the rule of law.

Rule of Law

The Crown's sentencing position relies on precedent and treats this breach of the injunction as if it were like any other breach of an injunction. That is why the Crown's authorities include Justice Grist's 2007 opinion on the Eagleridge Bluffs injunction,[9] the most recent authority in the Crown's Sentencing Guidelines. Justice Grist gives examples of noble causes that citizens might be tempted to defend by breaching an injunction:

> I have no doubt that the individuals before me sincerely believe that their cause was just. However, we have many individuals and groups in society who are passionately committed to what they view as just causes. Poverty, homelessness, health care immediately come to mind. If each individual or group chose to

break the law and breach court orders to enforce their view of a correct response to a just cause, our democratic society would quickly fail. This is not a frivolous or theoretical concern. . . . When a group of citizens chooses to publicly defy the order of the court, they encourage each individual to disobey court orders which they do not like. It is this defiance which undermines the rule of law and brings the administration of justice into disrepute.

All the noble protests Justice Grist considers are indeed worthy causes that seek to protect and improve life. But that is not the nature of the cause that is motivating me. Far from it. I have accepted the science that says that life as we know it will not survive climate breakdown. If climate breakdown breeds societal chaos and collapse, where there is no rule of law, no health care, no food aid, no housing advocacy—in short, none of the welfare institutions of society—then all of these causes will be irrelevant.

The climate crisis is a winner-takes-all war with planetary physics. If we lose, there is no second chance to rectify the situation. Whatever the outcome of the examples cited by Justice Grist, there will be another day to try again to improve people's lives. Not so for climate breakdown.

We are facing something unprecedented at an unprecedented scale. Emergencies the world has encountered until now have all been limited and repairable. The damage the climate breakdown brings is neither limited nor repairable. It represents the end of the rule of law, the end of society as we know it, and perhaps the end of human history.

The charge of criminal contempt is the court's way to defend against a specific attack on the law. By obstructing what I believe to be a suicidal fossil fuel project, I feel I am defending the rule of law not in the specific manner of the Crown but in the general manner of preventing complete climate breakdown.

Fossil fuel companies have lied to the public, manipulated governments and public opinion, and knowingly geo-engineered the earth in a way they knew would kill. No rule of law stopped corporations from putting profit over planet. Injunctions are being used now by corporations to protect their interests. No injunction protects the victims of climate breakdown.

I acted on my very real fear for the future. My panic is, however, intermittent. I am just as often distracted into blissful ignorance, as we all are, but then I am slapped back into awareness by the heat dome, crop failures, wildfires, floods, and tornadoes. That is also part of the unprecedented nature of the climate crisis. It is the greatest emergency we have ever faced and yet it only intermittently looks like an emergency. The climate emergency has not yet found its way into our laws because it is a singular slow-moving emergency. Repeated emergencies are addressed by precedent. The climate crisis does not repeat; it is one continuous wave of destruction.

I cannot ignore the legitimate fears of our young people. When Greta Thunberg received death threats at her home, her parents asked her to stay at home and not attend her speaking engagement at a climate conference. She said she would go nevertheless because she was less afraid of death threats than what it would mean if she did not continue to work towards a livable climate. A sixteen-year-old should not be more afraid for her future than the death threats she has received in her home.

I am motivated to act on what I see as the barbarism of a world without the rule of law. Simply, I find myself at odds with the Crown's understandable focus on the here and now and on what is specific and local rather than on what is general and foundational. I have a legitimate fear of worldwide collapse. I have to act to avoid that outcome.

Emergency

My fear may seem alarmist, but it is officially recognized at all levels of our government.

Vancouver and 515 other municipalities in Canada have declared a climate emergency. Canada's federal government, the owner of the pipeline expansion, has declared a climate emergency. The UN has declared a climate code red for humanity. The intermittent effects of the climate crisis have meant that while the Province of BC has not declared a climate emergency, it has declared several states of emergencies for fires, a heat dome, and floods.

Since 2019 our governments at every level are saying that we are in a new state of the world. The 2018 sentencing guidelines, which predate these declarations of emergency, rely heavily on the MacMillan Bloedel cases of 1994, which are twenty-eight years old, and even include cases going back to 1970, fifty-two years ago. Even the most recent authority of 2007 is still fifteen years old and a pre-emergency authority.

I understand that court orders must be obeyed even during an emergency. That is why I have pleaded guilty. In sentencing, however, I would ask that the predictable and normal response to the pressures of an emergency not be discounted. The psychological effect of the peril persists, whatever the order. Discretion in sentencing is one way to recognize the emergency rather than sweeping the most monumental threat to humanity under the rug.

Ecocide

The threat of climate breakdown has triggered a moral shift in how society sees resource extraction. We are in an abolitionist moment, where this time it is society's relation to nature that is being promoted rather than the humanity of slaves.

The concept of ecocide is another evolutionary step in how people understand justice. The general public live their lives according to basic principles of respect for each other. The habit of that respect naturally grows out to include other living things. Abolition of slavery was a shift in values. Seeing people as cattle became intolerable, and even cattle are now legally afforded some degree of humane treatment. The crime of ecocide is simply a recognition that it is unfair to destroy ecosystems that are the only home for species we share this planet with. Ecocidal projects are presently driving millions of species to extinction, at our own peril.

The pressure of a massively transformative new law, such as the abolition of slavery or women's suffrage, is felt in the public even before it finds its way into the written text of the law. In the court of public values, the crime of ecocide has already been legislated. It seems reasonable to me to adapt to this transition at this time in the only place the court has discretion, that is, in sentencing.

Conclusion: Community Service

Our society has been diagnosed with terminal climate breakdown with only a few years left to implement any kind of treatment. Last year the former chief UK science advisor Sir David King said: "What we do over the next three to four years, I believe, is going to determine the future of humanity. We are in a very very desperate situation."

Justice Grist worries, as do other justices, that the example of one breach of the injunction will inspire more. That was not the case for me. I was motivated by the death of my fellow citizens due to climate change impacts and the affront of expanding our fossil fuel infrastructure in the province where they died.

I'm asking to replace a week of the Crown's three-week jail time with one hundred hours of community service. This would meet the sentencing precedent set in 2018, while recognizing that the authorities of 2018 are no longer in line with an international shift in values created by the climate crisis. Climate breakdown is here, now.

Narrative: Arrest in the Time of Climate Breakdown

The Brunette River resistance to the Trans Mountain Expansion began in August 2020 with Dr. Tim Takaro occupying a portaledge high in a tree in Brunette forest in Burnaby, BC. A coalition of activists from several grassroots environmental groups came together to support Tim's tree occupation. Over a period of nearly two years, three permanent tree-sits with wooden platforms were built twenty to twenty-five metres high in the Brunette canopy. Pistachio and Kurtis Baute were the main architects of the first treehouse, known as Eagle, and the sits were supported by many others from the group that came to be known as Protect the Planet. Eagle was overrun by TMX and dismantled in December 2020. In the following week, Pistachio and Cauliflower built the second treehouse, Hummingbird, still in the path of construction but farther into the forest. The third, Blue Jay, was constructed near Hummingbird in the summer of 2021. A rope bridge connected the two, and together they became the main point of resistance against TMX construction in Burnaby.

Over the summer of 2021, Tim and Pistachio taught me and others how to climb up a rope to the treehouse, and coordinated a group of sitters who maintained a constant occupation in Hummingbird. Protect the Planet maintained the ground support that brought food and water to the sitters.

By September 2021, Trans Mountain began cutting down the forest on the way to the treehouses. To slow the cutting, Nugget,

Peanut, and Raccoon helped me get up and set up in "skypod two," one of two hammocks we installed in the top of two cottonwoods on the path of construction. The forest was good cover for sneaking past TMX security at dusk, after the workers were gone, but I was not prepared, mentally, to meet a bear on the way. I ran. Peanut knew to stand his ground and the bear moved on. Peanut commented, impassively, and a little condescendingly, I think, "They are just big raccoons." I didn't entirely agree.

Beyond bears, security patrols, and setting up a hammock in the tree in the dark, the windstorm was the worst. Cottonwoods are known to snap in the wind. Tall trees litter the ground in the middle of the forest. The risk was heightened by the hammock, which became a billowing sail in the wind. So, in the dead of the night, pelting rain, and wind I came down the rope. It was too short and I was left dangling ten metres from the ground, like a stranded parachutist. After about eight days of mostly lying down in the hammock, I was (surprisingly, again) too weak to go back up to lengthen the rope and too far from the ground to jump. Ground support saved me by installing another rope and switching me over to that. Everyone was drenched and exhausted. It was another embarrassing moment that confirmed that I was clearly out of my depth. Most activists are. It isn't a profession we train for.

The skypods were supported day and night by a team of activists on the ground who sent food and water up on a rope and protected us from TMX security. TMX and the RCMP allowed us to block construction for two weeks because the Liberal government did not want its pipeline to become an issue during the September election. The day after the election, on the 22nd of September, the "tank" moved in and I was arrested; the skypods were dismantled. Other anti-TMX activists—Janette McIntosh, Ruth Walmsley, Catherine Hembling, and Zain Haq—blocked construction machinery on the ground and were ultimately arrested as well.

Tim Takaro, the last and also the first of the "Brunette River Six" in the trees, was arrested later that year in another portaledge occupation at another site along the construction path. The six of us were the latest of about 250 people who had been arrested for breaching the injunction that protects the Trans Mountain Expansion.

From Locked On to Locked Up

When I found myself locked up in a Canadian jail, I wondered how I'd gotten to the point of having a cell door shut me in for my twenty-one-day sentence. On the surface, it's simple enough: I was in an urban forest in Burnaby, BC, up twenty-five metres in a tree blocking the Trans Mountain Expansion construction for nine days when a team of tactical RCMP came in a massive cherry picker (the "tank") to cut the cable that secured the bike lock around my neck to the tree, pluck me out of the tree, and plop me to earth. (The bike lock remained a fixture around my neck for a few days until a locksmith sawed it off—see photo with my bio.) I signed the RCMP's form saying I would not go within five metres of the site and would appear in court on November 5, 2021, for breaching the injunction issued by Justice Affleck against any and all interference with TMX construction. Others have wound their way through the BC Supreme Court for similar acts of civil disobedience against TMX. The cell doors have closed on others in much the same way, though now we are facing a different judge, Justice Fitzpatrick.

That's the story the news might tell if the story were newsworthy. Protest arrests have become a bit ho-hum for the media. More than 1,100 people were arrested for violating an injunction at Vancouver Island's Fairy Creek. Who can keep up?

A news story would not explain what led me to block TMX, even though I knew I would go from the top of a tree, looking out as far as I could see across Burnaby, to the four walls of a Canadian jail cell. Why block TMX? Why me? Why not complain and protest to my MP? (I did.) Why not vote for the Green Party? (I did.) Why not protest in the streets? (I did.) Why in a tree? (It works, for a while.) Why in Burnaby? (It's close.) Why get arrested? (Later . . .) Why now? (Desperate times.)

Six Lessons

Lesson 1: Motivation to act has many curious layers.
Layer #1: Outrage at the incoherence between talk and action. I was protecting the trees and protesting the Trudeau government's self-contradicting plan to fight climate change, which is, in a nutshell: Declare a climate emergency, chop down forests, ignore UNDRIP

while expanding fossil fuel infrastructure, pump more oil, and then sometime in the yet-to-be-determined future use oil money to plant trees and finance climate change mitigation in Canada. If there is any oil money. The government itself (Parliamentary Budget Officer, Canada Energy Regulator), and an independent source (Canadian Centre for Policy Alternatives) said there won't be. Meanwhile, $35 billion or more of taxpayer money will go to propping up (often foreign) fossil fuel companies, when it could go into made-in-Canada renewables for Canadians—wind, tidal, solar, geothermal, energy efficiency, and more—and into a just transition for fossil fuel workers. Things that would have an immediate effect. In an emergency, time is of the essence.

Layer #2: Climate change is in our faces and is killing us. This summer's heat dome should have been reason enough for being in a hammock at the top of that cottonwood tree. It killed 619 people directly in BC alone, and indirectly a further 121 for a total of 740. The trees were brittle from drought and heat. Broken limbs littered the canopy and fell in strong winds. The wooded tract encompassing the tree-sits became a somewhat dangerous place to hang out.

Layer #3: I've read the science and it is alarming. Many things I have read encouraged me to act for the climate in spite of the threat of jail. I knew about the UN's code red. I read IPCC commentaries and summaries. I followed the scientific literature on specific topics like the retreat of Arctic ice or methane released from melting permafrost in Siberia. The most recent horror story is that the IPCC's estimation of the temperature increase at which there is a high risk of tipping points has shifted from 5°C in its 2001 report to as little as 1.5°C in 2018. In only two decades, the IPCC has come to understand that its estimations of climate sensitivity are far too conservative.[10] We are presently at 1.6 degrees above pre-industrial averages.[11]

Lesson 2: Don't get stuck in the past. Reinvent yourself.
The story of political interference with the truth strikes the nerve of a deeper reason for protesting TMX. My birthplace in the southern state of North Carolina was the strangest motivation for my protest.

The South refused to recognize the simple fact of the humanity of their slaves because it was a threat to their economy. Canada is equally unwilling to accept the simple facts and consequences of a fossil-fuel-induced climate emergency. Canada can't imagine an economy without ecocidal fossil fuel projects, no more than the South could conceive of an economy or a way of life without slaves. It seems obvious today to condemn slavery unequivocally. Young people in the throes of a climate catastrophe see the destruction of nature with the same disgust as we have come to see slavery. We are on the cusp of recognizing internationally the crime of ecocide. In that case, Canada and Canadian mining industries would be the defendants, with no moral excuse for their disregard for life on the planet.

Lesson 3: Corporations will literally kill you to make a profit.
Winston-Salem, the city where I was born, is another reason for my tree-sit protest. It was founded on the tobacco trade and inspired two flagship cigarette brands—Winston and Salem. When it became clear that cigarettes cause cancer, the tobacco industry would not take medical science's no for an answer, and like the Confederates before them, banded together and went on the offensive. This time with a massive disinformation campaign, which became the model for oil companies' tidal wave of self-serving dishonesty in the US that peaked under former president Donald Trump.

The Canadian oil and gas industry is playing the same game as the slave-era South. Alberta—Canada's Alabama—has its war room and its threats of secession. It is the same game as the tobacco industry. Deny, delay, spread disinformation, and ignore the death toll their industry is causing.

The Canadian public is mostly standing idly by, as it did during the horrors of the residential school period.

Lesson 4: Direct action is a necessary response to government atrocities.
Indeed, the most compelling reason for risking arrest was the thousands of Indigenous children whose bodies are lying in unmarked graves around residential schools throughout Canada. They are silently looking up at us, eyes wide with disbelief: Why didn't you do something? Future generations are watching too, even as the present generation of children are being buried because

of climate-induced famine (as in Madagascar and Kenya). Where was the protest when the RCMP were ripping children from their family and their way of life? Where was the government's duty of care? The extractive industries took the land and left the bodies of children.

Canada continues to clear Indigenous people from their land. Extractive industries continue to use the courts to take whatever they like. The Wet'suwet'en are displaced by militarized RCMP. The Secwépemc are surrounded by man camps where Indigenous women and girls disappear. Indigenous stewards of ancient forests are pushed aside by logging companies and their injunctions. Should the public let an industry-captured Canadian government use settler law to commit crimes against humanity? If the story of residential schools does not inspire enough shame and disgust to push us to protect future generations, what will?

Lesson 5: Written law is a blunt instrument; justice depends on an engaged public.
We turn to citizens' assemblies and to juries to find our best answers to difficult questions. Greek courts had large juries, with as many as five hundred citizens. Democracies depend on juries to deliver justice, because the lived experience of ordinary people counterbalances the overly abstract and absolute pronouncements of written law, which is overwhelmingly crafted and preserved by the powerful to protect their own interests. Books should not judge people; people should judge people.

Injunctions are unfortunately modelled on the single Pontius Pilate judge, not a jury of twelve peers. When juries hear the defence of necessity for nonviolent direct action against climate-destabilizing projects, they increasingly overrule written law and find the defendant not guilty. For example, in the UK, Extinction Rebellion activists were in court in April 2021 for criminal damage to Shell Oil's office building.[12] In the Southwark Crown Court, the jury delivered a landmark not guilty verdict for each defendant, despite the judge ruling that five of the six had no defence under the law. In another example, in the US states of Washington and Minnesota, the "valve turners" set the precedent of the defence of necessity for climate action.[13] This group of climate activists closed all the tar sands pipelines going into the United States from

Canada. In the case of one of the valve turners, Ken Ward, the Washington State Supreme Court ruled that an earlier trial judge had violated Ward's Sixth Amendment rights by refusing to allow him to present evidence of the necessity of his actions to a jury of his peers, including expert testimony from climate scientists and civil disobedience experts.[14]

Neither written law nor judges as the voice of written law can keep pace with the climate and social change we are experiencing. Injunctions are a disjunction of the law because they circumvent the countervailing force of ordinary people's lived experience. Judges peer into their books to decide what is lawful; people look out into the world to decide what is justice.

Lesson 6: Sacrifice is the lifeblood of a society; greed is the poison.
Justice is now on the front lines, in the hands of young people. They have done their homework. They understand science. They have no investments in oil, gas, and coal to protect. They have no other investment than their future and the planet itself. They are asking us to save the planet.

We have a political and legal system that has grown old and hard of hearing. Our legal system does not hear science, it does not hear reason, it does not hear young people fighting for their future. It only hears money, loud and clear. Who can stand by and let young people try to fix this code red emergency on their own? I am in the best position to support their fight for survival. I am not poor. I am not marginalized by my race or background. I am educated. I have no job to go to or to protect. My future is already determined. The best thing I can do with my time left is work to safeguard young people's future.

People like me have to step up to the front lines, wherever those lines may be.

ZAIN HAQ,
Student Activist

Biography

Zain Haq grew up in Karachi, Pakistan, and witnessed his fellow countrymen's poverty and deaths as a result of the climate emergency. Zain sees that if we don't act now, we will become the most hated generation in history.

Zain came to Canada to study history as a student at Simon Fraser University. His study visa was revoked due to nonviolent civil disobedience actions. He has been arrested a number of times in the past few years. Not because he wanted to be, but because he no longer sees another option. His hunger strike with other students at the SFU campus in November 2021 resulted in a decision by the SFU administration on day one of the strike to divest completely from fossil fuels by 2025. Zain knows that in times of extreme negligence by our governments, we are obligated to participate in our democracy with enthusiasm.

———

Zain was arrested for blocking TMX work in October 2021, and sentenced to twenty-one days' incarceration, of which he served fourteen days in February 2022.

Narrative: Responding to the Climate Crisis from a Global Perspective

I write now having finally fought off my pending deportation from Canada, as a result of my non-consent to the Trans Mountain Pipeline Expansion and my subsequent arrest and detention. I am awaiting the outcome of my spousal sponsorship application for permanent residence. The campaign to stop my deportation succeeded due to people's willingness to write to their members of Parliament.

About a month after I arrived in Vancouver to study history at SFU, I learned about an Extinction Rebellion event to block Burrard Bridge. I went at first just out of curiosity but quickly got more involved. Soon after, I went to a Heading for Extinction talk with about two hundred other people and decided to sign up as a resister against the Trans Mountain Pipeline project. At first I thought, well, I won't really be that involved—just show up from time to time for a few events—because I obviously can't get arrested, given my status here on a study permit.

I personally felt indebted to Canada. I love this country's espoused values with respect to human rights and equality, even if they are not always lived up to, because there are countries in the world that don't have these values to begin with, like Pakistan. It is easy to take these values for granted if you are born and raised in Canada, unlike me. My actions, although controversial, were motivated by a deep love for the people of this country and the land. I do not wish to see the level of social breakdown in Canada experienced by the people in Pakistan brought on by ecological disaster. I saw on the news while I was jailed for participating in a march with Wet'suwet'en Elders, that 30 million Punjabis and Sindhis in Pakistan were displaced due to extreme flooding, and the primarily agricultural country lost 90 percent of its crops.

In a recent heat wave in India and Pakistan temperatures and humidity came very close to producing a "wet bulb" effect. This is a critical condition where the human body can no longer cope; there is a sudden binary transition and people just start dying in great numbers. It's inevitable that something like this will happen, if not this year or the next, then very soon after, and when it does it will be like an ecological 9/11. People will wake up and become aware that all our lives are at risk.

I think Canadians down the road will see my past actions as patriotic, similar to how Henry Morgentaler, who was jailed for performing abortions, was later given the Order of Canada. Times change, and people's attitudes change with them.

During the COVID lockdown, I saw climate activism collapse as people retreated back into their silos. As I saw others dropping out, I felt even more the need to take initiative and organize. I also felt compelled to step up because I saw that some activists lacked clear knowledge and understanding of nonviolence, as espoused by Gandhi and others. I was deeply troubled by the hateful and confrontational attitude toward police, government, and pipeline workers I found among some activists. I believe that hate is quite poisonous, not only intrinsically, but because it is strategically counterproductive. It distracts us from the purpose of the work and is bad for the mental health of activists, making them more likely to burn out when their orientation is that of "fighting" rather than promoting peace. And because it just doesn't get us anywhere.

Gandhi's lived example shows us how he was able to become good friends with his most intense enemies, especially in the struggle in South Africa for the rights of Indians, a fact that I find uncontroversial and very easy to understand and relate to. During my divestment efforts at SFU, there wasn't a word of hostility exchanged between myself and the administration. We didn't succeed just because we were right and were doing a hunger strike; we won because we were good people and acted as good people. During my time organizing in the past, I am proud to say that I maintained an authentically friendly relationship with members of the police and now with members of Parliament. Good faith goes a long way, and it is important that we provide this type of leadership and advice to young people in universities and high school; otherwise, we will start seeing levels of hate and violence that will be heartbreaking, especially since they are completely avoidable through good leadership.

Even though the pandemic lessened people's involvement in some ways, it also created an opportunity for global connections established through the internet to develop a movement with countries that included Canada, the UK, and Germany working together. This makes it possible to have a meaningful and proportional response to climate change and establish the groundwork for mass involvement. But we still have a lot of work to do, and the time we have to avert global catastrophe from climate change is very short.

I decided to take action with others regarding the Trans Mountain Pipeline by showing up to get in the way of construction of a temporary road at the Brunette Conservation Area by Brunette Creek. The road was being built so trees could be cut down to make way for the pipeline. Along with other tree-sitters there in October 2021, I blocked construction by appearing to be locked into a device, though in fact I was not. It took four hours to remove me and others from the site, and because it was a long weekend, the action also ended up stopping construction for an entire week. Officers from the Burnaby RCMP made the arrest. The arrest procedure itself was very calm and uneventful. I wasn't put in handcuffs or taken into detention, just taken to a police car and made to sign a release form right there on the back of the car before my release. Eventually I was taken to another entrance to the park and released. I was charged with criminal contempt of court, like hundreds of other citizens.

A few months later, I appeared in court along with my fellow resister Bill Winder. He was given a twenty-one-day sentence, and I was given fourteen days in detention along with him. We were held at the North Fraser Pretrial Centre in Coquitlam. It sounds like it's only for people awaiting trial, but it's also for people serving less than two years. If you have to go to prison, it's best if you can do it with another resister. It makes it feel like less of a gamble. Bill and I were cellmates and became friends. We learned we had a lot in common and talked about philosophy and literature and everything else while we were there.

Prison itself didn't seem so bad, though it's stressful to feel you are always being watched. It was especially hard not to have access to sunlight. We only got out for one hour each day in a small court-yard, and even then there wasn't that much light.

We had access to pen and paper, so I spent some hours writing up the account of my time in prison to give to others on my release. I could make one phone call a day, and that was usually to the Save Old Growth office. Save Old Growth is another environmental organization I did a lot with, and they were always there to talk with me during the time I was detained. We had a television and watched a lot of episodes of *Seinfeld*. The rest of the time, we often slept when there was not much else to do. We didn't have any caffeine in there to help keep us awake. When you are in prison, you learn about the experiences of other people in prison, and that is very humbling. I am lucky to have a family who, though they worry about me, accept what I am doing.

Sometime after my release, Canada Border Services detained me again for two days and put a removal order in place. They tried to make the argument that I was a public security risk, but I was lucky to have a sympathetic immigration judge and I was released under certain conditions. One of them was that I had to move from where I was living at the time to stay in East Vancouver with the bondsperson who put up the surety for my release. I can no longer attend SFU, because my study permit was revoked. If my application for permanent residence is accepted, I will legally be able to study and engage in public life and even public service in and for Canada.

The only other thing I can say right now is that people have to follow their conscience, align their actions with common human decency, act when they feel called upon, for the right reasons, and do so with love at the centre.

JANETTE MCINTOSH,
Presbyterian Elder and Educator

Biography

For Janette McIntosh, climate justice is deeply rooted in her personal, spiritual, and professional learnings and practices of more than thirty years. Her career began in environmental health. She then worked in community health, sustainability education, and research. Later, after studying theology, her focus has remained on justice, eco-theology, and reconciliation. Janette is a mother of two young adults, married, and she continues in faithful action for climate justice.

She is a KAIROS Blanket Exercise facilitator and was the KAIROS BC-Yukon representative. Janette is a member of the Earth Witness Circle that started gathering by the Watch House on Burnaby Mountain in the summer of 2018, which became the Prayer Circle Action Group in the fall of 2020, an affinity group of Protect the Planet: Stop TMX. Our interconnectedness with one another and being a part of a larger ecosystem shapes her actions—ideally for prevention, but sometimes, inevitably, as a reaction. In September 2021, in a prayerful and peaceful act of civil disobedience, Janette sat in front of the workers' gate blocking a big machine in protest against TMX.

Janette was arrested on September 8, 2021, sentenced to fourteen days (serving nine days) at the Alouette Correctional Centre for Women (ACCW) in February 2022.

Statement to BC Supreme Court to Justice
Shelley Fitzpatrick, February 14, 2022

Madam Justice,

Thank you for this opportunity to speak. I stand before you with sound mind and calm heart. I do so while acknowledging that we are on the traditional, unceded lands of the Musqueam, Squamish, and Tsleil-Waututh Nations. As a settler living in Vancouver, which I now call "home," I remain indebted to the Original Peoples of this land and its surrounding waters. I am grateful for their stewardship over the many years past, continuing in the present, and into the future, for generations to come.

Today, on February 14, on this thirty-first annual Women's Memorial March Day, I especially wish to honour the many women from the Downtown Eastside who have died due to physical, mental, emotional, and spiritual violence, and the women and girls who have gone missing or been murdered.

I do not contest the facts that Crown counsel outlined. I take full responsibility for my action and I've pleaded guilty at the earliest opportunity. I will abide by Crown counsel's recommendation for a fourteen-day custodial sentence.

In this submission, I will share my personal background and other factors that are relevant to sentencing, to help you to understand who I am and why I did what I did.

I am fifty-eight-years old and have dedicated thirty-five years of my life to ecological justice, both as a professional and as a volunteer. My specialty is environmental and community health. I have degrees in:

- Environmental Health (Ryerson University, recently renamed Toronto Metropolitan University)
- Community Health and Epidemiology (Faculty of Medicine, University of Toronto)
- Master of Arts in Theological Studies (Vancouver School of Theology)

I was born in Japan. My late father was a minister with the Presbyterian Church in Canada. My mother was an English teacher. They spent forty years in Japan with the Korean Christian

Church in Japan. Both of them learned to speak Japanese and Korean. I grew up in a minority Korean neighbourhood in Osaka. I went to a Korean Church and a Japanese school through grade nine. I speak fluent Japanese. I have three siblings, one of whom was born in Canada and another born in Japan.

My third sibling, a younger sister, was born in Korea. She was adopted by my parents at age three. As her older sister, I've felt the pain she's endured in Japan from cruel and harsh systemic racism, solely for being Korean. Many of my friends experienced the same.

In Japan, many laws—including the notorious Alien Registration Law—legitimized the harsh treatment of minority Koreans, including my sister and friends. Their experiences are relevant to my action at the Trans Mountain gate because they were my first tangible and personal lessons in law and justice. Witnessing what they went through helped me recognize systemic patterns and practices that favour one person over another. More particularly, how some laws may be used to discriminate and oppress, much like Canada's colonial laws have with Indigenous Peoples.

My sister's and friends' experiences taught me how law and justice may, at times, differ. That justice is more complex and more subtle than a methodical following of rules. Justice requires questioning whether the rules themselves are just. Justice requires fairness, inclusion, compassion, and understanding. It requires a willingness to consider all sides of a dispute and the consequences of decisions to everyone concerned. Justice requires the recognition of power and resource imbalances between ordinary people and big corporations.

Justice requires everything that was absent from the Trans Mountain expansion decision:

- Voices of concerned people were excluded from the National Energy Board process, including many of the people who live close to the project site and are directly impacted by its life-threatening risks.
- The impact of the pipeline on climate change and health was excluded from the process.
- The public and the media were excluded from the process. Legitimate questioning and scrutiny of what was going on behind closed doors was forbidden.

- Truth was not told fully, and this has compromised justice and democracy.

This deficient process enables politicians and Trans Mountain to act above the law, with impunity.

I do understand and I do appreciate the importance of the rule of law and of following judicial decisions, including this court's injunction. Throughout my life I've been a law abider and I'll continue to be. My action on September 8, 2021, was in protest of Trans Mountain, not of this court. I did not mean to disrespect the court.

Until my arrest I'd used lawful channels to voice my concerns. I met and wrote to MLAs and MPs. I organized and attended rallies. Professionally and voluntarily, I've engaged in scientific work, community outreach, research, education, public awareness, and policy development.

One of my most notable accomplishments was being among the team of researchers who developed the Ecological Footprint,[15] a scientific tool that measures the impact of human consumption on the earth's finite resources. We were an interdisciplinary team of doctors, nurses, social workers, epidemiologists, and planners, members of the Task Force for Healthy and Sustainable Communities at the University of British Columbia. I was the team's research coordinator for the five-year project from 1991 to 1996.

At a personal level, the Ecological Footprint helped me to evaluate my own way of living and my own wasteful habits. It made me acutely aware of the ecological limits in which we live.

As we developed the Ecological Footprint, which includes a Carbon Footprint measure, we calculated averages and concluded that if everyone in Canada were to continue their high-consumption lifestyles, we'd need two planet Earths to sustain our habits. Even in those early years, the science was clear that if we did nothing then the consequences to humanity would be grave and irreversible.

We piloted the Ecological Footprint with the City of Richmond, and I had high hopes that governments would rely on it to make informed and responsible decisions that could have averted the climate emergency we now find ourselves in. Unfortunately, the opposite happened. Although scientific knowledge and tools have been available, political will has not. The window of opportunity to reverse the course of climate change since the early 1990s has shut.

This is not my subjective individual view. It is a scientific view, backed by hard evidence and an international consensus. Governments have known this for a long time, and on June 18, 2019, Canada's House of Commons declared a national climate emergency. But on the next day, the same government approved TMX.

They have failed to protect.

In the few months before my arrest, the consequence of that failure became real and profound in British Columbia. I became increasingly concerned and ethically compelled to act after:

- Unprecedented, record-breaking heat threatened our health and our lives.
- The town of Lytton was destroyed by fires. News of this went viral around the world.
- Over six hundred people died from the heat dome.
- Livelihoods were lost and people were displaced.

These were not isolated events. There was unanimous recognition, even among politicians, that this was climate change in action. And more personally, around the same time, a garage next to our home caught fire. I felt the hot, dry and thick air; and how quickly fire takes hold, at uncontrollable speed.

A few weeks before my arrest, the IPCC issued its August 2021 report, which was described by the UN Secretary-General as a "code red for humanity." I'd like to file the Secretary-General's two-page statement about the IPCC report as an exhibit for my sentencing hearing.[16]

The secretary-general highlighted the following main points from the IPCC report:

- Many of the global heating changes have become irreversible (para 2).
- We are at imminent risk of hitting the 1.5 Celsius threshold in the near term (para 3).
- Extreme weather and climate disasters are increasing in frequency and intensity (para 4).
- The viability of societies depends on leaders from

government, business, and civil society uniting behind policies, actions, and investments aimed at limiting temperature
rises (para 5).

- "We need immediate action on energy. Without deep
  carbon pollution cuts now, the 1.5°C goal will fall quickly
  out of reach. This report must sound a death knell for
  coal and fossil fuels, before they destroy our planet. . . .
  Countries should also end all new fossil fuel exploration
  and production, and shift fossil-fuel subsidies into renewable energy" (para 7).
- "There is no time for delay and no room for excuses" (para 10).

In that unprecedented context of escalating dangers and heightened warnings—based on uncontestable facts—I felt a deep moral
and ethical responsibility to act. Despite the heat domes, despite
the fires, the lost lives, displaced people, and a UN code red warning, it was (and is) business as usual for Trans Mountain workers.

My act was peaceful and nonviolent. I co-operated with
the police.

I sat silently in prayer with my prayer circle friends, as a
mother, an aunt, a sister, a spouse, a friend, a neighbour, a scientist,
an educator, a citizen, a volunteer, and a committed advocate for
enacting UNDRIP and the Truth and Reconciliation Commission's
Calls to Action.

My motivation was driven by faith, hope, compassion, and
love. My prayers, hopes, and actions had only one goal in mind
that day: for all life to flourish.

Thank you for listening.

Narrative: Challenging Power with a Heart of Compassion and the Strength of Community

Throughout my days leading up to and during my incarceration,
I never felt alone. A big part of that was thanks to our sisterhood
and "buddy system" supporting both individual and collective
action. Our community members' thoughts and prayers were always with me.

On September 8, 2021, I sat prayerfully in front of the gates with
my Prayer Circle friends, not wanting to let the big backhoe inside.
The machine would create a path to the tree-sitters, resulting in

their extraction and the laying of the pipeline. My nonviolent direct action was prayerful and peaceful civil disobedience. As a mother, aunt, sister, and guardian of a few young children, I take a stand for our future—that it be protected for our young. I also remain committed as an advocate for enacting UNDRIP and the Truth and Reconciliation Commission's ninety-four Calls to Action.

On this day, I was able to remain strong and calm as I prepared to take action, knowing the love and support given me by my dear prayer circle sisters Ruth and Catherine, and Christine Thuring too. We had "practised" for arrest during other actions, starting in March of 2021. This was not a planned day of action, but that quickly changed in response to the machine that was present and waiting to be let in. I was called in from a distance (at Hume Park) where I was giving direction to the people who had signed up for the tree-sit tour, and was expecting to be at my mothers' place later that morning. Thankfully I reached my mother by phone, and although she has mild dementia that often leads to confused communication, she understood clearly the action that I was taking and blessed me for doing so. I was also thankful for Anglican priest Laurel Dykstra's calming spiritual presence, to Jessica and her son for bringing prayers and good medicine, and to my friend Brynn, who stayed right by my side until just after the injunction was read to us.

The constable that arrested me was a sympathizer. He was so nervous he was sweating buckets. If I'd had a handkerchief, I would have offered it to him. I felt compassion for him. After walking to the police car for documentation, I looked back and saw the big backhoe being trucked in. I was disheartened. I felt sick, angry, and sad. I saw this as the beginning of the end in this small corner of a forested patch along North Road. Had I let down our tree-sitting friends who would now be extracted? The trees and the forest, the blackberry bushes, hummingbirds, the frogs? This machine was going to open the way to destruction—Lost Creek, truly to be lost forever.

My prayer circle sisters were arrested for similar blockades in the days following my arrest. The three of us were tried and sentenced together on February 14, 2022. To be honest, I was more nervous about the sentencing trial and procedures in the court than going to jail. The court system—so formal, patriarchal, rigid, legalistic, and detached—is a colonial system made for and by lawyers. It was not meant to be friendly nor welcoming.

After the judge delivered her sentence (two weeks at ACCW), we were taken to a holding cell in the basement of the courthouse. It was damp and cold, and the slams of doors echoed through it. We started to sing, our voices blending in harmony—for warmth, reassurance, and spiritual lift!

After a time we were handcuffed and shackled at the ankles, then loaded into cages in the back of a police van. All stainless steel, with metallic mesh and Plexiglas between us. No seatbelts. I had a small meshed window to my left. As we drove up the ramp from the courthouse and into traffic, I saw the city bustling outside and wondered, can the people out there see me? Do they have any idea of what it looks and feels like inside this police van? The sun was going down. I had to pinch myself; is this for real? This is when it hit me. I was going to jail.

After one, two, three van changes, we arrived at the correctional centre around 7 p.m. I had been concerned for Catherine because she had to sit sideways for part of the trip and we were unable to communicate with each other, but we all arrived without physical injuries. A brown bag lunch was waiting for us in each of our stalls. Still cold and damp, we rekindled warmth and connection by singing again. We were given forest green sweatshirts and pants.

Due to COVID precautions, the three of us plus one stayed in one area for the first three days, but in separate cells, overlooking the central guards' station. We had a shared hall space where we could eat meals together. Our individual cells were approximately 1.8 by 4 metres, with two narrow slits of "window" for natural light, a toilet and sink, surveillance cameras on the ceiling, and a television high up on the wall. I struggled with the images on the television screen, in juxtaposition to my own reality: The truck convoy in Ottawa demanding "freedom," the escalating tensions in Ukraine, and the Olympics—all happening while we were in jail.

My cell had a canvas on the wall with an image from the former occupant of a red heart (perfect for Valentine's Day!) on the left; on the right half an upside-down cross burning. This image spoke louder than words; it was a humbling reminder for me throughout my stay at ACCW, especially as a Christian—a reminder of how and why close to 50 percent of incarcerated women are Indigenous. I immediately asked for pencil/pen and paper. Writing and doodling is something I sought for comfort and to help pass the time. It was delivered by the next morning. I don't know how I lucked out with this request; I know now that such simple asks by the other resisters were conveniently ignored.

After our stay in the segregation unit, we were transferred to the induction unit as a cohort of twelve women—five white, five Indigenous, and two South Asian women ranging in ages from early twenties to late seventies.

I prayed often for peace and understanding throughout the nine long days and nights.

The lights were always on, and a loud fan and heavy unit doors randomly slamming shut throughout the night made it difficult for light sleepers. Aside from this we were well cared for, and the guards were well trained to handle the mental health challenges, including nightmares, that some inmates struggled with. I prayed for peace for the inmates and guards every night. Even though there were scheduled times for meals, time in and out of our cells seemed random, but it was often a pleasant surprise to be "let out."

At the core of our climate activism is nonviolence. Nonviolent civil disobedience is a peaceful and powerful practice that can bring about profound change. It is a call to conscience and prophetic witness. It is intended to expose the violence in a situation, and to challenge the legitimacy of the systems of power which perpetuate that violence.

Sacred duty calls us to faith-full action, in solidarity with Indigenous friends near and far, and to protect all of God's creation. We the resisters will not let colonial ways dictate, because these ways can eradicate our connections and interdependence. We act together in faith, with active hope, and with love. My small action was but one of many arrests (240+ before me), and there are likely still more to come.

To quote the late Desmund Tutu: "If you are neutral in situations of injustice, you have chosen the side of the oppressor. I wish I could shut up, but I can't, and I won't." Tutu also reminds us that "We are each made for goodness, love and compassion. Our lives are transformed as much as the world is when we live with these truths." Yes, I believe this, and I trust others do too, and pray that we will have the strength to live out these truths fully, together. We must.

RUTH WALMSLEY,
Quaker,
Environmentalist

Biography

Ruth Walmsley graduated from Sheridan College School of Crafts and Design, Ontario, in 1985 with a major in ceramics, and from Simon Fraser University, BC, in 1990 with a BA in fine and performing arts. She has worked as a ceramic artist and as an organizer and teacher of fine arts programs. Singing and sharing music with others is a central theme in her life. Ruth and her husband co-own a family business, Harmonic Functions Inc., specializing in research and development of digital audio equipment used mainly in live theatre environments.

Ruth is a member of the Religious Society of Friends (Quakers), and is actively involved in multi-faith work, including with the Prayer Circle Direct Action group and KAIROS: Canadian Ecumenical Justice Initiatives.

Ruth is a passionate activist and advocate for social and environmental justice, as well as a strong community organizer and networker. In 1993, she was one of about nine hundred people arrested in the movement against clear-cut logging of old-growth forests in Clayoquot Sound on Vancouver Island. In 2012 she co-founded BROKE—Burnaby Residents Opposing Kinder Morgan Expansion, a grassroots organization dedicated to stopping the Trans Mountain Pipeline Expansion. Her work involves building strong alliances with First Nations Peoples in resisting large-scale fossil fuel extraction projects in their territories. Ruth attended the Tar Sands Healing Walk in 2014 as part of this witness.

Ruth was arrested on September 9, 2021, and served nine days of a two-week sentence in February 2022.

Statement to BC Supreme Court Justice Shelley Fitzpatrick, February 14, 2022

Dear Madame Justice,

I'd like to begin by acknowledging that we are here on the unceded and ancestral territory of the Coast Salish Peoples, and by expressing my gratitude for their stewardship of these lands since time immemorial.

I appreciate this opportunity to state my reasons for having breached the injunction order issued by Justice K.N. Affleck and therefore having committed criminal contempt of court.

On September 9, 2021, I was arrested, as part of an inter-faith Prayer Circle nonviolent direct action. On that day, a group of us entered an active work zone in a forested area in Burnaby, BC, effectively stopping tree cutting in preparation for construction of the Trans Mountain Expansion project (TMX). We sat in prayer and meditation, and sang songs honouring the sacredness of water, in order to make the statement that this desecration of Mother Earth must stop.

As a person of faith, I am mindful of the moral imperative for us to think seven generations into the future when making decisions which affect us today. I consider it to be my sacred duty to do whatever is in my power to ensure that I leave the world in a condition that will continue to support life as we know it, for present and future generations. The continued expansion of new fossil fuel infrastructure, such as the Trans Mountain Expansion Project, during a declared climate emergency, is in violation of this moral imperative. It will result in an increase in fossil fuel emissions, at a time when the science is abundantly clear that we need to be transitioning away from burning fossil fuels as quickly as possible, if we are to maintain a livable planet.

We are in uncharted territory. Climate change is threatening the survival of life on Earth. I am a mother of two adult children. Access to the basic requirements of life such as clean water, air, and food is their birthright. Yet they are part of the first generation ever to be facing the reality that this birthright is being stolen by a system which allows greed and profit to take precedence over people and planet. The shameful tragedy is that we have known for decades that we are extracting and consuming fossil fuels at a rate which far exceeds Earth's capacity to maintain a stable climate, yet this has been allowed to continue. I refuse to stand by and do nothing while over one million animal and plant species are threatened with extinction within decades—more than ever before in human history—as a direct result of human activity.[17] ENOUGH IS ENOUGH! Too much has already been lost.

I believe in the rule of law as a principle which defines the rights and responsibilities of people to coexist peacefully in society. I do not take lightly my decision to break the law. However, over the past nine years, I have pursued all available legal avenues to express my opposition.

In 2012, I co-founded the community organization Burnaby Residents Opposing Kinder Morgan Expansion, which is still active to this day. In 2014, I applied to be an intervenor in the National Energy Board hearings, on the basis of my deep concern about potential adverse impacts this project would have on myself and my family, given that my home is in close proximity to the Trans Mountain Westridge Marine Terminal. The board rejected my application to participate as an intervenor, and even denied my standing to submit a letter of comment.

In 2016 I spoke before the ministerial panel appointed by the Trudeau government following their election in the fall of 2015. I have met with my MP, written dozens of letters, and signed countless petitions urging the government to cancel this project.

I have organized and attended numerous marches and rallies in protest of this project.

With construction of the Trans Mountain Expansion proceeding unabated, my conscience compelled me to act in the most powerful way I could, to prevent any further erosion of the possibility of a livable world for my children and all future life. I am witnessing to the truth that Earth is a finite planet, with a limited capacity to sustain life. I have learned that life on Earth involves a reciprocal relationship, and we have forgotten how to attend to this balance.

The action I have taken is also in solidarity with the Indigenous Peoples of this land, who do not give their consent to this project.[18]

I recognize that this place where I live has been the home of the Coast Salish People since time immemorial. Canada is a signatory to the United Nations Declaration on the Rights of Indigenous Peoples. The UN declaration sets out an explicit requirement to obtain free, prior, and informed consent. It affirms the rights of Indigenous Peoples to make their own decisions about their lives, territories, and futures, and to decide according to their own laws, customs, and traditions whether a project should proceed, be modified, or be rejected.[19]

Madame Justice, I know that you have children of your own, and I'm sure you care about the future of young people today as much as I do. I ask you to put yourself in my position, and consider my decision to breach the injunction through the lens of my concern for the survival of my children, their children, and all life on Earth. My heart breaks with the knowledge of the damage which has already been done, for the lives we can never bring back. I grieve the reality that life as we have known it is not something my children and future generations can be assured of. I ask you to look into the future, and consider how the choices we are making today will be judged seven generations from now.

Just this morning, on my way to the courthouse, I received a message from my daughter Thea Walmsley, who is twenty-four years old. I would like to share an excerpt with you of what she wrote to me:

> Growing up, I always wanted to be a mother. To bring curious, open-hearted children into this world; to create safe and loving places for them to explore and experience all of the beauty and wonder it contains. And, in recent years, like many in my generation, I have been forced to confront whether this is an ethical thing to do, because of the deep uncertainty about whether the planet will be livable. I am being forced to consider how much will be robbed from them in the name of profit—how much of their clean water, their ability to grow healthy food, to experience biodiversity, to live without conflict, to exist in livable temperatures. How much anxiety they will be subjected to at the real possibility that their life will be upended by a natural disaster. I am being forced to reckon with the depth of the greed of those in power when making decisions as personal as whether

to have children. We all are. And it's infuriating. It's even more infuriating because it doesn't have to be like this. Those in power are making conscious choices at every stage, crafting the kind of world that we will eventually inhabit. We can make different choices. But those in power must be forced to listen.

Even amidst all of the deep injustice, I hold tremendous hope in the knowledge that people like my mother have brought up an entire generation of activists to follow in their footsteps. We are coming of age and entering the world, becoming writers, organizers, scientists, politicians, artists. And as the climate crisis deepens, we are poised and ready to take up the fight alongside them. And make no mistake; we're just getting started.

My decision to engage in peaceful civil disobedience was motivated by my love for this creation, and my concern for the future of my children and life on Earth. I am at peace with this decision, and am fully prepared to accept the consequences of my actions.

I know that many strong and courageous people have walked this path before me. They have stood before the National Energy Board, ministerial panel, and courts of law, and brought compelling evidence to bear on the dangers and folly of proceeding with the Trans Mountain Expansion. I am aware that it is the duty of this court to enforce the rule of the law, and that your only concern is to determine whether or not we are guilty of breaching the injunction.

However, this injunction leads directly to the worsening of the climate crisis, and violates the birthright of present and future generations to a healthy planet on which to live and thrive.

I hope and pray that my words and deeds, as well as those of my fellow arrestees here in court today and tomorrow, and the more than 240 concerned people who have been arrested for breaching this injunction prior to us, will serve to raise more public awareness about the climate emergency and what is at stake, and why the Trans Mountain Expansion project should be stopped.

Narrative: My Response to a Call of the Spirit
When I reflect on the motivations for my decision to engage in nonviolent civil disobedience two main influences leap out.

Firstly, my decision came from a spiritually rooted place.

Through my Quaker faith and practice, I experienced what I would call a spiritual leading to engage in nonviolent civil disobedience, as an expression of my profound concern about the harm being caused to the earth by the expansion of new fossil fuel infrastructure and the increased carbon emissions which result from that.

My Quaker faith gives me strength in doing this work. When I feel discouraged, I remember that I am only responsible for living up to the light that is granted to me. As someone who has a tendency to feel compelled to carry the weight of the world on my shoulders, it is a relief to remember that I am not solely responsible for the outcome, but only for being true to that which I am called to do. This allows me to let go and let God.

Secondly, I'm motivated by the reality that we're in a climate emergency. In February 2022, the IPCC issued a "stark warning about the impact of climate change on people and the planet, saying that ecosystem collapse, species extinction, deadly heatwaves and floods are among the 'dangerous and widespread disruptions' the world will face over the next two decades due to global warming."[20] Building new fossil fuel infrastructure, such as TMX, will contribute to global warming and worsen the climate crisis. This knowledge of what is at stake is part of what empowers and motivates me to stand up and do what I can to make a difference.

António Guterres, the UN Secretary-General, recently stated that "the truly dangerous radicals are the countries that are increasing the production of fossil fuels. Investing in new fossil fuel infrastructure is moral and economic madness."

My willingness to face jail time reflects my deeply held conviction that we need to act immediately to curtail fossil fuel expansion to prevent catastrophic climate change. Recent deaths in BC alone due to heat domes, wildfires, and extreme flooding, along with the recent code red for humanity, clearly indicate that we are in a climate emergency. We cannot afford to build new infrastructure in support of a carbon economy that is fuelling this crisis.

My decision to be arrested was also based on my conviction that there is a higher law than that of the colonial courts. I consider it my sacred duty to do whatever is in my power to ensure that I leave the world in a condition that will continue to support life as we know it. My hope is that in taking this action, others will be inspired to get involved in similar actions, in order to stop the development of new fossil fuel projects and the cutting of what is left of our old-growth forests.

My sentencing hearing was combined with those of Janette McIntosh and Catherine Hembling. During our sentencing, Judge Shelley Fitzpatrick pronounced us guilty and told us we "needed to be punished"' for breaking the law and in so doing, showing public disrespect to the court and for the rule of law. In response to my mentioning that I am the primary caregiver of my ninety-one-year-old mother, Fitzpatrick commented, "If there are any hardships to your mother resulting from your sentence, it is entirely your fault." The heartfelt arguments expressed by us and the other the defendants before us were ignored by the colonial "justice" system, which is set up primarily to protect the interests of corporations and profit at the expense of people and the planet. As frustrating as this is, I think it is imperative that arrestees continue to speak their perception of the truth, both for the public record and in hopes that as public opinion shifts in the direction of prioritizing climate action, and leaving fossil fuels in the ground, eventually the courts will follow. It will take time, but just as water will eventually dissolve stone, I have no doubt that society will shift toward prioritizing survival.

The experience of going to jail, sacrificing my liberty, personal autonomy, and choice, was definitely outside my comfort zone, but it was bearable. For one thing, I knew I'd be free in two weeks at most. I can only imagine how soul-crushing it must be for long-term inmates. The first day was the hardest. It was physically uncomfortable. I was transferred to the ACCW, still handcuffed and ankle-shackled, riding in three separate police vans. When I arrived I was strip-searched, X-rayed, and placed in another cold holding cell for several hours. I was locked into a cell separated from Janette and Catherine. However, we were in the same unit and shared a common space for several hours every day, where we ate meals together, had yoga sessions, and practised our three-part harmonies, revelling in the acoustics of the joint. The time spent with my two sisters made prison bearable.

Time was measured by the thirty-minute rhythm of the guards opening and slamming heavy metal doors, and of their faces peering through the narrow windows in my cell door to confirm that I was still alive in there. This continued throughout the night, making sleep a challenge. I could hear nothing of the outside world in that concrete cell—no traffic, no birds, no voices. However, the TV in my cell told me that in the world out there, the Olympics were being staged and the truckers' convoy had strangled Ottawa. After the first four days, we were occasionally let outdoors into a courtyard for inmates, with thirty-foot surrounding concrete walls that blocked out the view of the surrounding trees. But at least we could see the sky!

It got easier for me as the days went on, partly because I was able to make phone contact with my husband Tim, my friend and fellow arrestee Elan, and my mom. I adjusted to the conditions, I was able to slowly get more of what I needed, by way of blankets, a second mattress, books, and a yoga mat. I quickly learned that verbal requests, even when met with assurances that they would be acted upon, usually did not result in any action. Everything had to be put in writing, and there were forms for everything! For the most part, I found the guards to be respectful and felt like I was treated decently.

I have no regrets about having taken this action. Being arrested and doing jail time feels like a small sacrifice for me to make in the face of what is at stake. As an older person (sixty-one at the time of my incarceration), I feel that stepping up to take this kind of action is something I can do at this stage in my life, without having to worry as much as younger folks about my job or my reputation.

Did my civil resistance and going to jail have impact? Yes, it did get a lot of attention and contributed to getting people to think about why we would choose to make this sacrifice. It also helped that we got an op-ed published in the major Vancouver daily newspaper days leading up to our sentencing.[21]

Going to jail as a prisoner of conscience is a powerful act of sacrifice that touches people deeply. The idea of becoming vulnerable to the whims of captors who have great power over us captures our imagination with a sense of horror. These nine days of confinement are now part of my life story. But the arrest and imprisonment of the Brunette River sisters was never about us. It is about giving voice to the voiceless—orcas, spotted owls, and other relations who are suffering due to ecosystem collapse. It is about all we can yet save if we can turn off the taps from the tar sands.

My main hope in taking this action was that it would raise more public awareness of the climate emergency and what's at stake, and inspire more people to become engaged. I believe that massive civil resistance is necessary at this point in history, if we are to bring about the kind of change we need to avoid the worst effects of climate catastrophe.

Since our release from jail, my Alouette sisters and I have continued our activism with many speaking and singing engagements, mostly for various faith groups, to share our story about what motivated us to engage in peaceful direct action. We have also frequented gatherings before the sentencing trials of fellow re-sisters outside the courthouse in downtown Vancouver, and other protest rallies. On several occasions, we have occupied the lobbies of the Royal Bank of Canada to raise attention to RBC's role as Canada's leading financier of fossil fuel extraction, as well as the primary funder of the TMX and the Coastal GasLink pipelines.

These events provide an opportunity to educate the public and spur action by others. The Prayer Circle Direct Action Group that I started six years ago outside the Burnaby Mountain Watch House is thriving and growing. Spiritually rooted nonviolent resistance is alive and well!

CATHERINE HEMBLING,
Teacher, Unitarian, and Buddhist Practitioner

Ruth Walmsley, Catherine Hembling, and Janette McIntosh at their release from jail. Photo: Cynthia Materi

Biography

Catherine Hembling has been a Unitarian for forty-five years and a Buddhist practitioner for fifteen. She has a lifelong passion for the outdoors, which she credits to her parents, who took her hiking, berry picking, skiing, and boating from the back door of her childhood home in West Vancouver. After graduating in science from UBC (with a second major in mountaineering from the Varsity Outdoor Club!), Catherine spent two and a half years as a CUSO volunteer science teacher in Eastern Nigeria. She married a field geologist and became a prospector, a camp cook, and a mother of two boys. She has two delightful granddaughters. Catherine retired in 2000 as a special education teacher in French immersion. Since retirement she has become a music maker, artist, and an activist.

Catherine was arrested in September 2021 and sentenced to fourteen days' imprisonment (serving nine) on February 14, 2022.

Statement to BC Supreme Court Justice Shelley Fitzpatrick, February 14, 2022

First I want to acknowledge that we are meeting on the unceded historical territories of many Indigenous groups: the Musqueam, the Squamish and Tsleil-Waututh. Over in the area of the tree-sits, where I was arrested, the Kwikwetlem and the Qayqayt.

I want to acknowledge their leadership in this struggle against the construction of Trans Mountain Pipeline, in terms of legal cases, past and ongoing ceremonies, arrests, and inspiration to stand up for this planet. I am very grateful for their courage and persistence. So many defendants before me have made eloquent sentencing statements outlining the rational reasons why they opposed the building of this monstrous pipeline. They have covered the biological, engineering, economic, ethical, and environmental reasons. I do not intend to repeat them here in court.

The economics have changed since 2014, the early days of the proposed Trans Mountain Expansion project. However, the scientific facts and ethics of the matter have not changed. What has changed in that eight-year timespan is the mounting urgency of the calls of the international science community to stop putting more carbon into Earth's atmosphere. However, I want to address the court personally, not argumentatively.

What I do want to communicate to the court is my personal motivation. Why would I, for the first time in my eighty years, deliberately break the law, as it is represented by this injunction, and in this public manner, as a member of a prayer circle? I am not crazy, I am not malicious, I am not a saboteur, I am not disrespectful. I am an old lady at the end of an active and blessedly privileged life.

This is who I am: I was trained as a scientist, BSc, 1964. I taught science as a CUSO volunteer in a secondary school in Nigeria. I appreciate cause and effect; I love clear observations. I hate double standards. I have a great aversion to hypocrisy. I examine my life—I have been doing that consciously for many years as a Buddhist practitioner.

I try to live out my values. And what are my values? They are the values of the community of my church. I am a forty-five-year member of the Unitarian Church. We are a small progressive church with roots going back five hundred years.

We do not have a creed. Instead we covenant with each other to affirm and promote eight principles. We add principles periodically. In 1985, after two to three years of discussion and exploration, we added the Seventh Principle: "We covenant to affirm and promote the interconnected web of all existence of which we are a part."

That principle motivates me to civil disobedience.

So, let's look at it: The interconnected web of all existence of which we are a part—that means the connections between the plants and animals, and the effect of weather on them, us, the rocks, and the planet. Inter-being of plants and animals, and us, the climate, the heat, the cold. Interdependence when we think about the distribution of water, or about the balance of gases in the atmosphere, or about the pull of gravity of the moon and the planets, the distribution of metals in the stars—the interconnected web of all existence of which we are a part.

And it goes both ways—this interconnected web. The collective health of all the plants and animals on Earth is affected by humanity; their activities, their appearance, and their disappearance. Will the stars miss us—not so much! But if we change our activities, the air and the waters will slowly change. We already have plenty of evidence that species will repopulate protected natural preserves. There is real hope in that.

A second motivating value is that I treasure a life out of doors. All my life, from earliest childhood, I have been active outdoors, hiking, climbing, backpacking, skiing, berry picking, sailing, paddling, and all close to home on the North Shore, all part of what my family did. I was so blessed. I have kept up most of these activities into my old age.

When I became too old to take arduous week-long kayak trips, I continued to paddle in Indian Arm; day trips, slowly along the shores, pausing to just sit, with my paddle resting across my boat, to listen, to feel the rise and fall of the water under and around me, lifting me quietly, gently. It was the familiar feeling of being rocked in the arms of a beloved, and it is the peace I sometimes, rarely, achieve in meditation. When I recognized that, I knew I had to protect those waters. I had to line up with those already active protecting the inlet from the destruction of inevitable oil spills.

That was when I started to become active, attending National Energy Board hearings, writing letters, attending rallies, meeting with my MP. There was a growing rage in me, which did not improve my life. I discovered the Prayer Circle in 2019, and it offered a much-needed respite from anger and a way to be active, peacefully.

A third motivating factor is that I am blessed with good health. My good health may be part of my privilege, that I always had clean water, good food, good education, parents who taught me to live large parts of my life out of doors in the mountains and on the water. Perhaps my good health is a genetic gift. Other tendencies may be genetic too—the tendency to work for the good of my larger community runs in the family.

Let me explain.

My grandfather, a Montreal surgeon, decided at age fifty-three, in 1914, to move his family to England so he could join the British Medical Corps. He served out World War I in France, Belgium, and England doing army surgery and then returned to Montreal. My father, in 1939, joined the Royal Canadian Navy Volunteer Reserve, at age thirty-nine. He served on corvettes across the Atlantic for the duration of World War II. Neither my grandfather nor my father knew, when they decided to stand up for the good of their communities, what would be the outcome of those conflicts. They didn't know which side would win.

I have known for years the short-term consequence of standing up against this pipeline. I will serve my time, without complaint. However, I don't know what will be the long-term outcome of standing up for the safety of my community, for the benefit of my children and my grandchildren. I will not live to see the results. I am doing it anyway. I believe I am on the right side of history.

I am healthy, I have no job to lose, no fear of being blacklisted. I have no ambitions to travel internationally. I am a mother and a grandmother. I am painfully aware of the inevitable climate changes that lie ahead for my granddaughters.

Considering all that, and my values, I would be ashamed on my deathbed if I had spent the last years of my life sitting on the sidelines, closing my eyes, merely amusing myself, and doing nothing to stop this monstrous pipeline expansion pouring carbon into the earth's atmosphere. I do this peacefully, nonviolently, and full-heartedly.

Narrative: My Commitment to Defend the Land and the Children I Love

My arrest, September 23, 2021, was long in coming. The Trans

Mountain Expansion project (TMX) had become more and more illogical and threatening, as I learned from attending many meetings sponsored by both TMX and environmental groups. By the autumn of 2019, I was a member of the Prayer Circle associated with Protect the Planet: Stop TMX, meeting beside the Tsleil-Waututh Watch House on Burnaby Mountain.

Beginning in December 2020, I had been bringing food to the tree-sitters, always part of a team, arriving early in the morning in the dark, before the TMX crew arrived for work. But security was usually present even at that early hour, and we often played "duelling cameras," taking grainy dark pictures of security guards while they recorded us in photos and videos as we clambered up the steep bank from North Road to the Trans-Canada Highway. From the top of the bank, our route followed a worn rut outside the concrete barrier that separated us from the highway. The roar of traffic was so loud that communication was impossible. After about five hundred metres, we'd dip down onto a footpath into the forest that meandered to the base of the tree. We'd use our cell phones to connect with the person camping out high above, and they would lower a bucket on a long rope to receive hot home-cooked food. While on site we also acted as observers, photographing the gradual demolition of a forest rich with life, clearing an open-air warehouse for pipes and drilling equipment.

This area impinges on the greenway along the Brunette River between New Westminster and Burnaby, where salmon runs of four different species have been restored and frogs and crayfish thrive. There are blue herons and kingfishers, and at least one family of otters. The steep sandy benches of a former meander of the river are covered with cottonwood trees full of insects. There are wave after seasonal wave of wildflowers and butterflies. It is rich with many berry bushes, and consequently many birds. It has rare wild hazelnut trees which support squirrels, mice, voles, and many jays. As well, there are rabbits, a lynx, and a transient bear.[22] All this natural richness is within a built-up city. The area also sheltered many homeless people. Their tents and belongings were deliberately destroyed by TMX security, with impunity.

The decision to take nonviolent action and be arrested came out of meditation, sitting still and open-hearted in the green space near the Watch House in the early spring of 2021. The decision was made with others in the Prayer Circle team: Ruth, Janette, and Christine Thuring, essential allies and "sisters." We had to choose an opportunity to attract the most publicity possible with our arrest. There were several actions when we sat down with many supporters in front of machinery or access gates, but actual arrest was not that easy.

TMX didn't want to be arresting little old ladies, especially members of prayer circles! Sometimes they threatened to call the RCMP but in fact didn't follow through; they just mobilized their own security forces. With lots of aggressive bluster, they would claim as "prohibited" what turned out to be highway and railway property. Sometimes TMX security called the RCMP, but arresting officers didn't show up in time. Sometimes RCMP officers arrived, but found no reason to arrest. On one occasion the RCMP defended us from the harassing actions of TMX security.

In late April 2021, the nesting hummingbirds and enforcement of the Migratory Birds Convention Act provided more than four months of reprieve for the forested corridor along the Brunette, but once summer was over and the federal election behind us, September brought a concentrated effort by TMX to clear the corridor. The tree-sits had been set up to protect the trees, but it became obvious that TMX would take them out very quickly using a hydraulic cherry picker, a high platform for loggers with power saws, mounted on a tracked "tank." Fences went up quickly to outline the area prohibited by injunction. A troop of power-saw-wielding loggers on the ground cleared swaths of undergrowth to clear the way for the tank, and a rough road access was completed almost to the base of the tree-sits. It was now or never!

In the aftermath of arrest, court appearances, guilty pleas, and nine days of incarceration, I have renewed interest in singing in harmony! The "Alouette Sisters," Ruth and Janette and I, discovered in the resonant cement cells and ranges of the Alouette Women's Correctional Centre that we could sing in three-part harmony. We sang by request to the guards, and to our fellow incarcerated women inside. Now we sing by request to communities of faith and protest communities. It gives us centring and grounding. Harmony is magic! It opens up and encourages others. Singing provides us with an entry to speak to others about hope and agency in dark times.

I take inspiration from a quote by Thomas Homer-Dixon from his book *Commanding Hope: The Power We Have to Renew a World in Peril*: "We have to find a kind of hope that has muscular character, that sense of agency."

His summary in a July 13, 2022, CBC interview:

> I articulate a theory of hope . . . that commands our attention. It has a force in itself, but also we have the capacity to make hope do our bidding, to turn it into an emotion that's enormously powerful, that can allow us to change the world in favourable ways. The right kind of hope is the source of our sense of possibility . . . It allows us to get out of bed in the morning and keep going and keep trying, even when things look very grim . . . We can develop it, command it, make it into something that is powerful and that helps us prevail in this difficult world.

I would call that kind of hope "commitment": muscular commitment to limit global warming. The way I am exercising commitment is by doing what I can to stop TMX, to stop the production of tar sands bitumen to be sold to the world for profit and for burning. And so by singing with sisters in harmony, I continue to declare my commitment to my cherished natural world of plants and animals on this little piece of earth, and to future lives of beloved friends and family, to the future lives of my children and my children's children, and to all the future children of this precious green planet.

Part 5

Resistance through art

Painting of a street protest by Danaca Ackerson

GEORGE RAMMELL,
Sculptor

Biography

George Rammell was born in 1952 in Cranbrook, BC, and grew up in New Westminster. He studied at the Vancouver School of Art (now Emily Carr University of Art + Design) from 1971 to 1975, and has been active as a sculptor and art instructor since 1975. Throughout the 1980s, he worked as a studio sculptor for the contemporary Haida artist Bill Reid. He taught sculpture at Emily Carr over an eight-year period, and sculpture and drawing at Capilano University from 1990 to 2014. In addition to four European sculpture symposia, he participated in twenty exhibitions, including solo exhibitions at the Burnaby Art Gallery and the Charles H. Scott Gallery in Vancouver. Working with gravity, kinetic energy, and imagery, Rammell creates works with an intense sense of three-dimensionality. He is based in his new studios on Gambier Island, northwest of Vancouver. From 2018 to 2023, Rammell dedicated his work to the resistance against the Trans Mountain Pipeline and the injustice of the courts that are enforcing injunctions against land defenders.

George was arrested March 22, 2018, for protesting at the gates of the Trans Mountain oil tank farm in Burnaby. His sentence was a $500 fine.

Statement to BC Supreme Court Justice Kenneth Affleck, June 18, 2018

I'm pleading guilty to the charge of criminal contempt. I risked arrest along with my fellow educators, scientists, doctors, students, and citizens from all walks of life who, like me, had never been arrested before. We were there because we saw a multitude of injustices perpetuated by our prime minister and Kinder Morgan to push this reckless pipeline expansion forward at the expense of Aboriginal Nations, animal species, and the environment. Our actions at Kinder Morgan's gates were necessary to help press the pause button until real justice is restored.

I invested a decade of my formative years helping the modernist Haida artist Bill Reid, working with him as a studio sculptor. I valued the relationship because of his wisdom and willingness to share ideas throughout our ten years in the studio.

In 1986, Bill Reid stopped his work on *Spirit of Haida Gwaii*, his spirit-canoe for the Canadian Embassy in Washington, in protest of clear-cut logging on Lyell Island on Haida Gwaii. He then joined a blockade and was arrested with seventy-two other Haida.

Our federal government was ignoring Haida land claims and supporting a logging company that was planning to clear-cut 70 percent of the old-growth forest. This clear-cutting would have destroyed the island's salmon streams. The eventual successful protection of Lyell Island became instrumental to the launch of the co-operatively managed Gwaii Haanas National Park and contributed to self-sufficient and sustainable resource policies for the Haida Nation.

Bill Reid often spoke of Indigenous West Coast cultures that didn't write documents. The Potlatch is the heartbeat of those cultures; it's the equivalent to our western court system. The Potlatch is where title of land and names are proclaimed orally and through regalia, art, and dance. Our government's Potlatch prohibition was still in place during my lifetime, when Indigenous people had no right to vote and any Indigenous person caught potlatching could be sent to Oakalla Prison for two years.

It was under this Canadian apartheid system that the first pipeline was built from Alberta to Burrard Inlet in the early 1950s. The Tsleil-Waututh were vehemently opposed to it then, as they are to Kinder Morgan's current proposed expansion. Many Aboriginal Nations in BC were not adequately consulted or warned of the dangers of the proposed massive increase in dangerous diluted bitumen moving through their territorial lands and waters.

There were Tsleil-Waututh students in my classes at Capilano University, and I know how hard they've been working to restore their marine environment in Burrard Inlet from industrial pollution. They're finally re-establishing the kelp beds, but that will be lost in a matter of hours with a bitumen spill. Then what will they have to live for?

Justice Affleck, at the launch of your hearings you spoke of the freedoms we all enjoy in Canada and how our laws should not be abused. You spoke highly of our right to free speech and our right to protest, and how these rights exist because of our democracy. You spoke of the rule of law, and reminded us that when laws are broken, such as violations of your injunction that protects Kinder Morgan, there must be consequences and penalties to maintain civility.

Our federal government is supporting broad freedoms for Kinder Morgan, freedoms that don't apply to First Nations and nonindigenous citizens who, like myself, live on Burrard Inlet. Aboriginal rights are being violated while our federal government claims to be championing reconciliation.

I value our democracy and justice system, and I admire important judges with discretionary powers such as Justice Thomas Berger, who, when he was asked to assess the impact of the proposed Mackenzie Valley pipeline in 1974, invested three years to hear the concerns of First Nations and Inuit in more than thirty communities. He then understood the issues and he finally concluded (much to the dismay of the minister of Indian affairs, Jean Chrétien) that the pipeline should not proceed until Native land claims were settled.

Historically, judges have taken vastly different approaches to justice. Your first predecessor, BC Chief Justice Matthew Baillie Begbie, owned land in colonial British Columbia, yet he didn't believe any Indigenous people should own land unless the Queen bequeathed it to them. Justin Trudeau recently apologized for Begbie's hanging of Chilcotin Chiefs for defending their land during the gold rush. Today the oil rush has replaced the gold rush, and Trudeau has moved reconciliation to the back of the bus because it's impeding this corporate megaproject.

In 2014, all the arrested protesters at the drill site on the west side of Burnaby Mountain were exonerated because Kinder Morgan constructed their allotted work boundary with inaccurate GPS coordinates. This is consistent with this company's attitude of entitlement. Justice Affleck, I believe your injunction is a complicit part of the shield allowing Kinder Morgan, a filthy company with a horrible track record, to proceed without permits from municipalities. I believe this entire court process is placing the cart before the horse. Until the Supreme Court weighs in on outstanding Indigenous, provincial, and municipal court challenges and appeals, this whole process should be put on ice.

Please use your discretion to reserve judgment on our actions. Let's see how these legal challenges are resolved, then we'll know whether we were wrong in defending those whose voices are being ignored.

As Grand Chief Stewart Phillip states, "There is no social licence to proceed with the Trans Mountain expansion."

Narrative: Art as a Weapon to Expose the Injustice of the Colonial Courts

In 2018 I was appalled to hear that the Kinder Morgan pipeline would be cutting through the Burnaby nature reserve. This thousand-kilometre pipeline, pumping diluted, heated bitumen at 900 psi pressure, would be running along the Brunette River. This is where I discovered the magic of frog's eggs, tadpoles, and salamanders as a kid. I heard about the Kalamazoo River bitumen disaster and the terrible record pipelines have regarding ruptures and failed cleanups.

The Tsleil-Waututh Nation of Burrard Inlet was vehemently opposed to the project. I had sailed in the Tsleil-Waututh waters of Indian Arm as a teen, and I hold a deep respect for their kinship with their precious ancestral homeland. They had never given their consent to the pipeline's construction. They had worked to clean up their traditional waters of Burrard Inlet from industrial pollution and had recently celebrated their first clam harvest in decades. I wondered what they would have to live for when the inlet was spoiled with a spill.

I felt the need to take a stand, so I joined the growing ranks of allies sitting in the driveway of the Kinder Morgan oil tank farm on Burnaby Mountain. I was arrested with Ian Angus, SFU philosophy professor emeritus, and we were tried together in June 2018.

Ian Angus was the first of hundreds of defendants to plead guilty to breaking Judge Affleck's injunction, on the condition he could make a ten-minute statement. It was a brilliant move; a lot can be said in ten minutes. Affleck accepted the arrangement, hoping to set an expedient routine for convictions. Thereafter I began attending many of the resisters' trials. It became abundantly clear the judges are in over their heads, as they are not experts in the range of disciplines the defendants brought forward such as Indigenous law, environmental and health sciences, or engineering, and they are not working in a political vacuum. Just as the church did the dirty work for government during the residential school era, I saw judges relying on injunctions to clear the path for the energy sector. Their role was simply to enforce injunctions at the cost of Indigenous and environmental justice. I deplored their attitudes, which seemed to me racist, and their flawed understanding of climate science. I saw incarcerations of people who deserve awards for their outstanding work to seek justice. I saw those same extraordinary citizens return to the ongoing struggle as soon as they were free.

While drawing the proceedings of defendants' trials, I observed a stark difference between Indigenous Healing Circles and courtrooms that feature Baroque-style coats of arms that hang near the ceiling. Directly beneath them, judges are elevated on raised benches. They wear ceremonial black gowns and winged collars that date from the fifteenth century. When a judge enters or leaves the courtroom, everyone must stand or risk accusations of contempt. I also saw how court sheriffs attempted to prevent Indigenous defendants from carrying their ceremonial drums in court, referring to them as noisemakers.

During the proceedings, a young Indigenous defendant stated his ancestors had lived in the pathway of the proposed TMX pipeline "since time immemorial." The judge scoffed at the term, questioning its legitimacy; meanwhile, we defendants were trying to understand archaic legal jargon and courtroom protocols that were completely foreign to us.

Will George is one of the many Tsleil-Waututh Nation members at the forefront of the resistance. Referring to an event where he helped place an abandoned car in the driveway of the TMX oil tank depot in Burnaby, Judge Shelley Fitzpatrick asked him in court how he would feel if someone left a car in his driveway. Will responded, "They've been parking in my driveway for 150 years." This judge has repeatedly revealed how little she understands Indigenous culture and the legitimate reasons for Indigenous actions. During court proceedings, Judge Fitzpatrick made it clear she didn't even know where the Tsleil-Waututh reserve was located.[1]

Simon Fraser University professor and public health scientist Dr. Tim Takaro specializes in occupational and environmental health and the impacts of global warming. His warnings, as an intervenor during the review process for TMX, were ignored. He bivouacked high in the trees of the pipeline corridor for forty days while providing live educational seminars from his perches. He and UBC professor William Winder were each sentenced to twenty-one days' detention. The Anishinaabe activist Stacy Gallagher was sentenced to ninety days; he is still appealing. [Note from editors: Stacy's appeal at the BC Court of Appeals was rejected on June 19, 2024; his incarceration began that day.] Errol Povah, a former Sea Shepherd crew member, served forty days in jail. Indigenous Elder Jim Leyden was sentenced to twenty-eight days, his heart medications were delayed, and he suffered spider bites in jail that landed him in hospital on his release. He was later sentenced to an additional forty-five days, which he successfully appealed. Extinction Rebellion member Brent Eichler protested TMX and old-growth logging with a thirty-two-day hunger strike; he served thirty days in jail. Poet and author Rita Wong was sentenced to twenty-eight days.

The brilliant twenty-one-year-old third-year history student Zain Haq came originally to Canada on a study permit to attend Simon Fraser University. Through the threat of a hunger strike, he successfully worked with other students, faculty, and staff to have SFU divest from fossil fuels while encouraging McMaster University to do the same. Employing the civil rights movement as a model, he's been very active in protests to mobilize Canada toward climate action. He was threatened with possible deportation to Pakistan. Border Services said they considered him a national security risk. [Note from editors: Zain's deportation order was cancelled by the Canadian Border Services Agency in April 2024, though his future status in Canada is still under review.]

Haq questioned why his actions were deemed illegal while the government's failure to act in a global emergency is not. His court hearing was closed to the public and the press for "the benefits of life, liberty and security," which in the judge's opinion "outweigh the negative effect of limiting freedom of expression." Haq is an inspiration to youth suffering from climate anxiety, and his leadership skills are a threat to the status quo. He knows that life, liberty, and security are being eroded by climate change. He also knows that our social stasis is grounded in fear; many concerned citizens are fearful of the authorities, while the authorities are fearful of social change. His deportation would be an exercise of national cowardice, a transparent attempt to silence the kind of person that will stand on the right side of history.

Emily Kelsall and Maya Laframboise were jailed for frolicking in the mud of a pipeline construction site in their inflatable T-Rex outfits. This TMX site is adjacent to Burnaby Mountain Secondary School below the oil tank farm. Their hilarious actions engaged the public while raising the issue of species extinction exacerbated by oil-sands extraction and development. Their actions also portray the judges as dinosaurs.

Following her sentencing, Emily pulled on her T-Rex hood and tenaciously roared at Judge Fitzpatrick. The packed gallery of supporters was enthralled, but the judge showed no humour; she cleared the gallery and extended Emily's incarceration by seven days. The judge's attempt to thwart our youth seeking environmental justice was draconian. These young women were sent to the Alouette Correctional Centre for Women, but I believe it's Judge Fitzpatrick who needs correction in areas of treaty rights, Indigenous law, climate science, eco-anxiety, and judicial responsibilities to consider evidence in court.

Since 2018, my studio work has addressed the injustice of the Trans Mountain Expansion with expressions of resistance. I felt the best thing I could contribute to the cause is sculptural imagery.

We needed a contribution from every discipline that sustains our society to turn this fiasco around. Elders, kids, scientists, doctors, economists, engineers, artists, lawyers, donors; we needed everyone on board to turn the tide of public opinion. I made many carving tools for art auctions to raise funds for legal costs for Indigenous resisters. I created many pieces of protest art, including a large knotted pipeline entitled *Notley*, a hummingbird sitting on her nest, a large frog with dead tadpoles, satirical Trans Mountain injunction signs, rows of RCMP officers, and burning planets.

My most extensive activist sculptural piece is now completed, entitled *The Chambers of Predetermined Outcomes* (see p. 241). It was financed through the BC Arts Council and involves three ventriloquist dummy judges shaking their heads and pounding their fists. Positioned above them is my satirical version of Canada's coat of arms, whose origins began in medieval Europe. Warriors preparing for battle tied their embroidered coat of arms over their armour so their bodies could later be identified on the battlefield. Their crests declared their kingdom and military rank. These emblems are now used to proclaim national authority and patriotism. The Canadian coat of arms was adopted from England; its white unicorn is a symbol of Scotland. The unicorn is bound in chains, captive, as a celebration of England's very first colony. The judges' mirrored eyes reflect weather disasters on their laptops. *The Chambers of Predetermined Outcomes* references the work of Hans Haacke and the late Robert Arneson, a prolific San Francisco Bay area Funk Art ceramicist who portrayed military generals during the Vietnam era.

This installation, which will be considered subversive by some, was unveiled in the Longhouse Church in East Vancouver on March 21, 2023, to a standing-room-only crowd. In addition to my talk explaining its inspiration and meaning, the event included a speech by Rueben George, manager of the Tsleil-Waututh Sacred Trust and de facto spiritual leader of our movement.

I intend to return to my studio work this fall, hopefully in tandem with the demise of this pipeline due to environmental and economic realities.

TAWAHUM BIGE,
Poet,
Spoken Word Artist

Biography

Tawahum Bige is a Łutselk'e Dene, Plains Cree poet and spoken word artist from unceded Musqueam, Squamish, and Tsleil-Waututh Territory (Vancouver). Their Scorpio-moon-ass poems expose growth, resistance, and persistence as a hopeless Two Spirit Nonbinary sadboy on occupied Turtle Island. In typical Aries-sun fashion, Tawahum completed the first-ever Indigenous Spoken Word residency at the Banff Centre in 2018 while completing their BA in Creative Writing from Kwantlen Polytechnic University in 2019.

They've performed at Talking Stick Festival, Verses Festival of Words, Canadian Festival of Spoken Word, and at over fifty different venues from Victoria to Toronto with a mixture of poetry and hip-hop. Past the stage and onto the page, Tawahum has been published in over a dozen different literary journals & magazines including *Red Rising Magazine*, *Prairie Fire*, *CV2*, *Arc Poetry Magazine*, the *Fiddlehead*, and the anthology *Beyond Earth's Edge: The Poetry of Spaceflight*. A prolific word-artist, Tawahum has three self-published chapbooks with poetry collections on the way, including a collection-in-progress funded by the Canada Council for the Arts. Nightwood Editions published Tawahum's debut collection, *Cut to Fortress*, and his music can also be found on all streaming platforms.

Beyond the page, Tawahum has battled the (in)justice system of BC including his land protection work against Kinder Morgan/TMX. Of course, this doesn't stop him from grabbing a boom mic to amplify his words of resistance and resurgence at front-line rallies, street performances, and more. Tawahum can be followed on Instagram, Twitter, and Facebook: @Tawahum.

Tawahum was arrested at the Westridge terminal August 14, 2018, and sentenced to twenty-eight days' incarceration on October 6, 2020.

there's a battle coming
by Tawahum Bige

sleepless hours on
    camping mats
with watchhouse warriors:
elders youth
women men thems

6 am wake and bolt upright
see a new face but familiar
nice to meet you
silent preparations
pre-action coffee
scones and a short
drive to Kae Tempest's
"Europe is Lost"
so what're we gonna
    do to wake up?

smudge prayer and upend
tents and chairs
to seat our blockade

the morning air is curious
forest fire smog
makes me asthmatic

contrarian elder
    smudges with me
prays with me
to flight with me

eagle feather fan
handed to me

this war is spiritual

we can't see
the other side

of the salish sea
in this fog of war
from fire

we mock employees
regretfully
they've chosen the path
down extraction
but are still human
we're filmed

more youth circle up
elders educate
gentle and critical
pinpointing
like tawaha—
bulls-eye

eagle feather brings
    youth to flight
we don't talk to cops

so when they arrive
we blockade with
    this banner made
from thousand-
    year thick cedar

ocean crashes on the shore
enveloping us in power
two spirits fly thru
around
and into us

american on the boom mic
reminds us what's right
what's just

a mermaid cries
so do i
so do we

boombox injunctions
and uncomfortable cops
averting eyes

honour
warrior
water
travellers
Chief Dan George
songs for these
as we iron our line

three drums beat
our heartbeats to one
my eyes sting
in sweat and tears
and blood

i am handed a tissue
but these streams
salting my cheeks
are honey and sweet
nourishing and curing
fear washing out of me

i am pulled for a moment
    from ceremony
a pig wants my feathers
but uncle keeps me
in prayer
in relation
in all relations
blanketed in warmth
from ancestors' breath
over my body
urging more tears

yellow vests arrest and i am
    on their left

our friend
you do not walk alone

i am next
i can't hear their harps
silked strings from tongues
wagging
but know when it is time
to stand

they do not take my eagle fan
held high as i march

Tawahum our friend
you do not walk alone

eyes avert
DNA
date of birth
name
address

the cops try to get my
    phone number
i'm tempted to tell him
*we haven't even gotten to
    know each other yet*
but my eyes remain on
    smoky waters

do you understand?
do i understand?
avert eyes
Avery on my right
and we're processed
and they're removed
i am interviewed
but pray for their safety
*they should've told me it was
    their second time*

85-year-old rolls in
this sinister senior
joins the blockade
restarts boombox injunction

marsi cho

chats
boom mics
and stacks of injunction
as the smudge
    smoulders further
and the third arrest

*Noah our friend
you do not walk alone*

*Joanne our friend
you do not walk alone*

Avery is released

with medicine
we are soothed
smoothed
and again I am interviewed

the work is delayed
    for five hours
with all eyes on us
and that is our warrior power
and objective complete
as the campaign continues

ELAN ROSS GIBSON,
Actor

Photo: Ruth Walmsley

Biography

The city where Elan Ross Gibson was born—Medicine Hat, Alberta—was known to have "all hell for a basement" (quip by Rudyard Kipling), as it was built on a subterranean gas field. As a child, she was exposed to the DDT spraying of alleyways as a means of mosquito control. Thirty miles north is the Suffield Experimental Station, where there were experiments to combat World War I nerve gases, as well as nonatomic explosions in the vast "vacant" prairie of the 1950s. These things inform her decisions today.

In 1966 she graduated with a BFA in Drama from the University of Alberta. This was the first degree of its kind offered by a Canadian university. Exciting moments as an actor included being cast in big productions like *Circle of Two, Small Sacrifices,* and *Jurassic World Dominion.* But the satisfying projects were small Canadian plays like *The Blues* at Passe Muraille in Toronto and *Great Canadian Women* at an Edmonton Fringe Festival. The most rewarding feedback was from work in *An Unexpected Christmas*—a Hallmark film. Closer to home, she worked with Mairy Beam on two plays for the Vancouver Fringe Festival, as the narrator in Mairy Beam's play *Irreparable Harm?,* based on some of the TMX-resister court cases of 2018; and as dramaturge and co-producer in *The Judge's Daughter,* which addresses the conflict between pipeline activists and their trial judge.

Elan became aware of climate change and the concept of unceded land after attending events in Burnaby (where she had lived since 1993) with Bill McKibben and Rueben George of the Tsleil-Waututh Nation. She attended some of the Truth and

Reconciliation Commission hearings at the Pacific National Exhibition. Her awakening was amplified when she attended a town hall sponsored by BROKE—Burnaby Residents Opposing Kinder Morgan Expansion—and she has been resisting the expansion project ever since, for three fundamental reasons: climate change; Indigenous rights and title; and risks to her community, friends, and family.

———————

Elan was arrested at the tank farm on May 16, 2018, and was sentenced on December 6, 2018, to fourteen days in jail, serving nine.

Statement to BC Supreme Court Justice Kenneth Affleck

Your Lordship,

With respect for you, the Crown, and the court's time, I don't know how to plead. My actions on May 16, 2018, were a desperate act of self-defence for myself, my loved ones, and the community where I live.

I am a retired professional actor and along with other concerned citizens, I have tried to get the attention of the federal minister of public safety and emergency preparedness and have been ignored, even having the door locked against us during a peaceful demonstration to present a letter of our concerns.

Our then deputy fire chief of Burnaby has published an extensive report on the serious risks of the tank farm expansion and lists a 5.2-kilometre radius as a "High Life Hazard Area" in the event of a fire or explosion at the site.[2] The Concerned Professional Engineers put out a report on the unacceptable risk of a tanker collision at the railway bridge and Ironworkers Memorial Bridge which span the inlet.[3] I live five kilometres from the Burnaby Mountain terminal and four kilometres from the Ironworkers bridge.

BROKE—Burnaby Residents Opposing Kinder Morgan Expansion—intervened with the National Energy Board concerning the toxic materials contained in the product as well as the risks of an earthquake in our area. The ministerial panel highlighted these concerns.

There have been five events of local seismic activity between Squamish and Mission in the last month. The 1999 Izmit Bay earthquake in Turkey sparked a disastrous fire at a refinery with the same type of holding tanks as the thirteen tanks that will be left in use in Burnaby, along with twelve new, bigger ones on approximately the same footprint at the edge of a forest on the side of a mountain adjacent to a densely populated neighbourhood.

The collision of the *Sanchi* tanker with a cargo ship in January 2018 in the South China Sea, causing explosion and fire, and the Superior, Wisconsin, refinery fire and explosion in April 2018 left me with a feeling of hopelessness after the past five years of advocating against this project because of its risks to life and community.

Yes, the TMX project received approval from the government. The government also received an ultimatum from the company (Kinder Morgan) that they would pull out if they couldn't see the way clear to continue construction by May 31, 2018. The decision by the Federal Court of Appeal on a court challenge by the Tsleil-Waututh, Squamish, and Cold Water Nations from last fall hasn't been made, and yet our prime minister says this pipeline will be built.

I don't understand how the system can work like this. My rights as a citizen and the expectation of a safe life are being violated.

Narrative: The Trials and Tribulation of Self-Representation

On May 16, 2018, I took part in a "die-in" at the Burnaby Mountain terminal organized by BROKE. I planned on breaking the injunction that barred protesters from blocking access to work sites. I was arrested with four others and was "processed" on site. My first appearance was on May 28 at the Supreme Court of BC, where I read my statement and did not make a plea. My next appearance to make my plea was on June 12. At this time I pleaded not guilty. Over the summer I conferred several times with colleagues and a lawyer, got affidavits, spent hours in the law library at the courthouse, and requested the aid of three witnesses to appear at court for me. I went to trial in November, self-representing and claiming *force majeure*[4] against the federal government for buying the Trans Mountain Expansion project.

On November 16, I dropped off a bound copy of my affidavits and other material to the Crown prosecutor, who seemed quite confused by it. I also registered a copy of this same book with the court registry, thinking it would be at trial. The lawyer who advised me was a criminal lawyer and therefore directed me as it would be appropriate for a criminal trial. However, it appears that although I was charged with criminal contempt, my judicial process was to follow the requirements for a breach of the civil code! Furthermore, regardless of being a civil matter, the records are kept in the criminal section of the court. How is a poor civilian trying to do her moral duty expected to understand all this?!

I went to trial on the 19th of November. By this time I had evolved from an arrogant and self-righteous individual, first to a humbled woman due to the support and kindness of the lawyer, friends, and witnesses, then to a bundle of nerves on the day. The judge, as is his duty for self-represented defendants, instructed and guided me. My trial lasted four days and it had its ups and downs.

In court I did not do a thorough questioning of the police who had arrested me and had appeared to testify. I was more intent on bringing my points to bear. But what followed was a series of mishaps. First, my affidavit from the then deputy fire chief in Burnaby was not admissible because he was not appearing in person to defend his report to the NEB in 2015. I did not know that was a requirement of affidavits. My ignorance led me to believe that one or the other would be enough.

Secondly, I had offered the Crown a list of my witnesses, which the prosecutor, Mr. Rattan, said wasn't necessary. But when I called my first of two expert witnesses, that was a different story. I guess I hadn't mentioned that they were "expert" nor presented their testimonies earlier so that the Crown could prepare questioning! Oops! Then there was the fact that one of the witnesses had also been arrested! Her charges had been dropped, as she hadn't been read the injunction, a requirement for arrest at that time, and the judge allowed her to proceed. Her testimony was on the toxic atmosphere around the tank farm from escaping gases when she had worked there. The second expert was a cancer researcher and professor who explained the risks to our health. There were no questions as I remember for either of these witnesses. My third witness was a member of the community who lives on the mountain at UniverCity. I am still embarrassed to this day that the judge allowed her to enter the room with a walker and mount the stand only to be dismissed without testimony! She was to testify about the effects she already felt from occasional emissions from the current tank farm.

The judge's familiar refrain had been, "Try to change the law, don't break it." I did supply him a list of all the things that BROKE and I had done to try and stop the construction of this expansion project, which had no effect, and so I'd taken the only option I believe I had—civil disobedience.

At the conclusion of my trial and the summations, the judge gave his conviction on November 22, 2018. I have to admit he took great pains to explain to me why *force majeure* did not apply. Not only because my death isn't imminent from the threat, but also *force majeure* is in the Criminal Code and I was being tried under the common law or civil code. Again, how is a poor citizen to understand all this!

Sentencing was held over until December 6. I was told by the Crown's assistant to expect fourteen days to be recommended, but was asked if I had any mitigating factors that would warrant a house arrest and community service? My home is my sanctuary, and I was not about to turn it into a jail. So I replied, "No mitigating factors" and faced jail-time. Also, I considered that my civil disobedience was in fact community service, so a sentence of more community service would not be a penalty. I was sentenced to fourteen days on December 6.

The jail experience really depends on one's frame of mind, I think. I was proud to stand for the cause, not accepting guilt for any wrongdoing.

We were in maximum security during that first weekend, after which my fellow inmate left. I was moved to medium security, which was another ball game. The inmates do have the opportunity to learn skills. As I was there only for a few days, I was given the task of making Christmas decorations for the staff craft sale. Again, I learned a lot about humility. White, privileged older women have a lot to be grateful for.

The most gruelling time was the ride out to the institution—nothing to hold onto, no visual clues to the outside, and a terrible orange light that emanates a horrible glow. And the food—lots of starchy carbohydrates. Finally, hard sleeping platforms and cement walls that suck the moisture out of you.

For me, my arrest and conviction and sentencing was a choice, and I never felt threatened. Other women I met in jail were there not by choice, or if by choice, their life circumstances did not serve them well. I was honoured to be treated with their respect and acceptance and to this day am affected. Some offered their stories and they have left their mark on my soul. I was even blessed to share in the sushi night that some of the women have after their canteen supplies arrive.

EARLE PEACH,
Musician

Biography

Earle Peach is a musician, composer, arranger, conductor, and teacher. He grew up in Aylmer, Quebec, and came to Vancouver in 1975 to study creative writing at UBC. He has written music for theatre, film, and dance performance and has worked as a food co-op coordinator, music program organizer, stained glass fabricator, and musical director. In the fall of 2017, Earle won the Mayor's Arts Award for Community Engaged Arts. Currently he directs three choirs, performs with five musical groups, organizes a monthly community coffee house at Mount Pleasant Neighbourhood House and a weekly singalong at Kitsilano Neighbourhood House. One of the choirs he directs, the Solidarity Notes, has been involved in protests against Kinder Morgan / TMX since 2014 and continues its involvement in the protests to this day. His chief role in opposing TMX has been to bring song to the fight.

Earle was arrested on March 4, 2021, for climbing over the fence at the TMX site on North Road in Burnaby. On May 17, 2021, he began a sentence of fourteen days' incarceration at North Fraser Pretrial Centre in Maple Ridge, and was released after nine days.

Excerpts from Statement to BC Supreme Court Justice Shelley Fitzpatrick, May 17, 2021

I'm grateful to be before you today. This is a moment I've thought about long and hard, as I'm sure it's been for many who have come before me. We are deeply privileged to share this moment by which we shape our own lives, but also in a small way, the future of our existence on this planet. It's a moment in which you, the judge, and you, Mr. Prosecutor, play a crucial part, in providing the incentive to correct myself. I'll say more about this a bit later. First I want to speak about justice.

Madam Judge, you and I share a common belief in justice, although we may interpret it a bit differently. I know you only as a representative of the law, so it's presumptuous of me to speculate about your opinions; suffice it to say that in one view, perhaps one you share, justice represents the product of a vast edifice of jurisprudence over time, modified by changes in society and legislation, but always aimed at preserving the collective will of the people. I don't deny that it is that, but for me in a more basic sense justice is not a legal framework but a universal concept, representing the protection of rights and duties.

Now by a right I mean a state which confers upon the holder the privilege of dictating, or limiting, the actions of others, and the flipside of a right is of course a duty, which compels the holder to act or limit their action in accord with the rights of others. The most basic right is the right to exist, and this right is inherent to all living things *a priori*, in other words simply because they do exist. Plankton has a right to exist. Other marine creatures have a right to exist. Plants have a right to exist. And humans have a right to exist. This right is limited only by the need for survival of another creature. In the case of humans, if we remove the right of an individual to exist we generally call it murder, although of course there are exceptions such as self-defence. If we remove the right of a class of humans to exist we call it genocide, and this is considered a much worse crime, for which "self-defence" is an imaginary excuse.

Strangely when we cross the human boundary, this right seems to evaporate in human estimation. Of course the notion of plankton having the same rights as a human is absurd; however, the right of plankton as a class to exist, and the duty of humans to honour that existence is, in my view, not an artifact of our imagination but is absolute. This duty is multiplied exponentially when the existence of plankton is understood to be integral to the survival of many other species on this planet, including humans. And yet there is nothing in the law which protects the right of plankton to exist, nor for that matter the right of anything but humans to exist. This is where your view of justice and mine part ways; for if the great legal framework you represent fails to accommodate these basic universal rights, we thereby lay the groundwork for our own imminent destruction.

Consider the fact that plankton are responsible for more than 50 percent of the oxygen produced by plants. They provide the most basic food source for all life in the ocean. If the plankton disappear, ultimately all life in the ocean will cease, and humans will be forced to live in artificial climates, never stepping outside into an atmosphere which will not support them. Most of the plants we live on will cease to exist. Most of our population will die. This is not speculation, it's supported by the most sophisticated modelling we can come up with. It's not something to worry about in the future: it's happening now.

You may not be familiar with a study by scientists at Dalhousie University published in 2010 which estimated that on average since 1899 the amount of plankton in the oceans has dropped by 1 percent annually.[5] It's not rocket science to understand that this represents an existential threat to all the creatures in the ocean and the land, including us.

Why is this happening? Of course, the answer is changing ocean temperature due to anthropogenic climate change, caused by the use of fossil fuels. This is the crisis which our national broadcaster tells its employees they are not allowed to refer to as an emergency or a crisis; those are "opinions," which will alienate some portion of CBC listenership. Climate change is, you know, political. Lots of people think it's a hoax, just like they think COVID-19 is a hoax.

Companies like Exxon, Enbridge, Chevron, and the rest pay hundreds of millions of dollars to spread lies and uncertainty about this impending nightmare, and they've been very successful. They have obtained legal status as individuals, with even more rights than the average person. Internal documents from Exxon clearly show not only that the company has known and lied about climate change since the late 1960s, but that they are banking on it to open up new areas for drilling like the Arctic Wildlife Refuge and the Northwest Passage, once all the ice is gone. And these companies have co-opted governments into accepting their agenda, putting public money into projects which will perpetuate the use of fossil fuels well into the remainder of this century. To put it bluntly, the future of the world is at stake and we as a species are doing next to nothing to halt the roller coaster to oblivion.

Why are we doing so little? Because despite the law's claims to dispensing justice equally, or even wishing to do so, the evidence points in a different direction. Far from offering justice to all creatures alive, which one might think would be appropriate if we truly considered ourselves stewards of the earth, our societies don't even offer justice to the majority of human beings

The TMX project fails the test of justice on myriad levels. I know many others have brought the particulars of this pipeline before you, and I know it makes no difference to you: a law's a law, you obey it or break it, and if you break it you suffer the consequences, period. And I'm not expecting any different. However, I consider it my right to strain your patience by simply pointing out that if there is any natural justice in the world, justice which recognizes the right of species to exist, this project is an offence against it, and as such it must, it simply must be fought.

Now my concept of justice and yours cross paths in the legal system you represent. Over time, principles like the recognition of the rights of living creatures have filtered into the body of law, sometimes through legislation but most often through struggle or collective horror.

The rights of someone not to fear simply because they are a Jew, or a Palestinian, or a homosexual, or a woman, or a worker, or a child, or poor, or disabled, or Indigenous, have found their way into the law, and these rights limit the power of society and even of rich corporations. Witness the ability of a little hummingbird to stop a pipeline, even temporarily! What better example could there be of the recognition of natural justice in jurisprudence? It says, in effect, that the designs of corporate executives or a political machine to appease a desired constituency do not trump this creature's inherent right to exist. Would that the law also protected plankton!

The question then is, how does the law evolve to more closely resemble what I'm calling natural justice? And the answer is, most often, through violating unjust laws. I know you know that throughout western history laws have changed primarily when there is a public mood for them to change, and that mood is primarily expressed through civil disobedience. John Rawls in 1971 described civil disobedience as "a public, non-violent and conscientious breach of law undertaken with the aim of bringing about a change in laws or government policies. On this account, people who engage in civil disobedience are willing to accept the legal consequences of their actions, as this shows their fidelity to the rule of law."[6] I am indeed willing to accept those consequences.

And it is for this, more than anything else, that I firstly have to thank you as a representative of the legal system; for representing a system which is not immune to change, and not simply the justifying arm of tyrants and criminals. I could climb over the fence on North Road, say no to two nice police officers when they offered to walk me out without charges, and not end up riddled with bullets, or having my home burnt down, which could well have been the case in the 1930s. I could enjoy all the protections of the law afforded presently to a nice, articulate, reasonably well-educated white, male, middle-class settler when they commit an act of civil disobedience.

Unfortunately, the Original Peoples of Turtle Island have experienced nothing like these protections. The law has allowed them to be cheated, assaulted, and murdered, dispossessed of their languages, families, cultures, livelihood, in short, their identities. It is not anything like an understatement to say that this legal system has overseen and enabled genocide, and although some changes have occurred they are woefully inadequate. It will take a lot of civil disobedience from people like me to bring more meaningful changes to this state of affairs, and one danger is that people like me will imagine that this is someone else's fight, not theirs.

Secondly, I have to thank you for offering us a way to finally stop this pipeline. We are at the nexus of a place of real possible change. Once people understand that being sent to jail as a form of civil disobedience is effective in, even essential to, changing the system, you have lost the war. There comes a point in every struggle when too many people have been arrested and the case against them collapses.

In Clayoquot Sound, on which much of the current paradigm of punishment is based, it took only 900 arrests. It's perfectly obvious that if 5,000 people were arrested and imprisoned for violating the TMX injunction, the project would stop permanently. Even 2,000 would do it, and this is the Achilles heel of the punitive paradigm: At a certain point incarceration is not a deterrent, but rather an inducement, an incentive to action, as people realize that their swelling numbers bring the status quo ever closer to its knees.

The prosecution has to rely on the fear and complacency of citizens to maintain "order," and when that fear and complacency evaporates, so does the project. All that is necessary is for us to recognize our own power, and to act according to principles embodying a worldview we wish to bring about, a world in which all creatures are respected and protected equally.

There remains only to tell you how I will use my time in jail fruitfully. I intend to read some books I've already ordered for North Fraser Pretrial, so I certainly hope you're sending me there; to write music and songs, which is my lifelong journaling habit; and to reflect on how I can be a better, more effective activist: how I can respond to the parts of myself that want to give up, sit back, and wait for the end to come.

Years from now, if I live that long, how would I ever justify my capitulation? I'll tell you that around me I see people who are tired of attempting to bring change by allowing harm to be inflicted on themselves. They act nonviolently and conscientiously, aware of the likely consequences of their actions; they take stands based on the highest principles our society can aspire to. Many of these people have worked much harder and for longer than I have, and I confess that their diligence is both an admonishment and an inspiration to me and, I hope, to others. For now we need others, people willing to put themselves out, even a bit. People willing to say, I will do what's necessary even if I suffer for it. And I want to point out to those people that thanks to Justice Affleck, one consequence of arrest people need not fear is a criminal record. As you know, Justice Affleck declared that all arrests in the matter of TMX will not be written into an offender's criminal record, for which I can only offer him thanks. And with that, I've said all I have to say. Thank you for your patience.

Narrative: Notes from Jail

First, I must acknowledge that this narrative reflects my privilege, including the fact that I could consider the option of going to jail in the first place. The fact that I could prioritize procuring paper and a working pencil, the fact that I am by choice vegetarian and could insist on my right to be so, the fact that I could meditate to support my spirit, that I could not lose hope when so many others in that prison had already done so in the face of the unforgiving system they were subject to, the fact that I could use sound to measure my cell or weep while listening to Ravi Shankar playing, the fact that I could look at the other people I was incarcerated with from the perspective of someone not already defining myself as a loser or a bad person . . . essentially everything which made this experience individual to me reflects my privilege.

May 18

I'm writing this on a paper towel, since (so far) writing paper has not been provided to me. I've had a decent rest, and enjoyed the rays of sun which filtered in through this east-facing window. Well, not a window exactly; more like a slot, with an exterior metal wall perforated by holes. Nevertheless the sun was an immense gift, a sign of the life which continues outside of this artificial environment.

This place is all about control, perforce; how could it be otherwise? The food is, as advertised, awful. Supper consisted of two "sandwiches" of white bread with a couple of slices each of industrial cheese. Breakfast: a plastic wrap of something resembling corn flakes, three slices of bread, a muffin, two Styrofoam cups containing apple juice and skim milk. I was offered coffee, but strangely none appeared. Everything (naturally) in plastic packages; the detritus accumulates.

There is, of all things, a television in this cell, although it has a habit of randomly losing signal. On it, along with the predictable bottomless pit of dreck, I can watch BBC, CBC, and perhaps most interestingly, APTN.

On the wall behind me is written: "Lord, I ask you to keep my loved ones safe, and grant us another day, another chance to make things right, with our past, our present, for our future, so we can live in peace with each other and ourselves, and with you. In your name I pray dear Jesus—Amen." Above it is written four times: "bail will happen." On the door someone has written in pen: "___ ___ is a rat." Ghosts.

I was informed by the guard who led me to this cell that for vegetarian meals and writing paper I should fill out special request forms. She then brought me those forms, and I dutifully filled them out; however, no one seems interested in actually taking these forms. The gentlemen who brought my "breakfast" informed me that this was the job of the duty officer, who supposedly checks in on prisoners every forty-five minutes. I did see one face flash by the window a bit later, so I knocked on the window of the door. He approached with that upward tilt of the chin which conveys contempt, and when I made my request, walked away shaking his head. It's all about power and control, no?

Yesterday, on leaving the courtroom (and I did hear the calls of people singing and telling me they love me), I was led, or rather directed, by a taciturn young man down some cement hallways and (after being handcuffed) up some stairs, then down in an elevator, to a hallway with holding cells, into one of which I was placed.

Quite shortly thereafter I was led to an "interview room" divided into a Their Half and a My Half by a plexiglass window with a slot in it. Two typical young sheriff types appeared on the other side of the glass (truly notable how, while the prosecutors and judges are almost exclusively white, almost all the guards and sheriffs are people of colour, mostly South Asian), and took my particulars including date of birth, eye colour, and so on. All my personal effects were taken: my wallet, keys, glasses, money (carefully counted and signed for), and jacket. After this I was trundled to another waiting cell where I was searched. Then another interview, this time with two younger women, one of whom was a justice of the peace. The undertaking in question was my agreement to the terms of probation—naturally it raises the question as to what would have happened had I not agreed!

Back to the holding cell, and now leg manacles, and then a police vehicle with a cell. A red overhead light. I found I could block the unpleasant flow of cold air into this space by leaning against it. This vehicle proceeded to the police station on Main Street, where I was placed in another cell, searched again, and then transferred to a second vehicle for the drive out to Port Coquitlam. This time the driver was a young blond woman, exhibiting the seemingly standard indifference (another day of transporting criminals, ho hum). I couldn't see her in any case: my little cell was now at the rear, larger but with cold air pouring down from the ceiling, and thus unblockable. I could see out the back of the van, where rain was falling as she took Cordova through the Downtown Eastside. I began to sing, starting of course with "Have You Been to Jail for Justice!" Then I sang the "Internationale" in three languages, as much as I could remember of "El Pueblo Unido," and "Bright Star." I also sang the harmonics of the space.

The drive was surprisingly short; on arrival I was led into North Fraser, where the real dehumanization begins. Yet again I was searched, then fingerprinted. During this process I noticed a group of guard types behind me swearing their heads off about something. I was then unclothed and given prison garb, which is uniformly red. Also as advertised, I was required to demonstrate that I was hiding nothing under my testicles or between my butt cheeks. My interactions with these people were not uniformly impersonal; I observed flashes of humanity on a few people's parts.

I'm not quite sure of the order of things, but I was interviewed about my mental health by an older woman named Sue (the only official to introduce themselves in the entire process); she wanted to make sure I wasn't in a mood to harm myself or others (I wasn't). She was pleasant, in an egalitarian sense. After Sue I was visited by a nurse and his assistant, who took my blood pressure. I was dismayed to learn that it's quite high, complete news to me. Finally, I was led through a series of doors into this unit, which contains thirty-three cells on three floors. I am on the second floor, numerically in the middle, number 15.

There is sugar in every meal, at the very least in the form of juice. So far my attempts to deliver a request for vegetarian meals have been fruitless, but I did manage to contact Barbara by telephone on the third try, and filled out yet another form to add her to the list of possible "visitors" online. A younger duty officer also saw fit to give me some writing paper, and even allow me to sharpen the several pencils I've already accumulated; however, the computers are nonfunctional, the items I've ordered from the canteen (writing papers, a pen and some envelopes) supposedly won't arrive until Friday or Saturday. The sugary food is giving me a constant headache, and tonight I had to throw out a perfectly good pork chop.

May 19
As I stepped through the door to the outside area (before being

locked down) the duty officer asked me whether I was here for a pipeline protest. When I responded that I was, he muttered "that seems wrong" and walked away.

May 20

Yesterday I felt ill enough that I requested a COVID test. Now I feel OK but have been placed under COVID isolation protocol until my PCR test comes back negative. This means no more outdoors, no shower, no leaving the cell. I passed on the request for veggie meals both to the duty officer and the doctor, both of whom said they would do something about it; but again tonight I had to throw out the main dish. I've requested several times to be able to take a shower, with no result.

Some understanding of the actual situation here: the game is psychological, designed to induce resentment and reaction; my response must be independence. If guards can engender lots of requests they are powerful; if I don't need them, I am powerful. Thus, rather than request clean laundry I can wash mine in the sink; I can even bathe, using paper towels. As far as the books and veggie meals and mail goes, I will request to see the chaplain. By the very institutional nature of this place, the guards are psychologically primed to act disrespectfully; thus, I hear cellmates down the block pounding on the bars and screaming. That is a game I can't afford to play. I will, however, turn down dinners which are not vegetarian.

Quite paradoxically I continue to feel good. I can meditate, watch old movies, write music, sing, stretch, and rest.

Some folks I've met here: First, the unfortunate gentleman from Korea who is stuck in a room where the light has broken, so he spends his days in semi-darkness. He speaks very little English and wanted to try to use the phone, and he asked me to help him. Of course the guards would never do that! I attempted to guide him through the slightly byzantine phone system which requires you to put your "CS" number, which is how prisoners are identified; but you also have to repeat your own name, and the institution's, several times, and when this man tried, the system kept claiming he wasn't "loud" enough. Of course he was, but in truth he couldn't pronounce "North Fraser Pretrial" so he was out of luck. In sympathy I offered him paper, an envelope, and a pencil, suggesting he might like to write to someone—his wife, perhaps? He shook his head and said "wife no good." I had the sense that this feeling may have something to do with his presence here, but I didn't inquire. His family is mostly in Korea, but no, he didn't want to write to them from North Fraser Pretrial.

Then the young fellow with a tiny ponytail. He often smiles with a kind of bland, open innocence. He's here on breach of parole, having tried to steal a catalytic converter. He tells me his brother is a vegan animal activist, his mom a vegetarian. His basic issue is addiction—to a variety of things, but clearly to something which requires cash to support. He shakes his head sadly as he speaks about staying clean for six months, getting his old job back, almost putting his life back together.

The nurse just appeared to check my temperature and blood pressure again. From what I could see my blood pressure is still high. I told the nurse and his assistant that I feel as well as I've ever felt in my life; the decision to experience joy and optimism, as well as the absolute luxury to dispense my time as I see fit, have conspired to bring me a growing state of grace. Naturally this is predicated on the knowledge that this will have an end, and that soon enough I will feel the sun and the breeze, smell flowers, walk on grass. I've moved my cot to the top bunk, to take advantage of the early morning sun which continues to make an appearance until 9:30 a.m. or so.

This morning the chaplain dropped by as requested, and we communicated through the door. He wrote down my requests for mail and a veggie meal, and hey presto! A vegetarian lunch was delivered. Still no mail nor books, however. I also requested sharp pencils from the nurse's assistant, who assured me he would pass it on. (I've heard that one before.)

May 21

Breakfast is served around 7:30. Today I decided to eat some of the muffin they brought, but ate the porridge with no milk or sweetener (very nice). I will climb back up after this and continue to enjoy the lovely sun, perhaps sleep a bit more (certainly can't fault this experience on the basis of access to sleep!).

Blessedly, mail has arrived and I've spoken with Barbara on the phone. Several of the letters brought tears to my eyes. The phone was brought by a fellow who described himself as the "phone dude" and stood outside the cell holding the phone while I spoke on an extension. B's voice kept breaking up, as apparently did mine; but our message of love and connection was certainly clear enough.

May 22

Still no release from what feels close to solitary confinement—I haven't showered since Tuesday, no access to fresh air, the only conversation is brief interactions with the guards.

Note at 4 p.m.

I have cracked the code of this room's harmonics, which had puzzled me—but of course, it being a rectangular box, there are two sets (width and height are the same, so the higher set is reinforced, except that there are intervening objects on the walls). Lengthwise the harmonics are based on A 55 Hz; height and width are at F 88 Hz, meaning the ratio of length to height is 8/5, or 1.6. Of course then I had to measure the walls, using my height as a basis. They are close to 220 cm tall by 365 cm long, for a ratio of . . . wait for it . . . 1.64!

May 23

8 a.m.

Contemplating the features of a hunger strike. Of course this constitutes the ultimate power of a prisoner, and it's also extremely difficult. I have refused breakfast today and yesterday; yesterday's lunch was a white bread sandwich of industrial cheese, an apple and something resembling Kool-Aid. I swapped the white bread for some whole wheat (I'm generally not eating the bread they bring), but if today is a repeat performance I will refuse that as well. All of these meals are served in Styrofoam boxes, with the inevitable plastic packages of canola margarine (inedible), Coffee-Mate, sugar, stir sticks, and (I presume) some kind of sweetener; I've not enumerated the contents, but simply stack the Styrofoam boxes with the others (there are now eight in the stack, plus maybe another one or two in the wastebasket, and thirteen Styrofoam cups at last count). I have since Wednesday been unable to shower, experience fresh air, remove garbage from my cell, enjoy reading material, make a telephone call, have access to a sharp pencil.

These, especially the first five, are basic to the rights of incarcerated people. The trope of each official to whose attention I bring this fact is that they'll get back to me, and they never do.

11:30 a.m.
I've just spoken with Barbara and been let out of my cage. I walked around outside and had an interesting conversation with a gentleman who claims to have died three times and been outside his body. The newspaper had already been appropriated by someone else, but I've been able to sharpen these pencils and acquire more writing paper. The guy in 13, unfortunately, is still locked in his room—today is his fifth day. Another inmate slipped a small community newspaper under his door saying "at least you'll have something to read." For now, the violations of human rights in the lockdown remain a concern, but my own experience is less onerous.

I want to remember some details about the man who died three times—tall, bearded, with hair shorn almost off and a scar on the side of his forehead. His bottom teeth frequently show when he speaks, and they seem unnaturally perfectly spaced and even—was that a hint of gold caps? He loves to garden, collects and propagates heritage seeds, had some quite sharp observations about the system, prides himself on never taking handouts and being taught by his father to be as self-sufficient as possible. He has studied maps of historical Vancouver, tracing the routes of hidden streams almost as an energy map of the land (although later he claimed that protrusions on the trunks of trees resulted from the trees consuming the bodies of creatures which had died under them, and represented those bodies). He mentioned how much of the shoreline historically was mud flats.

Later
At last, a real writing pad, and real pens! Be still, my beating heart.

8 p.m.
Interactions with some others here. A very polite younger Korean man who gave me a packet of chamomile tea is in for second degree murder, looking at a life sentence with possible parole in ten years. A short, heavier man with many tattoos tells the story of beating up someone who had slept with his girlfriend while he was in jail

(to the enthusiastic "yeah, bro" and high-fives of another listener). He now claims to have renounced sleeping with other women because his girlfriend is "gold"—they've been together for five years. This guy and the other one are both Trump supporters. "Fuckin'" is a simple term of emphasis, liable to turn up virtually anywhere, in any sentence. They were also kind enough to warn me about whistling in jail, so I won't do that anymore! All these folks manifest a degree of normality, but all but one (a tall, gangly kid with one eye, who is new to the system) have been in multiple times. The tattooed man has maybe $200,000 saved up and is trying to imagine a different life; but the suggestion of possible school didn't impress him. He claims to have "oppositional defiance disorder," rendering him incapable of dealing with a classroom environment.

May 24

I've spoken to two of my fellow prisoners about meditation. They seemed interested. The tattooed man is also something of an artist, making interactive sculptures with glue sticks. The gangly kid read me his statement to the judge, an earnest plea promising that this is a road he doesn't want to go down. His primary issue, at least at this point, is addiction. The man who died speaks of his younger sister with venom; ever since they were children they were treated differently by their parents, frozen roles crystallized to lifelong rage against the opposite sex. He has damaged himself in his struggle not to inflict violence on others, hitting himself in the head with a hammer until he was permanently scarred and possibly brain damaged. In meditation I've been struck several times with grief for these people's trauma and a wish for their healing.

Worth saying that one of the central survival techniques I've developed in here is a return to meditation, several times a day. Many years since I've had a consistent practice. While locked down I also exercised by walking the perimeter of my cell twenty times three times a day, and doing modified exercises using the bunk beds to pull myself from a bent to a straight position.

May 26

I was informed that I was being released after nine days of a fourteen-day sentence (for good behaviour). The release was just as ridiculous, formal, officious, and pointless as the initial processing.

I was taken by a taxi to the nearest bus stop, which was some miles from the nearest SkyTrain station. I remember being conscious of the ordinariness of the things and people around me . . . or rather, their unconsciousness of the dream they swim through daily. I was intensely aware of having recently been in a state different from what most people around me would ever experience. I was eager to see Barbara. I was looking forward to rejoining the fight to stop us from destroying our own world.

I was free.

RITA WONG,
Poet, Professor, Social and Environmental Justice Supporter

Photo: Heather Menzies

Biography

Rita Wong is a poet-scholar who attends to the relationships between water, justice, ecology, and decolonization. She teaches at Emily Carr University of Art + Design, on the unceded Coast Salish territories, also known as Vancouver. She has co-edited an anthology with Dorothy Christian entitled *Downstream: Reimagining Water*, based on a gathering that brought together Elders, artists, scientists, writers, scholars, students, and activists around the urgent need to care for the waters that give us life. A recipient of the Dorothy Livesay Poetry Prize and the Asian Canadian Writers' Workshop Emerging Writer Award, Wong is the author of *Current, Climate* (Wilfrid Laurier University Press, 2021), *Beholden* (Talonbooks, 2018, with Fred Wah), *Undercurrent* (Nightwood, 2015), *Perpetual* (Nightwood, 2015, with Cindy Mochizuki), *Sybil Unrest* (Line Books, 2008, with Larissa Lai), *Forage* (Nightwood, short-listed for the 2008 Asian American Literary Award for Poetry, winner of Canada Reads Poetry 2011), and *Monkeypuzzle* (Press Gang, 1998).

Wong works to support Indigenous communities' efforts towards justice and health for water, having witnessed and participated in such work at the Peace River, the Wedzin Kwa, Ada'itsx (Fairy Creek), the Columbia River, the Fraser River, the Salish Sea, and the Arctic Ocean watershed. She understands that when these waterways are healthy, life (including people) will be healthy too, and that we cannot afford to endanger and pollute the waters that sustain our lives.

Rita was arrested at Westridge shipping terminal in Burnaby on August 24, 2018, and sentenced to twenty-eight days on August 16, 2019, serving eighteen days.

Statement to BC Supreme Court Justice Kenneth Affleck, August 16, 2019

I'm grateful to be here alive today with all of you on sacred, unceded Coast Salish territories, the homelands of the Musqueam, Squamish, and Tsleil-Waututh Peoples.

On August 24, 2018, while British Columbia was in a state of emergency because of wildfires caused by climate change—breaking records for the second year in a row; putting lives at risk, health at risk, and displacing thousands of people—I sang, prayed, and sat in ceremony for about half an hour in front of the Trans Mountain Pipeline project's Westridge Marine Terminal.

I did this because we're in a climate emergency, and since the federal government has abdicated its responsibility to protect us despite full knowledge of the emergency, it became necessary to act. We are in imminent peril if we consider the rate of change we are currently experiencing from a geological perspective—we are losing species at an alarming rate and facing mass extinction due to the climate crisis caused by colonization. This is the irreparable harm I sought to prevent, which the court, the Crown, and corporations also have a responsibility to prevent.

Everyone has the responsibility to respond to this crisis. We are on the global equivalent of the *Titanic*, and this industrialized ship needs to change direction. We also need to build lifeboats, healthy places that can support resilience in the future, such as the sacred Salish Sea.

I acted with respect for the rule of law, which includes the rule of natural law and the rule of Indigenous law and the rule of international law. Under the rule of law:

I have a responsibility to my ancestors and the ancestors of this land to protect the lands and waters that give us life with each breath, each bite of food, each sip of water.

I have a responsibility to reciprocate to the salmon who have given their life to feed mine, to reciprocate to the trees that produce and gift us the fresh air from their leaves through the perpetual song of photosynthesis.

I have a responsibility to give back to the great Pacific Ocean, the Salish Sea, Stalew (the Fraser River), and the many water bodies on which human life—and other lives—depend.

I have a responsibility to hold our politicians accountable when they persistently breach their international legal obligations to protect us. They should be enacting policy to reduce greenhouse gas emissions, not to increase them in ways that jeopardize a stable society.

In breaching the injunction, I had no intention of reducing respect for our courts. I do intend to ask the court to respect Coast Salish laws that uphold our responsibilities to care for the land and waters that make life, liberty, and peace possible for everyone. I sincerely ask the court to take our reciprocal relationship with the land and water into consideration because we are on Coast Salish lands, where everyone is a Coast Salish citizen.

I'm one of over two hundred citizens of conscience who were arrested because, unlike our federal and provincial governments, we take the climate crisis seriously. We take the need to protect society seriously. We did what we could to maintain respect for the justice system:

We co-operated with Indigenous spiritual guardians, nongovernmental organizations and the police.

We waited patiently for decades before determining—at a moment in history when time has almost run out to act—that orthodox ways of getting the federal government to act were doomed to fail.

The police were informed in advance and they appointed people to liaise and communicate with the NGOs to maintain order.

All of this is evidence of the rule of law working.

I respect the court's concern for the rule of law. I do appreciate that obeying court orders is part of the rule of law. There are more aspects of the rule of law that I would ask you to consider before sentencing me.

Natural law and Indigenous law rely on mutual aid and co-operation, qualities that require maturity and a deep love for one's community, recognizing that we are all equal. It is a rule of law that works primarily from a place of love and respect, not from fear of authority and punishment. This is the aspect of rule of law that has moved the hearts and spirits of the thousands of people who've shown up to care for the land and waters of this place. Such an understanding of the rule of law, as coming from a place of love and courage more than fear, could strengthen our sense of democracy. It could make our commitment to reconciliation a sincere one.

We can all learn from natural law and Coast Salish law that we have a reciprocal relationship with the land; and that we all have a responsibility to care for the land's health, which is ultimately our health too. My ancestors teach me to act responsibly, to honour the water, the land, and my relatives. I feel their teachings in my blood and guts, my bones that carry their spirits within them, my heart as it closes and opens again and again with each beat.

The morning of my arrest we hung red dresses to honour the missing and murdered Indigenous women, the sisters who are made more vulnerable and victimized by the man camps that accompany pipeline expansion and massive resource extraction. We sang the women warriors song, over and over again, for each woman who should have been there but wasn't. We sang for our grandparents, for people from all four directions of the earth.

Our ceremony that morning was an act of spiritual commitment, of prayer, of artistic expression, of freedom of expression, an act of desperation in the face of climate crisis, an act of allegiance with the earth's natural laws, and a heartfelt attempt to prevent a calamitous future for the human race.

As I see it, one shows respect by speaking honestly, a view shared by Canada's Truth and Reconciliation Commission. To speak the truth is not to show contempt, but to hold those in power accountable for failing to protect us and for instead knowingly choosing to inflict systemic harm and violence upon us and upon the land and waters that give us life.

I pray that the urgency of the climate crisis and our responsibilities to be good relatives living on Coast Salish lands, under Coast Salish laws, will help to guide this justice system as it encounters land defenders. As land and water defenders, we do what we do for everyone's sake.

Narrative: Lessons from Prison

My work for the past decade as a writer and a scholar has been to learn with and from water—to follow the teachings of rivers and watersheds. I love the bodies of water that have been called the Bow River, the Fraser River, the Peace River, the Columbia River, the Pacific Ocean, the Arctic Ocean, and all the watersheds that British Columbia and Alberta are part of.

I was born on Treaty 7 territory in what is also known as Calgary, and spent half my life there before moving to the unceded Coast Salish lands known as Vancouver. I love both places. I oppose pipeline expansion because I love the land known as Alberta, and see the urgent need to make a transition from fossil fuels.

How do I express this love?

I feel that the best way to repay my debt to the people who built the oil industry is not to automatically assume that oil is the only way Alberta can survive, but to lovingly assert that there are at least two things more important than oil: water, and life itself. As former lieutenant governor of Alberta Grant MacEwan pointed out in his last book, *Watershed: Reflections on Water*, 75 percent of the water in the Bow and Elbow Rivers comes from snow melt. When we accelerate that melting beyond a certain rate, we are guaranteed to melt the ice caps. Surely we are smarter and better than this.

I believe that everyone who lives on unceded Coast Salish lands has a responsibility to uphold Coast Salish laws,[7] which entail respecting and protecting the land that gives us life. This is why, since March 2018, I've spent a great deal of time up at Burnaby Mountain. It is why I was arrested and sentenced to time in prison.

On August 24, 2018, while BC was in a state of emergency due to wildfires, I sat in ceremony in front of Trans Mountain's Westridge Marine Terminal. For this act of opposition to fossil fuel expansion that no one can afford, on August 16, 2019, I was sentenced to twenty-eight days in prison by Judge Kenneth Affleck in the BC Supreme Court, as recommended by the Province of BC's Crown prosecutor, Monte Rattan.

After I left the courtroom, I was handcuffed, shackled, and transported in a chilly van with fellow political prisoner Will Offley. He, like me, had argued that our actions were motivated by necessity due to the climate crisis. As I wrote in my sentencing statement, since the federal government has abdicated its responsibility to protect us despite full knowledge of this emergency, it became necessary to act. Our arguments were rejected by Judge Affleck.

Will was incarcerated at North Fraser Pretrial Centre, while I was moved into an overly warm vehicle that ended up in the Alouette Correctional Centre for Women in Maple Ridge. The combination of heat and sliding around on the metal seat gave me motion sickness, so I had vomited by the time I arrived at the prison.

My first night at the ACCW was spent in maximum security. My cell (Charlie 9) had a bulletin board, on which a previous prisoner had left words: COURAGE & SERENITY. The lights never went off completely in my cell. I threw a sweatshirt over my eyes and slept from sheer exhaustion after writing a letter to friends and watching a bit of APTN on the television. It was a surprise and a pleasure to see Sharon McIvor on TV, talking about the regaining of status for Indigenous women who'd had it taken away by colonial legislation. In the morning, I was moved to medium security after breakfast. Though my stay in maximum security was short, I was treated kindly by my fellow inmates, one of whom gifted me a hair tie and another who showed me how the phone system worked.

In medium security, Birch A5, I had a cellmate who showed me the ropes around the prison and even made us prison candy, a confection melted from creamer, sugar, and peanut butter packets salvaged from the dining hall.

Many of the women I met were struggling through various experiences of addiction, trauma, and poverty. Prison is not the best place to address these problems. One woman was a survivor of residential school abuse, another had been attacked on the Highway of Tears as a young teenager, another was four months pregnant and constantly hungry because the meal portions in prison were inadequate for someone who is eating for two. Many other prisoners were also hungry much of the time. Some women who didn't need as much food shared what they could with others who felt hungry. The dining hall served food ranging from bologna sandwiches to chicken to hot dogs, and for breakfast, toast, muffins, and porridge. Prisoners can supplement dining hall meals with food purchased from the canteen. For a while, we could eat vegetables from the prison garden, though that privilege was arbitrarily withdrawn.

Prison was hard but bearable, and actually very educational for me. I noticed how people navigate a systemically violent structure by helping each other endure the system with compassion and kindness in all kinds of ways, big and small, notwithstanding personal and interpersonal dramas that come and go. In the spirit of sharing whatever gifts I could, I facilitated a creative writing workshop while I was in prison, for the women there have powerful voices, stories that need to be shared.

More programs are needed to support healing and empowerment of inmates. Systemic discrimination results in the overrepresentation of Indigenous women and low-income women among the incarcerated.

I had the opportunity to work outside, tending the prison's grounds, pruning trees, and so forth. Prisoners who work are paid a starting wage of about $2 a day. I was fortunate to have funds put into my account by friends so that I could buy rice, cheese, popcorn, and junk food that I shared as much as I could. But if I'd relied only on the $20 that I made for working ten days on horticulture in prison, I would not have been able to buy much. Indeed, I spent half of that $20 on a $10 yoga mat that I passed on to another prisoner when I left ACCW.

As the time passed I kept thinking: Imagine what we could do if we diverted fossil fuel subsidies—and billions wasted on destroying forests through disasters like the Site C dam—towards regenerating forests and the carbon sinks we need to cool this earth? What if we invested in local food security, regenerative agriculture, and diversifying genuinely renewable energy? Though our systems are currently failing us, I believe that the transformations we need are both possible and necessary.

I had the privilege of being as well prepared as one might be for going to prison—I'd visited prisons as a volunteer for several years as part of Joint Effort[8] and Direct Action Against Refugee Exploitation. I also had information from previous prisoners who'd spent time at ACCW for their principled opposition to this pipeline expansion, women like long-time social justice activist Jean Swanson, who became a Vancouver city councillor in 2018.

This helped me imagine what to expect and how to prepare for incarceration.

I wish I could be as well prepared for the climate crisis. I'm not, although I'm trying my best to get prepared. For starters, I got arrested because of the urgency of the climate emergency. The courts' and the Crown's failure to address the climate crisis is made clear by contrasting my four-week prison sentence with the few pitiful fines paid by Trans Mountain Corporation that has had a much larger destructive impact on the land than my small action at the Westridge Marine Terminal.[9] Government agencies that should be enforcing environmental protection laws are failing us, and when I and other land and water protectors point this out, they penalize and scapegoat us, instead of holding to account the criminal damage that the Trans Mountain Pipeline has inflicted as its contractors cut down many thousands, possibly millions, of trees and destroy wildlife habitat. This disproportionate enforcement against individuals trying to prevent harm while ignoring corporations harming the land and water is systemic injustice.

It's surprising to find myself in the unexpected position of having spent time in a Canadian prison as a political prisoner, punished by the petro-state for asserting my responsibility to care for the health of the land and water. Spending time within the prison's walls taught me that there are good people caught in terrible systems, and that systems change is a necessary response to the climate crisis. The women in prison are a microcosm of the larger challenges we have with addiction as a society. Where poor women addicted to drugs are criminalized through policing that targets vulnerable individuals, other forms of addiction found in powerful, wealthy circles, that are arguably as deadly or more deadly for humanity, have been given a free pass by the federal government.

I think addiction to oil is something we as a society need to face and get over together. I understand that the transition off oil is hard, yet it is technically possible, as the Solutions Project demonstrates.[10] Greta Thunberg and George Monbiot, too, have alerted us to the urgent need to support natural climate solutions at the scale required.[11]

We urgently need to return ourselves to health and balance,

to what the land can teach us when we listen to the lessons of the rivers, the ocean, the forests. We can be better relatives to one another. Now is the time to stop poisoning the earth and to create jobs that care for and renew the land instead of destroying it, as efforts such as the Green New Deal in the US are trying to achieve. Now is the time to make that leap.

Instead of rearranging chairs on the deck of the *Titanic*, we need to be building lifeboats. First Nations organizations like the Tsleil-Waututh Sacred Trust articulate the cultural shift needed to reduce our carbon footprint, helping us to make those lifeboats. As protectors of the Burrard Inlet, they do their sacred work for all our sakes. The very least we can do is reciprocate by contributing whatever gifts and skills we each bring towards the urgent goal of climate justice and the move to a renewable society.

Almost every day in prison, I would take the time to sit outside, watch the trees, and sing songs to thank the land. Gratitude, respect, and reciprocity with the land were what I decided to focus on while I was in prison. My body was restricted, but my heart, mind, and spirit were free. One time, we smudged briefly in the prison, standing in a circle and singing the women warriors song, the bear song, and a song for the eagles. It was a quick ceremony before we had to get back to our unit for count and lockdown, but it reminded me of the healing walk for the tar sands that I participated in years ago.[12]

In the first year of that healing walk through the brutal devastation wrought by Suncor and Syncrude near Fort McMurray, immersed in gross, carcinogenic air, somehow we saw a bear that day and an eagle above us. The next year of the walk, the organizers made T-shirts for the healing walk with both the bear and the eagle on them, and I often wear this shirt to remind me what the healing walk has taught me. The bear and the eagle represent love and courage, both of which guide us when we honour our reciprocal relationships with the land and water.

I was released from Alouette Correctional Centre for Women after eighteen days for good behaviour. I walked out with naloxone training, more mail than I've ever received in my life, and a renewed commitment to uphold natural and Indigenous laws. I went right back to the Coast Salish Watch House at the perimeter of Trans Mountain's tank farm, where I continue to be active with the Mountain Protectors working group.[13]

People have asked me: What can I do? I say, Don't give up. Find creative ways to stop the pipeline expansion and turn it into a stranded asset. Spend time with and protect sacred places like the Burrard Inlet, the Peace Valley,[14] your local creeks and forests. Our future depends on these acts of care and attention. Don't look away from the violence that Trans Mountain is inflicting. At the same time, keep an eye on the solutions we need to build together, the life boats that are in the making.

The narrative by Rita Wong was adapted from an article she published in the Tyee, *September 4, 2019,* thetyee.ca.

George Rammell's Artwork: George (lower right) with his "Teeter-totter" at a downtown Vancouver rally. Photo: Pia Massie

The Chambers of Predetermined Outcomes, sculpture by George Rammell

Above: Danaca Ackerson's Protest Protest Art; Marching down Vancouver's streets with the Carnival Band. More images at danaca-ackerson.weebly.com

Opposite (clockwise): Indigenous Chiefs lead the March up Burnaby Mountain on March 10, 2018 (Rogue Collective#Protect the Inlet)

Arrest of Elizabeth May and Kennedy Stewart at the TMX gates on Burnaby Mountain. Photo: Jimmy Jeong

Resisters at the TMX pipe staging ground near the Brunette River. Photo: Donna Clark

Rueben George speaks. Photo: David Favrholdt

Drone shot of a small section of resisters participating in "Hug the Mountain," May 7, 2022

Arrest of Janette McIntosh, in orange shirt; one of the Brunette River Six. Photo: Laurel Dykstra

Brunette River Six on Sentencing Day, February 14, 2022. Photo: Cynthia Materi

Part 6
Resisters fighting for their future

T-Rex duet at the TMX staging grounds near a Burnaby high school.
Photo: Tim Takaro

EMILY KELSALL,
Storyteller

Emily tree-sitting in
Hummingbird.
Photo: Ian Harland

Biography

Emily Kelsall is a storyteller and activist from unceded Squamish territory, colonially known as West Vancouver, BC. Emily has published pieces about her experience with the anti-TMX resistance in the *National Observer* and *Chatelaine*. She's been involved in politics and activism since the age of fifteen. She is active in the Vancouver arts scene, engaging in comedy, poetry, and rap-battling. Above all, she's passionate about telling great stories that do good. She is currently studying documentary filmmaking at Capilano University.

Emily was arrested with Maya Laframboise in May 2022 and served a twenty-eight day sentence in February 2023.

Excerpts from the Statement to BC Supreme Court Justice Shelley Fitzpatrick, January 27, 2023

Dear Honourable Justice Fitzpatrick,

When I was a little girl I was terrified of climate change in the same way some kids are scared of monsters under the bed. I'd look at the temperature gauge on my mom's minivan and ask for reassurance: "Is the temperature normal?" Late at night on my bed, I'd use my iPod Touch to look up phrases such as "Global warming hoax" and "Climate change not real." Anything to quiet the panic in my young mind.

The people around me grew adept at sensing my anxiety and putting a plug in it. "The weather outside is normal, Emily. Global warming isn't as bad as people are making it out to be. The government is taking care of it."

My first bouts of activism were when I was in kindergarten. I put together a petition that I circulated at recess to save the trees. Then I organized a few kids to pick up garbage during lunch. When I was in grade 8, I wrote to every premier in Canada expressing my concern about climate change.

In grade 10 I worked with a campaign called Our Horizon that had the brilliant idea of putting warning labels about climate change on gas pumps. I spent hundreds of hours getting endorsements from local businesses, and presented the idea to the cities of West Vancouver and North Vancouver. North Vancouver accepted the idea and I thought my job was done, but oil lobbyists intervened so that the warning labels were transformed into small stickers encouraging drivers to check their tire pressure.

Last summer I was in Stanley Park when I noticed that some of the trees looked dead. Immediately I panicked, thinking "The warm temperatures are killing the trees," and then as I'd been taught, I reassured myself: "That's not true. You're worrying for nothing, Emily. It's all in your head." I instantly felt better. A few days later I came across a news story on CBC about how drought and moths are killing the hemlock trees of Stanley Park. My reassurances were wrong. The monster is real. No matter what people have been trying to tell me, the government is not doing enough to stop climate change. The planet is still warming and it's getting worse.

I've been to the trials of a couple other climate activists. Oftentimes these people are dubbed as "individuals who are passionate about the environment" by the prosecution.

We are not acting as "individuals." We are acting on behalf of a body of science with the backing of the UN Secretary-General, who called the expansion of oil and gas projects like this pipeline "moral and economic madness." Calling climate activists "passionate about the environment" is a watered-down, backhanded dismissal of the scope of our reality.

I am not "passionate about the environment."

I am not carrying my supplies for prison in a recyclable tote bag.

I am not praying that my cell block has a view of a tree.

When I write my daily letter to my friends and family, I'm not concerned about whether they'll recycle them or not.

I am passionate about survival.

We are told time and time again that we can protest peacefully as long as we're doing it within the scope of the law. The Crown is concerned with protecting the rule of law, but we're concerned with protecting life on this planet. If we stay within the bounds of law, because the law is always correct, then we ignore humanity's entire history—from women's rights to Black rights to human rights. People like Rosa Parks and Emmeline Pankhurst broke the law and were taken to jail. We wouldn't have the freedom and rights we have today if they'd never had the courage to defy the status quo. That's something I learned in civics class.[1]

I'm here today as someone who is advocating for rights that are not yet recognized as fundamental: environmental rights—the "absurd" idea that clean water, a breathable atmosphere, and abundant nature are not a privilege but a universal right, and that stripping us of this right robs us of our health, happiness, and humanity.

Within my lifetime, I will see the oceans acidify and rise. Species will go extinct and forests die. I will witness floods and famine. When I look to my future, I am many things. I am frightened. I am angry. But I am not sorry for the work that I've done.

I began working on T-Rex against TMX because I refuse to live in complacency. I want to stand up for what I believe in, in a way that resonates with every ounce of being. I accept my sentence and see it as a natural consequence of activism. I know I'll keep fighting, no matter the cost, as long as I live.

Above all else, I have only this to say in conclusion—an ancient T-Rex proverb that goes:

[At this point I reached into my shirt, pulled out the T-Rex mask I'd hidden there, and put it on.]

Rawr rawr rawr
Growl growl
Snarl
Rawr rawr.
Thank you.

Narrative: T-Rex Eats Pipelines for Breakfast

I want my contribution to this anthology to shed light on the importance of mental and spiritual well-being that is necessary to sustain the fight for justice. This includes some details about my depression and anxiety in relation to climate change. I want others who are struggling to know they aren't alone, and want readers to realize that dramatic and positive change is possible.

A special thank you to everyone who called or wrote while I was in prison. You were with me when I needed it most.

The Morning of My Sentencing Trial

On January 27, 2023, I pulled on my yellow blazer and glanced at myself in the bathroom mirror. The purple under my eyes was heavy. My skin was pasty and gaunt. My hair was short and unkempt. I had impulsively cut it just the night before with a pair of scissors, lopping off my ponytail until only a bob of brown hair remained.

I could hear my sister and their girlfriend stirring in the next room. I took a final look in the mirror, re-entered my bedroom, sat down and began furiously making amendments to the speech I was to give before a Supreme Court justice in three hours. I went over in my head what I needed for the day: ID, credit card, water bottle, a couple pencils, and cash that would pay for ramen noodles and paper when I was in prison. I made sure to remember to take the dinosaur mask I'd acquired a few days earlier. This was vital.

My stomach was churning as I headed out. Surprisingly, prison wasn't the main stressor. I felt proud to be going to jail for a cause that I believed in. The cause of my suffering was depression, obsession, and anxiety. I'd been haunted by these spectres my entire life. My worries growing up were wide and varied. They touched on the possibility of alien abduction, bridges collapsing, and cryptic creatures causing me harm. As I grew into a teenager, with the help of my family and psychologists, I determined that the aforementioned preoccupations were not true. One worry reigned supreme, though: climate change. This was the one knot no professional could undo.

We drove in my mother's car to the courthouse. When I arrived I saw a reporter already setting up a camera. My stomach twisted in anxiety. *What should I say? Will I say the right thing? What if I don't do the right thing, the brave thing, and the pipeline is built and it's all my fault?*

For the last two years my climate anxiety had been especially bad. In 2021 I had been part of a cohort of tree-sitters north of the Brunette River, a scheme that delayed progress on the drilling of pipes through Burnaby Mountain.[2] Despite the stress of avoiding TMX security, I was relatively well. Then I took a break from tree-sitting and volunteered with Indigenous communities, but after the heat dome in June my anxiety returned.

Around the time I conceived of T-Rex against TMX, I was deep in the throes of fear. T-Rex against TMX was a careful attempt to walk the middle ground; a way to be myself while still taking action to create change.

The idea might not have taken flight if it wasn't for my friend Maya.

T-Rex against TMX

One day, I went to a Stop TMX action and found Maya Laframboise dressed in an inflatable dino suit. I'd only just begun

Some concept art I drew months before the action.

to circulate the idea of "T-Rex against TMX," but Maya told me she loved it so much so that she'd secured "trexagainsttmx" as a handle on Instagram, Twitter, and TikTok. Thus, our partnership was forged.

Our first action was on April 26, 2022. Maya, myself, and two photographers stopped work at the marine terminal in Burnaby. We were all nervous, taking turns visiting a porta-potty before we attached our microphones, suited up, and headed down to the terminal. I'd brought with me a gaggle of rainbow helium balloons. I didn't know what we were going to do with them, only that they looked cool. I came up with a concept on the fly to hand them out to the workers driving in and out of the terminal. If they took a balloon, we'd let them pass. If they refused, we'd have no choice but to stop them. Of course, someone refused a balloon and traffic was stopped. (Photos from this event are available on our Instagram page: @trexagainsttmx.)

Our plan went swimmingly. The media team was phenomenal and did a great job taking pictures and videos for distribution on social media. We stalled work for about an hour until a few RCMP officers showed up. For a while they just stood there deliberating while Maya and I sang "Call Me Maybe" by Carly Rae Jepsen at the top of our lungs. Finally the officers approached us, asked for our names (which we refused to give), and informed us we had to leave. We'd gotten what we came for, so we did.

Thrilled with our success, Maya and I convened at a coffee shop and plotted further. So far our plan was going off without a hitch: we were blocking work on the pipeline, and doing it in a way that proved activism was accessible, fun, and funny. And so far, we were getting off without serious legal repercussions. We were sure that TMX and the RCMP would have to follow the five-step process before arresting us, which included reading the injunction and allowing us a chance to leave.

We giddily fantasized about T-Rex stunts that would gain us traction online and build an army of anti-TMX activists. Later that night I began to happily edit the footage from our action into our first fifteen-second video. The next morning I uploaded the video to TikTok and went to work. During my break, I checked the app and was floored. We'd amassed 100,000 views in a few hours! Comments were flooding in.

"The only way to beat pipelines is with cringe and memes," "I NEED 100 OF THESE VIDEOS PLEASE," and "Where is this and can I join you?"

Over the coming weeks, I shipped T-Rex against TMX stickers across Canada and the US. I continued to upload videos, and soon had 11,000 followers and 460,000 views.

On the morning of May 11, 2022, we struck again. On the outside, I orchestrated the action with confidence. Internally, anxiety paired with activism stress caused the borders of my reality to feel crumbly. Still, I didn't want to back out, especially with a small crew assembled to document our latest endeavour. I met Maya, our cameraman, and two supporters at a parkade in Burnaby near a pipeline construction site. One supporter brought a huge sign that read "T-Rex Sports Day" and an assortment of toy sporting goods.

The six of us made our way toward the construction site. We wove through the alleyways of warehouses, careful to avoid the direct sightline of security. Together, Maya and I peeked out from behind a corner and assessed the scene. A few metres away there was a large blue fence covered with mesh, and the standard green and orange TMX injunction sign that warned us to stay out.

We inflated our suits, approached, and scaled the fence before the dumbstruck guards could stop us. On the other side of the fence, a supporter handed us the badminton set and we began to waddle on the wooden walkway towards the stairs. A worker, armed with a 2005-esque camcorder, shouted at us: "You're not supposed to be here. You're on private property!" To which, giddy with adrenaline, we shot back: "Try not building a pipeline!"

On the rickety wooden stairs, leading down the slope into the work site, a dozen or so men in hard hats were staring up at us. I felt like a debutante at a ball. Gradually we descended the steps. No one tried to stop us as we waddled through the work site, searching for a suitable spot to set up a badminton net.

After a couple rounds of back-and-forth, we lost our birdie. So we improvised. Together we launched an imaginary target into the air and stuck it back shouting: "Here you go, T-Rex!" and "Take this, T-Rex!"

After about twenty minutes of uninterrupted play, I began to sense something was wrong. Still, we played on. Eventually a worker emerged from the group of hard hats watching and smiled,

"Hi, T-Rex," in a voice that was friendly and familiar. I wouldn't be surprised if he knew who I was. My years of pipeline resistance are dotted with memories of strange men in safety vests who inexplicably knew my name.

"You're breaking an injunction," he continued, waving a copy of it in our faces.

"What's an injunction?" Maya shot back. "We don't know what that is. We're dinosaurs. We don't speak English."

"We're holding you here until the police come," said the man. "If you try to escape, we'll use force to keep you here."

When he began to walk away, I gestured for Maya to come close.

"We've got to run," I whispered vehemently.

"Okay," Maya responded.

The worker with the injunction stood a few paces away, watching us closely.

"Help me take down the net," suggested Maya.

"Leave the net," I implored, already beginning to turn away. "Run! Go, go, go!"

Together we began to sprint away from our worker. We could hear him shouting from behind us: "Stop! Stop!" Never a duo to do so, we did not comply.

We sprinted up the hill towards the fence, condensation forming in the plastic window of our T-Rex suits. When I rewatched the video of our escape, I can hear the cameraman laughing.

I bolted up the fence and my suit tore in the leg as I hastily pulled myself over the top of the wire fence and landed on the other side. I could feel my dino-form deflating as I turned my attention to Maya, who was a few paces behind. "Go, go!" I urged her. She was still making her way over the fence. I was sure that if we were fast enough, we could hide near the warehouses and escape without being caught. Then I turned around. Five or six RCMP officers were gliding towards us. A police van big enough to transport two girls in T-Rex suits was idling behind them. There was no way we could escape.

"You're under arrest for mischief," the officer said. I felt calm as I unzipped my suit, revealed my face, and offered my hands to be cuffed.

On the short walk to the van my officer turned to me curiously: "How do you inflate those things?" he asked.

"Oh," I responded, "there's a fan!"

"Does it just take batteries?"

"Yeah. Double A's."

Throughout my activism, my propensity for believing the best in people has been my downfall, but it has also led to some of my most magical moments, from playing tic-tac-toe with a security guard by lowering a bucket from our tree-sit, to conversations with my detaining officers. I felt a camaraderie with the man leading me to the police van. He was a little shorter than me, and couldn't be much older. *(An important rule of activism I only incorporated recently into my practice: Don't talk to cops.)*

"What do you think about the pipeline?" I asked.

"Oh"—I could hear the diplomacy disc starting to spin in his brain, overriding the possibility of a candid answer—"I just do my job, go home and play video games and don't really think about it too much."

I felt a little indignant, a little proud, and a little fearful. What if I went home and played video games and didn't think too much about these things? Would I become complacent? Was worry a prerequisite for action? Was my suffering necessary to propel me towards change-making?

As the doors slammed behind me in the police van, I began to laugh. A new feeling was overcoming me: elation. Sitting in the police van in a T-Rex suit, hands bound behind my back, I felt like I had finally found the Goldilocks zone of activism: a sweet spot where the urgency I felt aligned with the action I was taking. I started to sing.

Through the barrier dividing us, Maya suggested silence. We were being watched. As much as I wanted to relive what had just happened, anything I said could and would be used against us.

When we arrived at the station, Maya was taken out and processed first. In the cold, hard police van, the buffer of joy that protected me from my anxiety began to erode. Every now and again an officer opened the door to check on me. Eventually I asked what his favourite colour was. (Blue.)

I was taken out of the van and led into the station where my information, photo, and digitally scanned fingerprints were all recorded. I signed an agreement stating I understood what I was being charged with and that I agreed to stay several football fields away from any TMX work site until a later to-be-determined date. I drove away with just enough time to make it to work.

Court

On January 27, 2023, after our press conference, Maya and I entered one of the courtrooms at 800 Hornby Street, accompanied by our lawyer Karen Mirsky and around forty supporters.

Judge Shelley Fitzpatrick went over the details of our arrest. She painted a picture with her judicious words of us donning T-Rex suits, hopping the fences, and playing badminton. These were the facts—strikes against us to be carved in the stone and kept in legal records for the rest of our life.[3] And they were hilarious.

When Fitzpatrick recounted Maya's observation to the TMX employee that "We're dinosaurs, we don't speak English," the gallery burst out laughing.

"The crowd will be quiet please," Fitzpatrick chided, "otherwise they shall be removed from the courtroom. This isn't a humorous exercise."

But it certainly wasn't a serious one either. And why should it be? Climate change is frightening enough as is. If we let figures of authority dampen our joy, what kind of movement are we?

Since I could remember, my struggle with mental health meant I had trouble telling which of many different inner voices belonged to me. But when my name was called, I rose, and through the act of standing I innately knew what I was planning was the right thing to do and the right time to do it. But my legs were shaking until the final lines of my speech when I pulled the foam and felt dinosaur mask from my shirt and slipped it over my head.

Rawr rawr rawr
Growl growl
Snarl
Rawr rawr.

Mayhem. The gallery erupted into thunderous cheers and applause.

"Take that off right now, Ms. Kelsall. Security! Security!" called Fitzpatrick. "Clear the courtroom."

I felt my upper arm grabbed by a security officer who pulled me to my feet. I quickly turned, pulled off my headpiece, and handed it to my lawyer. As the security guard guided me back to the booth where the defendants sat, I glanced at the audience and trepidatiously raised my fist to another wave of applause.

As people were herded out of the courtroom, I heard shouts of protest, the frustration and indignation that is bottled in proceedings like these finally being released. One man shouted, "Where's the justice?!"

The courtroom was now quiet except for murmurings between my lawyer and Fitzpatrick. Karen Mirsky approached me saying that I might be expected to apologize. I agreed to do so; after all, the damage had already been done, and it couldn't have gone better.

Mirsky approached Fitzpatrick: "I am instructed by Ms. Kelsall that she is prepared to apologize."

Fitzpatrick responded: "I find an apology coming from her at this stage to be uncredible."

She was right about that.

Over lunch I was glowing and my mind was clear. My only concern was that my "stunt" would bar the supporters from re-entering the court room. Luckily, everyone was allowed in to hear Maya's excellent speech.

There was a short break and then Fitzpatrick returned with her decision.

First she addressed Maya, then me. While she was speaking to me, my vision grew blurry. I reached over and grabbed Maya's hand. I looked right at Fitzpatrick. The reproach in her stare was magnified by her dark circles of eyeliner. She mentioned the letters submitted by my dad and my psychiatrist. Those letters touched on my mental state, gave my diagnosis in detail, and even suggested that my depression and anxiety had contributed to my decision to don dinosaur suits and break the injunction.

How could I make everyone understand that the actions I took as a dinosaur were some of the brightest, sanest moments I'd experienced over the past year?

I held Maya's hand tighter.

We were made to pay a fine of $1,240, the amount of money we'd cost TMX by delaying them for twenty minutes. The Crown prosecutors hadn't initially suggested a fine for our punishment.

This was Judge Fitzpatrick's idea. Maya received twenty-one days, and I received twenty-eight—an additional seven for my "courtroom stunt."

Finally, Fitzpatrick exited the courtroom. Maya and I were pulled to our feet and handcuffed. The gallery began to sing. I left behind my crying friends and family as we went through a door at the back of the courtroom and were led into the bowels of the building.

On the Way to Alouette Correctional Centre
Everyone knows it's not fun being a prisoner. The worst part is how you are treated by your captors. My ankles and hands were cuffed. I was shuffled between cells for a while until our ride was ready.

When I was asked to clear my pockets by a corrections officer, I produced one "Get Out of Jail Free" card from Monopoly. The female officer took one look at it and said, "That won't help you here. The sense of humour is appreciated, though." Her dry tone suggested they were starved for levity.

Eventually Maya and I were loaded together on a truck bound to the Alouette Correctional Centre. I sat facing backwards, and she sat facing forwards. As we began to make our way through the Downtown Eastside, my mind began to race about what I could have done differently in court. I tried to pull myself back into the present using schoolyard games from our childhood. With bound wrists, we played chopsticks and concentration. As we drew closer to the prison, the eerie red lighting on the inside of the van switched to a white iridescent glow.

Once inside the facility, Maya and I were separated. I sat in a holding cell, waiting for further orders. Inside I could hear the voice of a shrieking woman. The guards approached the door she was locked behind and spoke to her calmly: "Are you coming off anything right now? Are you withdrawing?"

Judge Fitzpatrick said a lot of things about me that weren't true, but one thing she was right about is that I come from a privileged background. Going to jail for me means different things than it would for someone who doesn't have the resources I have. A lawyer, money, and a supportive community made my experience manageable. It's unjust that the majority of people I met inside were not as fortunate.

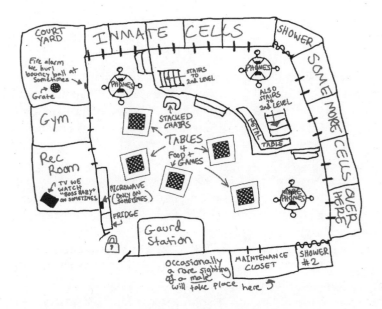

A floor plan I drew of Unit Charlie's main floor.

Once I'd had my first taste of prison food, I was ushered to a space with a shower where I was instructed to undress and do the infamous "spread-your-legs-and-bend-over" manoeuvre. I showered and then suited up in my prison-issue underwear and sports bra, grey sweatpants and shirt, and black Velcro shoes. Finally I went through a full-body scanner, before being transferred to the space I would call home for the next several weeks: Unit Charlie.

Charlie

When I was a little girl, I kept pet hamsters. On top of the basic hamster cage set-up, you could add plastic tubes and nooks to extend your hamster's habitat. The result was a contained environment that provided just enough stimulation for survival. That's what Unit Charlie felt like, right down to the white metal railings that resembled the bars of a hamster's cage.

Our cells were comprised of hard bunk beds, cubby space, a small collapsible writing table, and an open-concept steel toilet in the corner. I'd expected to be locked inside during the night, but I was rattled to find out we were trapped in our cells for intervals throughout the day. During my first lock-up, I felt I was losing

My "seg" attire.

what little strength I had left. When night fell, I kept biting until my skin turned purple and I drew blood.

I slid off my bed, went to the door, and waved a guard down. "I bit my hand," I told her. "Can I have a Band-Aid?" The guard unlocked the door and told me to come with her.

She took me to a holding cell and told me to remove my clothes except my underwear. She returned and handed me a padded dress. It was white, heavy, and had Velcro straps for the shoulders.

I was barefoot as I followed two guards. They buzzed us in through a series of doors and hallways. I was dropped off in my own private cell which featured a high ceiling and a long narrow window. The door closed behind me. I realized I'd unwittingly landed myself in solitary.

Segregation

In prison, I tried to compare my experience to being in a mental hospital. I drew a Venn diagram of it.

The guards slid a piece of paper under the door that informed me I was assessed to be a danger to myself. The idea behind putting me in solitary, or segregation (colloquially known as "seg"), was so I could be closely monitored to prevent me from hurting myself.

Mostly, I thought about was how cold my feet were. I didn't get normal sheets and blankets. I just got a few more of those "suicide prevention smocks." I laid one down as a mattress cover, one as a blanket, and used the third as a combined pillow and eye cover. The lights in our cells had two settings, and off wasn't one of them.

After my first night in solitary on the weekend, I asked when I could go back to Charlie. I was informed that a psychiatrist needed to assess me before I could be released, but he didn't come in until Wednesday. Just my luck, I'd picked the wrong day to have a mental breakdown.

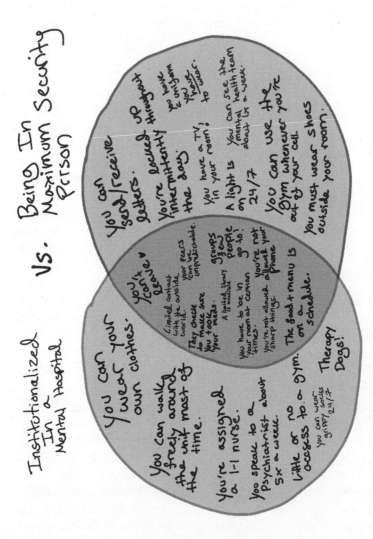

Institutionalized In a Mental Hospital **vs.** Being In Maximum Security Prison

Institutionalized In a Mental Hospital (left circle):
- You can wear your own clothes.
- You can walk freely around the unit most of the time.
- You're assigned a 1-1 nurse.
- You speak to a Psychiatrist about 5x a week.
- Little or no access to a gym.
- You can wear gripy socks 24/7
- Therapy Dogs!

Overlap (center):
- You can't leave.
- Limited contact with the outside world.
- They check to make sure you took your meds.
- A limited library is available
- You have to be in your room at certain times.
- groups you can people go to.
- your peers can be unpredictable.
- you're not allowed sharp things.
- You're not allowed your phone.
- The food + menu is on a schedule.

Being In Maximum Security Prison (right circle):
- You can send/receive letters.
- You're locked/intermittently throughout the day.
- You have a TV in your room?
- A light is on 24/7
- you have a uniform & uniform you must wear.
- You can see the mental health team about 1x a week.
- You can use the gym whenever you're out of your cell.
- You must wear shoes outside your room.

My Venn diagram of being in mental hospital / prison.

The book cart always seemed out of reach. I saw it get tantalizingly wheeled around the seg unit. Half a day later I was graced with a soapy paperback that tided me through many hours.

I asked to see a priest. He prayed with me that I would find clarity. A social worker told me I could make more of a difference alive than dead. I ate meals part of me wanted to refuse. Once a prison guard rolled an old TV in the hallway just outside my door. She played *Shrek 2*. I couldn't hear the dialogue through the thick door, so I knelt on one of my suicide smocks and watched through the flap that food was shoved through.

On Wednesday the psychiatrist came and I was sent back to Charlie. Over the next couple weeks, I wrote feverishly in my cell. Composing and discarding final letters to my family. I called my sister on the phone almost every day, checking in.

With my other inmates I played Sorry, Uno, and a card game someone made up as a child. Late at night, when my roommate was dozing off, I watched *BattleBots* on my cell's TV, pinning my future onto the fates of machines duking it out in pre-recorded episodes: *If Captain Shrederator wins, I'll find a way to die. If Whiplash wins, I'll go one more day.*

In a moment of awe for human ingenuity and resilience, I donated my oatmeal packet and apple to another inmate who promised to turn it into something great. While we were all locked in our cells, she peeled the apples and coated them with margarine from the tiny packets; later that night, she presented to us a delicious crisp, straight from the microwave.

Once a week, we were escorted round the corner and locked in another room with books on the shelves and smiling old women who wielded guitars. We sang about Jesus. The pastor who held my hand and prayed with me came in on Tuesdays and taught the women about healthy relationships. On Fridays a spiritual healer came and conducted a smudging ceremony. Sweet smoke covered our faces and escaped through the bars on the courtyard's roof.

Once a bunch of us inmates gathered outside in the concrete courtyard, aching for amusement. Someone brought out a long, thick skipping rope they'd woven from plastic bags. We spent a happy hour taking turns skipping, remembering songs and games from our youth. When we couldn't think of any new ones, I got to work composing the following:

Welcome, welcome, come and enter
Alouette Correctional Centre
Grey on the body
Velcro on the feet
How many pieces of bread will you eat?[4]

The song went over very well and I felt very happy. When we were done, the guard took our plastic skipping rope and put it back behind guarding station. We all went inside and were locked in our cells again.

Release

I left prison on February 14, 2023. On my way out the door, the guard said, "I hope we don't see you again." It was meant to be encouraging, but it felt hollow. Why shouldn't I come back? Why couldn't the officer see how much injustice was protected under the law?

After getting out of prison, my depression got worse. I felt like water being pulled down a drain; holding on seemed futile. In March 2023, I was admitted to a psychiatric hospital. Sometimes I could see the end of my life and it felt like the combustion of the sun: frighteningly bright and exquisitely final. In April, I was planning on leaving the hospital and ending things not too long afterwards. Just before I left, I had a chance encounter with a Buddhist monk. Over the course of our sixty-minute conversation, I could feel a light switch in my heart being turned from shadow to light.

The next morning I woke up, now at home, and saw light coming through my blinds—and the heaviness wasn't there any longer. Nor was it the next day nor the next. I spent hours on the couch, watching the rain fall onto trees and crying because I'd always assumed the world had gotten less beautiful over time, and I could ascribe its increasing dullness to climate change. But now I suddenly realized that the world had always been beautiful and it was me who for a time had lost the ability to see that.

I've accepted that I alone am not responsible for climate change, and that the earth is wise and powerful beyond my understanding. Just as I've learned to trust myself, I have to learn to trust the planet.

As of writing this I'm three months into a documentary filmmaking program at Capilano University. I'm very happy and healthy. My relationship with my family has healed. I don't hold on to anger as I once did. I feel like I can finally be a friend to the those around me.

When Maya and I get lunch, I'm able to listen to and hold her experience just like she held my hand in the courtroom. I used to be caught up in fantasies and nightmares, detached and dissociated. Now I'm wide awake—able to interact, grow, and love. I can feel the cold water on my hands and the weight of cotton on my skin. I can look at things that scare me—dying trees, tankers on the water. I feel the fear, sadness, and helplessness underneath, but I'm still able to love, laugh, and dance. I brainstorm and organize and imagine a future full of healing. I'm grateful, hopeful, and excited to work with the people around me to achieve exemplary things.

When I recount the story of my transformation, people usually ask me what the monk said that helped me. In truth, almost everything he said I'd heard before. It was more about how he said it. It was his presence that mattered most.

A lot of people have been alienated from activism because they don't feel heard, respected, or because they are pressured to be arrested. Sometimes activists haven't fully internalized the risks and consequences of their actions, and so they face them unprepared. Others burn out from anger and fear.

Activism means embodying the values we want to see in the world: kindness, compassion, justice, balance. If our motivations behind actions are misaligned with the society we want, how can we expect to create the world we've been dreaming of? Just as strongly as I believe radical change is necessary, I also believe in radical kindness and community building. By building the world we want in the present, we can ensure a better future. I'm excited to continue in activism, and even more excited to do so with an open heart. I now know, radical change can happen at any time.

Climate change is terrifying, but we don't have to let that fear own us. We can choose to cultivate joy and hope at every turn. We can choose to imagine a wonderful future. We can choose to act on those visions. We can start today.

MAYA
LAFRAMBOISE,
Community Organizer

Photo: Tim Takaro

Biography

Maya Laframboise is a community and labour organizer based on unceded Coast Salish territories in Vancouver, BC. She has been involved in broad-based climate justice organizing around pipeline expansions, Indigenous sovereignty, and divestment. She is passionate about education and public advocacy around the intersections of the climate crisis, colonialism, capitalism, and the economic growth paradigm. She believes that radical transformational change is needed to tackle the social, economic, environmental, and cultural crises of our times, and that community-based work is a powerful antidote to the fear and hopelessness that often accompanies an understanding of these monumental crises.

Maya's undergraduate thesis at McGill explored how Indigenous rights, title, and resistance create financial risk and liabilities for resource extraction companies operating on unceded Indigenous lands. She is also a contributor to the book *Enforcing Ecological Catastrophe: The Police and Military as Drivers of Climate Change and Ecocide*. Born and raised in the Lower Mainland as an uninvited guest, Maya is Red River Métis and a mixed white settler (Mennonite, Scottish, British, and Irish). In her spare time she enjoys mycology, working with plants, being outdoors, reading, painting, and spending time with her family (including her cat Fidel).

Maya was arrested at the TMX construction site at Lougheed Highway and Gaglardi Way in Burnaby on May 11, 2022, and she was sentenced to twenty-one days incarceration on January 27, 2023.

Statement to BC Supreme Court Justice Shelley Fitzpatrick, January 27, 2023

I am a twenty-four-year-old woman who is ready to take responsibility and accept the consequences of my actions. I write this letter not as a defence, but rather to provide insight as to why I did what I did.

My actions were not intended to attack the integrity or subvert the legitimacy of the court, but were motivated by my deep love and care for my fellow humans and nonhuman relations, and my understanding of the risks that this pipeline poses to our collective well-being. I was motivated to halt pipeline construction by my desire to stop the suffering that this pipeline's construction and operation will inflict. I was not acting with violence, but rather with the intention of preventing violence.

In 2021, I graduated from McGill University with a first-class honours BA in environmental studies and urban geography. I switched into this program midway through my degree after the release of the 2018 IPCC report because, after understanding the limited window of time humanity had to avoid the worst of the climate crisis, I felt motivated to contribute my life (or at least the next twelve years) to this.

After switching programs and facing a barrage of horrifying statistics about the likely state of our future world over the remainder of my lifetime, I began to experience an immense sense of doom, grief, and anxiety. This switch in my studies coincided with an abusive relationship, and as a result of these two simultaneous factors, I became depressed and suicidal. It was at this point that I told myself that if I could contribute in any way towards helping humanity avoid the worst consequences of the climate crisis, it was worth staying on this earth. And so I stayed, I received counselling, and I got involved with climate justice activism as my reason to keep going. Four years later, I am still in counselling. I have overcome addiction to alcohol, marijuana, and tobacco. I am healing, and I am just as committed to climate justice as ever, despite increasingly harsh reality checks and never-ending news about the oncoming consequences.

Following the release of the latest IPCC report on climate change, UN Secretary-General António Guterres said, "climate activists are sometimes depicted as dangerous radicals. But the truly dangerous radicals are the countries that are increasing the production of fossil fuels . . . investing in new fossil fuel infrastructure is moral and economic madness."

Canadians and the creatures with which we share the planet are dying from climate change caused by increasing GHG emissions. The difference between a 1.5°C warmer world and the current trajectory of 4° warming by the end of the century represents a preventable catastrophe for future generations of humans and other species. In 2021, BC was ravaged by wildfires that burned entire communities down (Lytton), a heat dome that directly or indirectly killed over seven hundred people, and flooding that threatened livelihoods, all as a consequence of rising global temperatures . . . and we haven't even hit 1.5° yet.

TMX will lead to increased emissions. It will pump an additional 890,000 barrels of fossil fuel every day and increase Canada's greenhouse gas emissions at a crucial moment in time when global emissions must decrease to avoid the worst of the climate crisis. The government needs to take the climate crisis seriously to keep people from dying and to offer young people like myself any chance at a safe and secure future that isn't marred by constant catastrophe, suffering, violence, and upheaval.

More immediately, the pipeline threatens key human and nonhuman habitats with destruction, including many endangered species such as orcas, salmon, caribou, and nesting birds. It virtually guarantees the extinction of the Southern Resident orca whales in the Salish Sea and seriously threatens the livelihood of salmon (on which over two hundred species rely) due to oil spills, pollution, and tanker traffic. A spill in the Lower Mainland would be catastrophic for our water supply, and millions of people could get sick as a result, more than our hospitals can contain. We could see people dying waiting for medical treatment just like we did during COVID-19.

It also crosses and threatens to destroy many sacred sites and waters for First Nations in BC. The Union of British Columbia Indian Chiefs (UBCIC) is against the expansion, along with many First Nations along the pipeline route, such as the Secwépemc and Tsleil-Waututh Nations. In 2010, the Save the Fraser Declaration against all expansion of the tar sands was signed by sixty-one First Nations along the Fraser River watershed. In 2014, the Salish Sea Treaty made the Kinder Morgan Expansion Project (now TMX) illegal under Coast Salish law. In 2017, the Treaty Alliance against Tar Sands Expansion was signed by 122 First Nations,[5] banning TMX specifically and other pipeline projects like it.

Pipeline construction poses a serious threat to Indigenous women and girls due to the relationship between resource industry "man camps" and Missing and Murdered Indigenous Women and Girls and Two Spirit Plus (MMIWG2S+). Man camps are temporary remote housing facilities for out-of-town workers (mostly men) in the resource extraction industry, and have been linked to an increase in violence against Indigenous women, including harassment, assault, sexual assault, and missing/murdered women cases. This link between man camps and violence against Indigenous women has been well known to women from these communities for a very long time, and was affirmed in the federal inquiry into MMIWG2S+ in 2019, which concluded that the crisis amounts to genocide. Are we supposed to sit there and accept the risks that we know these projects pose? In this way, TMX is genocidal.

The United Nations Committee on the Elimination of Racial Discrimination (CERD) has issued Canada three warning letters to cease construction of the TMX pipeline until free, prior, and informed consent has been obtained by the rightful Indigenous title-holders along the route, and to immediately withdraw all policing / military / private security forces defending the pipeline construction. Canada has ignored these warnings.

I am Red River Métis through my paternal grandmother Aprille Nault, and I am a citizen of Métis Nation British Columbia. I am a direct descendant of people that fought in, and some that were murdered by the RCMP during, the Red River Resistance of 1870 and North-West Resistance of 1885, including Andre Nault and Damase Carriere. Andre Nault was Louis Riel's first cousin (their mothers were sisters). The infamous events that kicked off the Red River Resistance in 1869, when Louis Riel stepped on the surveyor's chain and proclaimed they would go no further, occurred on the property of Andre Nault, River Lot #12. During the Battle of Batoche in 1885, my great-great-great-grandfather Damase Carriere broke his leg and was mistaken for Louis Riel, and the Canadian army tied a rope around his neck and the other end to a horse and dragged him behind the horse until he was dead. His battlefield torture is recorded as one of the most horrendous events during the struggle for the rights of the Métis in the Prairies, and he is buried with eight other Métis warriors who died in the Battle of Batoche.

The Alberta tar sands, the source of TMX bitumen, fall within the boundaries of the Historic Métis Nation Homeland. Many Indigenous people from Alberta are demanding a moratorium on further expansion of the tar sands. Cree activist Clayton Thomas-Müller explains:

> a moratorium on [tar sands] development is required until the concerns of First Nations and Métis regarding the many serious issues that have been raised by this breakneck industrial development are addressed. These include the human-rights abuses; the human and ecological health crisis; the climate-change implications; the water- and air-quality implications; the treaty-rights implications; the tribal sovereignty and self-determination implications; as well as the cumulative socioeconomic impacts on the health and way of life of Indigenous peoples. Each of these serious issues must be responded to, respected and protected in a permanent, traditional, Indigenous framework, in compliance with the spiritual and natural laws, treaties and inherent rights of Indigenous peoples.[6]

You speak repeatedly of our apparent disrespect of the rule of law. I do not mean to challenge the importance of the rule of law, Madame Justice, but only to point out that the emphasis on the rule of law in a colonial court on stolen land is a cruel and ironic hypocrisy. The spiritual and natural laws of this land, and the Original Peoples of this land, predate these colonial courts by thousands of years. Even your own mother law, British common law, was ignored in the founding of these courts by way of the failure to make treaties, a violation of the Royal Proclamation of 1763.

If we do not respect the rule of natural law, Madame Justice, the price we will all ultimately pay is far greater than a twenty-one-day jail sentence. The floods, fires, and heat waves are evidence admissible in court to this statement. I can think of no greater disrespect for the rule of natural law than to incarcerate those who uphold it, in a kangaroo court on lands for which your government has never acquired the legal title deed, in your effort to defend the most flagrant and egregious violation of this natural law—the continued expansion of fossil fuel infrastructure despite knowledge of the harm and violence it will cause to our Mother Earth and all her inhabitants.

I am an uninvited guest here on these unceded Coast Salish lands. The Squamish and Tsleil-Waututh Nations whose land we are on, who never surrendered their land to the Crown, and who are the rightful title-holders to the land where the incident in question took place in Burnaby, are opposed to TMX.

As Métis people, we are Otipemisiwak, the people that own ourselves, governed by the value of wahkohtowin, our kinship to all our relations. I have been taught by my Elders to always act with the next seven generations in mind. By allowing this pipeline to go through despite opposition from First Nations and despite the threats it poses to destroy our nonhuman relations and the lands and waters across BC, we are not living by the value of wahkohtowin. We are certainly not thinking seven generations ahead.

I am hopeful that in the future we will see change towards a better world. I now understand that my actions were not necessarily a step in that direction, and in the future, I would reconsider which actions would be most effective in bringing about systemic change in the deeply exploitative and unjust society that we currently find ourselves in. Our collective lives may depend on it, and I invite you with open little T-Rex arms to join us on the right side of history.

Narrative: Fighting Fossil Fuels with a Fossil That Roars
I initially got involved with the TMX fight towards the end of 2019 when I was living in Montreal. As an honours student in Environmental Studies at McGill University, one of the

requirements of my degree was the completion of an undergraduate thesis. I had grown up in BC and loved the lands and waters there deeply, and I had been following the pipeline resistance fights there from across the country, observing the news and social media with a perpetually heavy heart. I figured I could use the opportunity of my thesis research to contribute to front-line resistance movements in some way, despite being thousands of kilometres away. I ended up examining the undisclosed financial liabilities of TMX, building on the work of the late Secwépemc leader Arthur Manuel.

Less than three months after formally starting my research, the COVID-19 pandemic swept the world. I remember FaceTiming my parents (who both work in health care) on March 14, 2020; my dad said, "The world hasn't seen anything like what we're about to see in over a hundred years. You're coming home." Abruptly, I returned to my loving and supportive family, and also to a region that felt like the last frontier of unbridled resource extraction; the wild west of unceded land through which pipelines had to travel to bring Alberta's beloved bitumen to coastal ports for export.

Shortly after moving back, with only six credits remaining in my degree, I had to take two semesters of medical leave: the first was due to complications from a medication I had started, and then two months into the first leave I received a concussion, whiplash, and a herniated disc from the blunt end of a police baton to the back of my head at a peaceful protest of AIG insurance (one of the companies insuring the TMX pipeline), which extended my medical leave an additional semester into the summer of 2021.

After finally graduating, I knew I needed to get involved in the fight in some other capacity. In-person activities finally seemed to be resuming as the fog from the pandemic began to clear. People had been intermittently blocking access to the TMX work sites in Burnaby. A friend told me about a new group of people called T-Rex against TMX who were dressing up in inflatable dinosaur costumes, attending protests and solidarity rallies against the pipeline, in addition to occasionally blocking access to work sites, jumping the fences, and climbing on equipment in high-traffic areas to bring public attention to the pipeline resistance through absolute revelry.

The T-Rex would appear with signs bearing slogans like "Keep me in the ground" and "Leave my bones alone," a reference to the fact that bitumen from the Alberta tar sands literally contains fossilized dinosaur remains. In interviews, they would reference the fact that they had experienced a mass extinction before and it sucked, and they wanted to help humans avoid the same fate they had encountered 65 million years prior. Right before our arrest, the group went viral on TikTok.

I thought it was hilarious. And brilliant. People loved us, the cops had no idea what to do with us, and the suits always de-escalated intense situations. Plus, no face no case, or so we naively thought.

On May 11, 2022, Emily Kelsall and I donned the dinosaur costumes and scaled the TMX work site fence near the foot of Burnaby Mountain to set up a friendly game of badminton in the construction pit. We were under the impression that the RCMP had to go through a five-step process before arresting anyone for breaching an injunction, which included reading you the injunction aloud and giving you an opportunity to leave, only upon refusal of which could you be arrested; thus, our plan was to cause a quick and quirky disruption of construction and simply leave once law enforcement arrived.

After about twenty minutes of badminton, accompanied by supportive honks from passing traffic, TMX's private security surrounded us. They waved the injunction in our faces without reading it, telling us that the police were on their way and that any attempt to leave would be met with physical force. When the RCMP arrived, we were arrested for criminal mischief, our short little arms handcuffed and placed in a prisoner transport van (still fully costumed) to be taken to the RCMP detachment. We were released on conditions later that day which included a) not going within five hundred metres of a Trans Mountain work site or equipment, and b) only participating in "lawful and peaceful protest." The police insisted we keep our costumes on for our mug shots.

The mischief charges were dropped a few months later and replaced with criminal contempt of court for violating the injunction. It turns out we had been mistaken about the five-step requirement by the RCMP. While this is usually the case, unbeknownst to us, the court had granted Trans Mountain an amendment to their injunction that the five-step process was optional for TMX arrests. It seemed there was no way for us to avoid conviction and jail time.

On January 27, 2023, we both pleaded guilty. There was ample video evidence of us scaling the fence directly adjacent to the injunction sign, proving that we were wilfully violating it. Which, I mean, we were. But the pipeline itself is a violation of international human rights law, so the apparent unlawfulness of our actions was the least of my concerns.

I was sentenced to twenty-one days and Emily twenty-eight days at Alouette Correctional Centre for Women (ACCW) in Maple Ridge by Justice Shelley Fitzpatrick (Emily received an additional seven days due to her "T-Rex roaring stunt" in the courtroom). The gallery of supporters were horrified by Justice Fitzpatrick's conduct, which I found to be unprofessional, demeaning, and contemptuous towards us. There were multiple professional complaints filed about her through the Canadian Judicial Council following our sentencing hearing.

We were taken immediately from the courtroom in handcuffs to a holding cell downstairs, where we were required to remove all layers except our base layer before being frisked. Our belongings were searched and catalogued, then placed in plastic bags. After about ninety minutes in a holding cell at the courthouse, we were told it was time to leave for ACCW; we were handcuffed again as well as placed in ankle shackles, which was particularly dehumanizing, before loading onto the transport van. The drive there was especially rough when the driver went over speedbumps, because we weren't wearing seat belts and the benches are concrete, so you would fly up and hit your tailbone at a ninety-degree angle against the seat.

As we rode in the transport van through the Downtown Eastside, I was viscerally reminded that our government is not allocating resources in a way that supports the common good of society. The unhoused, marginalized humans marked by drug addiction and mental health crises only seem to matter to our elected officials when the ghettos become unconfined and the geography of poverty expands such that the signs of human misery creep into the adjacent financial and tourism districts, threatening profits and forcing those at the top to witness the consequences of their hoarded wealth. That's when the Vancouver Police Department comes in for violent street sweeps and tent city evictions. So long as the disadvantaged are exploited and contained, no one in power seems to give a fuck about their well-being enough to provide the resources and support that's needed to address the root of the problem.

Juxtapose this with Emily and me, here on our way to prison, costing taxpayers thousands of dollars to incarcerate, because a judge whose paycheque is signed by the state decided it was the fair and just price for us to pay for blocking work on a pipeline owned by the government of Canada. A pipeline that the government will spend over $30 billion to complete, which offers no economic benefits, threatens to destroy the water, land, and atmosphere and poison our water supply, threatens the safety of our women with man camps, and is adding megatonnes of carbon to our already suffocating atmosphere, killing our relatives.

In anticipation of my incarceration, my endocrinologist had written a letter to the prison and judge outlining my care needs with regard to type 1 diabetes. This letter had been discussed with a prison representative, myself, and a legal advocate on a conference call a couple of days in advance of my arrival so that they could prepare whatever was needed to follow the care plan stipulated by my doctor. Despite this, upon intake, the actions taken by the nurse directly contradicted my doctor's note, particularly when they took my glucose tabs away from me and said I would need to ask for them if I needed them. Towards the end of the medical interview, my blood sugar started going low, but my requests for glucose were denied. I was then taken back to my holding cell and locked up for about twenty minutes with no food or communication from anyone. Ultimately, I called a guard over and stated that I needed glucose or food immediately. They quickly arrived with a juice box and bagged dinner, and tested my blood sugar again; it had dropped even further to 1.9, which is low enough to put me at serious risk of a seizure or diabetic coma. Luckily neither occurred, but the fact that my health was unnecessarily put at potentially fatal risk is completely inexcusable—and unfortunately, not uncommon.

After this it was time to submit to a strip search, shower, and change into a grey uniform. Then I went into a Soter RS body scan, which is an X-ray just like the ones at the airport. At this point a new guard came in who was speaking about us in a pretty dehumanizing way, referring to us as "this one" (i.e., "bring this one over here" instead of "bring her over here"). They put me back in handcuffs and escorted me to the segregation unit, which I figured would just be for the first night for COVID protocol. I had to really advocate for them to let me keep glucose tabs in my cell, which was extremely frustrating given what had just happened, but ultimately they let me keep a tube of ten glucose tabs for the night.

I was so tired, I fell asleep right away in spite of the lights that stayed on. The next morning I woke up to staff knocking on my cell door to give me my meds. It was around 8:30 a.m. and light was coming in through the windows, so I could now see outside—the grassy courtyard, parking lot, all fenced, and lots of trees on the perimeter of the property. I could make out the tall yellow cedars with their drooping boughs intermingling with the more upright-pointing firs, with a couple of pines, birches, and I presume maples scattered throughout. I was so grateful for the presence of the forest in my view, and I would turn to these trees often for company, guidance, and calm over the course of the following fourteen days.

There was a notice slid under my door that I had been placed in solitary confinement because I had failed the Soter body scan the night prior and was suspected of carrying drugs or contraband. This shocked me, as I wasn't carrying either (I don't even use drugs). They swabbed my hands, and a few hours later they told me I had also failed the hand swabs, which had detected traces of narcotics. It made no sense! They told me to wash my hands really well, including under my fingernails, and to clean my cell (with what—toilet paper?), and said they would swab my hands again later; I needed to return three consecutive clean hand swabs before going through the body scanner again, and only upon passing could I be moved into the normal living units.

Time moved agonizingly slowly in solitary. It ended up being three more days until I was moved onto the regular living unit. The medium security unit at the correctional centre was closed down and has been since the beginning of COVID, so the only open units were maximum security. The biggest difference between medium and maximum security is that you get to go outside in medium. I was placed on Bravo, while Emily had been placed on

Charlie, so we didn't end up seeing each other the entire length of our incarceration. I wondered why they had separated us.

I was placed in a double room with a friendly woman in her mid-thirties doing five months for fraud. Almost all of the women were really kind and genuinely friendly; it was nothing like TV dramas where you have to worry about being jumped if you accidentally take someone's seat.

Outside the cells in the common area on the second floor (where my cell was located) there were chairs, tables, a kettle, sink, microwave, and fridge. On the first floor there were tables with chess boards on them, puzzles, cards, a "programs" room with a book cart and a TV for movies, a room with exercise equipment, three phone booths, showers, and an outdoor pen. My reputation on the unit became a) travelling down the stairs at an unusually fast pace, and b) reading books at an unusually fast pace; this earned me the nickname "Rocket."

The overwhelming majority of the women I met were there, either directly or indirectly, as a result of addiction. Most were incarcerated for property crimes, many hadn't even been convicted of anything yet and were only there because they couldn't afford bail; there were very few if any truly violent offenders on my unit. Even those who had committed so-called violent crimes (e.g., armed robbery) I concluded had mostly been driven to do so by their addiction. So many women had stories of being in abusive relationships and staying in those relationships despite the abuse, because they were getting something they needed from their partner (usually money, drugs, a roof over their head, or protection from others). And of course, it's unusual that those relationships are the start of one's traumatic experiences, but rather simply the cycles of trauma acting itself out.

I recently had someone ask me a question that I have encountered many times: Isn't it a distraction from the urgency of the environmental movement and our limited remaining window of time to be focusing on related but separate issues like Indigenous rights, capitalism, and police violence/militarization?

My answer remains unchanged, with the short answer being no, it's not a waste of time. On the contrary, I firmly believe that our success in fighting the climate crisis depends on it. We do not all need to be working on every single issue all the time (that's impossible), but we do need to understand each other's struggles so that we are able to stand together when the time comes. It is only by understanding the interconnected nature of our struggles that we will be able to challenge the systems that got us here and those who perpetuate them, including ourselves. It is only through solidarity with one another that we can build the critical mass necessary to win.

I can't think of a single successful social movement in history that did not use civil disobedience in some form. Disobeying unjust laws is a crucial ingredient in the recipes we are writing to create a more just future for all. There may be right and wrong ways to go about this, or at the very least, more and less strategic ways to go about this, but it will remain a crucial ingredient nonetheless.

As more young people come to understand the reality of what our future will look like without drastic global greenhouse gas emission reductions, we have less and less to lose. The looming question for me isn't whether the incidence and magnitude of civil disobedience will increase; I am certain that it will. Rather, the question is: Through what means and to what ends will this inevitable energy be channelled? And that is a question that we must all answer together.

CONCLUSION

The direct cost of the TMX pipeline project totalled $34 billion, and though the federal government is currently seeking a buyer within Canada to offset some of that cost to the public, it's unknown what entity, if any, will be willing to purchase it and for what price. Canadian taxpayers will likely bear a significant portion of the cost, sale or no sale.

There are the inevitable environmental costs for the pipeline, in that it expands fossil fuel infrastructure and increases global greenhouse gas emissions. Furthermore, it endangers those whose lands it traverses and adds to tanker traffic at the Port of Vancouver at the risk of a catastrophic spill.

This is $34 billion that could have been put to better use toward a green and sustainable future. With that amount, the government of Canada could install about two million heat pumps in homes or build more than a half-million public fast EV charging stations. It could replace fossil-fuel-burning power plants with sustainable sources of electricity. These are dollars lost to the expansion of rapid transit and subsidized, affordable housing. The number of potential clean energy jobs thus created would dwarf TMX's long-term employment potential.

And yet this ill-fated enterprise in wanton wastefulness was carried out with a disregard for land, water, air, and the well-being of people and other living creatures. In September 2023, as reported in *IndigiNews*, the Canada Energy Regulator approved TMX's request to drive an open pipeline trench through Pipsell—a Secwépemc Nation Cultural Heritage Site—over the Nation's objections. Trans Mountain requested the deviation because it encountered a hard rock formation along its original route and no longer wanted the expense of the microtunnelling it had agreed to with the Nation.[1]

The Trans Mountain project follows our country's long and well-worn historical path of breaking agreements with First

278 Standing on High Ground

Nations and ignoring their values and traditions. Still, land defenders Jim Leyden, April Thomas, and Billie Pierre, whose words appear in our book, continue to stand up to Trans Mountain every day for the rights of Indigenous Peoples to exercise sovereignty over their lands and preserve them for future generations. So do others, such as Rueben George of the Tsleil-Waututh Nation. We must remember and take inspiration from the victories of other Indigenous groups such as the Tahltan, who succeeded in creating the Sacred Headwaters in northern BC and protecting them from exploitation by Shell and other extractive industries.

Recently, one of us, walking along Vancouver's False Creek, saw the effects of an oil spill from a small derelict private vessel. A sheen of oil stretched kilometres, from Science World to the Burrard Bridge, and left a foul diesel odour in the air. One thinks of the possible harm from even a small spill to marine life and humans. Consider the increased risk of spills created by the TMX project. Have we forgotten the *Exxon Valdez*?

The stories told in this book show that those who will lead us into the future are often gripped by eco-anxiety, so vividly described in the words of Emily Kelsall, one of the T-Rex gals. But those fears are entirely reasonable, reflecting the reality of the climate crisis. This is not a pathology. It is normal and wise to be afraid when so much that we cherish in the world is in peril. When you know how to avoid peril but continue skipping merrily toward it, that's pathology! Emily, Maya Laframboise, and others in this book understand the situation clearly, and that understanding underlies their resistance to projects such as TMX that exacerbate the climate crisis.

While we honour here those who broke the law and often went to jail for justice, we are angered that the system so dishonours them. Why is it that, in the words of journalist George Monbiot, "those who seek to protect the living planet by democratic means are arrested en masse and imprisoned by the authorities, while the people and organisations trashing our life-support systems are untouched by the law"?[2] This is shockingly evident in the treatment received by the Indigenous resisters, who were forceful in confronting the racism of the judicial system.

Other contributors—such as Elizabeth May, Romilly Cavanaugh, Tim Bray, Tim Takaro, and Robert Hackett—leveraged their political and social status, and their legal, scientific, media, and technical expertise, to publicize the misdeeds of TMX and draw attention to the fight to stop the pipeline.

The motivations of the resisters were strongly grounded in a sense of ethical imperative. This is particularly evident in, but not at all restricted to, contributors driven by their faith-based convictions. Tama Ward and Emilie Smith are clergy, and three members of a Prayer Circle made up part of the Brunette Six—Janette McIntosh, Ruth Walmsley, and Catherine Hembling. It is clear from their words that their moral and spiritual ideals propelled them to take action and sustained them through the painful days in prison.

For Tawahum Bige, Rita Wong, Elan Ross Gibson, Earle Peach, Danaca Ackerson, and George Rammell, art was at the centre of their resistance, and, as George put it, they made that art a weapon against colonial injustice.

For many—including William Winder, Barbara and Robert Stowe, Tim Takaro, and Zain Haq—the protection of the health of people and other living beings, and the preservation of ecosystems, was at the heart of their determination to resist TMX. Hisao Ichikawa reminds us of the environmental and spiritual cost to all of us in the excessive consumption that TMX fuels.

Many contributors describe the moral struggle that ultimately led to defiance of a court order. In most cases, this was uncharted and difficult personal territory. For others, the decision seemed a logical response to a tragically idiotic idea—an appropriate response when all other means failed.

We as editors began working on this book driven by a desire to preserve for posterity the accounts given here of those who answered the call to stop TMX and mitigate the heating of the planet. We believe those who resisted TMX will be recognized as models and guides for how to respond to the climate crisis. They should be seen as among the leaders of today and the vanguard of tomorrow, as they work to redirect humanity's path away from collapse and toward renewal. They are working to ensure that those who come after us can thrive.

Construction of the TMX pipeline expansion continued with full support and funding from the Canadian government. The fight to push back climate change has been neither brief nor easy, but it is critical work that must continue. The need is urgent.

As this book goes to print, bitumen has begun flowing through the expanded pipeline. The pipeline went into use in May 2024. Will this mean that the actions of these folks were in vain and their stories of no consequence? Hardly. In ten years of resistance to the pipeline, the following have been achieved:

- Thwarted emissions: By delaying the completion by five years, a total of 60 megatons of emissions were avoided during those years.
- Reduced oil spill potential: There has been at least one less tanker trip per day through the Salish Sea during this time, or 1,750 fewer tanker trips in total.
- Climate policy evolution: The resistance put pressure on government for climate action, so that they can no longer ignore climate concerns in reviews of new projects.
- First Nations opponents have strengthened their power to direct energy infrastructure development in Canada through participation in hearings, direct action, and litigation.
- There is now a network of committed climate activists who have learned how to work collaboratively during the fight against TMX.

Through their acts of disobedience, the brave individuals who tell their stories of resistance and arrest in this book made the good trouble necessary for the evolution of justice. They have established that any project such as TMX will incur high legal and reputational costs. They called into question the rules designed to protect a company whose actions could be considered an assault on justice for a large swath of humanity.

Two thousand years ago, the Talmud admonished, "You are not obligated to complete the work; but neither are you free to desist from it." The greater fight to arrest and mitigate climate change and the heating of the planet continues. That fight is not yet won or lost—but it is far from over, and so we are obliged to keep on fighting.

In the Netherlands, in Montana, in Ontario, and elsewhere, young people and climate action groups are taking their governments to court over failure to provide for their security by establishing weak climate policy.[3] They won in the Netherlands in 2019 when the Dutch Supreme Court ruled in favour of the Urgenda Foundation's claim that the emissions reduction target the government had set was unlawfully low.[4] This was the first successful case in history in which citizens argued that their government has a legal obligation to prevent dangerous climate change. The court ordered authorities to further reduce emissions, and the Dutch government complied with a decision to shut down coal-fired power plants by 2030 and a 35-billion-euro package to conserve energy and develop renewable energy. In Montana a judge also ruled for youth in a landmark decision that the state had violated their right to a clean and healthful environment by continuing to approve fossil fuel projects.[5] A similar youth-led Ontario case was dismissed in Ontario Superior Court, but the court agreed that climate change is disproportionately affecting youth and Indigenous people. This case is being pursued in the Court of Appeal for Ontario as of January 2024.[6]

These legal victories sustain the possibility that a future court ruling may shut down TMX, but we could equally predict its demise based on economics as the world moves away from oil as a source of energy.

This book is a call to action from those who have put their bodies, hearts, and minds into the fight against expansion of fossil fuel infrastructure. We see how their passion, sound judgment, and commitment have fuelled nonviolent action to confront corporations and the Canadian government. Their demand is for a turn away from the march toward catastrophic climate change. How will we respond to their call?

APPENDIX:

Reflections on Civil Disobedience in the Face of Environmental and Colonial Injustice

D.B. Tindall, PhD, Department of Sociology, University of British Columbia

I spent much of my youth and early adulthood growing up in Victoria, on Vancouver Island, where I spent time outdoors and in the forests. I was also a precocious follower of the news and current events. As a young adult, several of the protests to protect old-growth forests caught my attention—partly because I had a strong connection to nature, and partly because civil disobedience seemed like very unusual behaviour. On the latter point, as a teenager at least, Victoria seemed like a pretty boring place. Seeing people in the news risk arrest for a cause they believed in was quite eye-opening.

I became aware in the 1980s of media reports on the protests over places such as Lyell Island (Athlii Gwaii) on Haida Gwaii and Meares Island in Clayoquot Sound (the protests had started in the decade before). Some of them involved civil disobedience led by Indigenous protesters, and there were numerous arrests at both sites. As a student, awareness of environmental issues prompted me to do a master's degree on the tragedy of the commons at the University of Victoria.

"The tragedy of the commons" refers to situations where there is a shared natural resource such as the ocean or the atmosphere, and there is a conflict between self-interest and collective interest. Individual people, groups, or countries may benefit from acting in self-interest, but the commons will become depleted and everyone will be worse off if a sufficient number of actors act selfishly. Actions that disproportionately increase carbon emissions in the context of a warming planet are a case of a tragedy of the commons. For example, Canada contributes about four times its share of carbon emissions to the global atmosphere relative to its population, while enjoying a high living standard. But globally, human and ecological welfare is diminished.

I moved on to PhD studies at the University of Toronto, became interested in collective action and social movements, and was inspired by the aforementioned environmental protests. My growing understanding of environmental issues led me to focus my research on environmental activism and, in particular, actions in BC to protect old-growth forests.[1] I have also studied some of the groups that mobilized to oppose the environmental movement.[2]

The Clayoquot Protests

The 1992–93 protest over clear-cut logging in Clayoquot Sound (also known as "the War in the Woods") provided a precedent for the civil disobedience actions opposing the Trans Mountain Pipeline Expansion. Civil disobedience involves engaging in an act of protest by violating a law.[3] Such actions are undertaken because of a deep sense that a given situation is morally unjust. People engaging in civil disobedience knowingly subject themselves to imprisonment, fines, and other punishments. Normally, as with the people whose stories are recounted here, they do not try to avoid these punishments, seeing them as part and parcel of the act of civil disobedience.

Clayoquot Sound is located on the west coast of Vancouver Island in British Columbia. It is comprised of remote islands, fjords, watersheds, and the largest nearly intact temperate rainforest ecosystem on Vancouver Island. Containing approximately 350,000 hectares of endangered ancient rainforests, it is considered by many as priceless natural heritage. The Clayoquot Sound region is home to the Nuu-chah-nulth First Nations and to the nonindigenous communities of Tofino and Ucluelet. These towns, and Port Alberni, are intricately bound up in the economics, culture, and politics of the region. Clayoquot Sound has been a site of concern for environmentalists and a symbol of wilderness preservation for over thirty years.

In the early 1990s, a conflict arose over the logging of remaining pristine rainforests in Clayoquot Sound, with Indigenous groups and environmentalists challenging industrial logging practices. Most of the territory south of the Sound had already been subjected to massive clear-cutting. Environmental groups and First Nations communities used a range of tactics to try to prevent this logging, including public talks and presentations, protests on the lawns of the provincial legislature, and blockades of logging roads in the vicinity of Clayoquot Sound. The campaign culminated with a mass protest in 1993, after the provincial government announced plans to open up two-thirds of the Sound to extensive logging. Over nine hundred people were arrested for engaging in civil disobedience by blockading logging roads leading into the Clayoquot Sound area.[4]

Both protesters and observers noted the connection of the Clayoquot protests to a larger tradition of peaceful civil disobedience. For example, the minister of the environment at the time, John Cashore, stated, "Coming out of my ethical and theological perspective, I'm a person who looked upon Martin Luther King as a hero. . . . Now I find myself in government and being on the other side of some of those actions I find, deep within me, a real challenge to work through some of those feelings."[5] The Clayoquot protest was the largest act of civil disobedience in Canadian history at the time; it was recently eclipsed by the protests over logging at Fairy Creek.

Notable outcomes of the Clayoquot protest included a government-ordered moratorium on clear-cut logging in the area for a period of time, and the creation of a scientific panel with an Indigenous co-chair to study uses in the region. Since that time, no large-scale industrial logging has taken place in the area. Several decades later, a number of the protesters involved in Carmanah, Walbran, and Clayoquot protests applied what they'd learned from these actions in the fight to stop the Trans Mountain Pipeline and the cutting of old-growth forests in Fairy Creek.

The struggle to protect Clayoquot Sound was an important precedent for the use of civil disobedience in British Columbia (though not the earliest instance of it). Civil disobedience has been employed in the past in other Canadian settings such as anti-nuclear protests, civil rights, Quebec sovereignty, and Indigenous struggles for their traditional land, resources, and title.[6] The 2012 Maple Spring protests over proposed increases to university tuition fees in Quebec are another example of a protest movement where acts of civil disobedience played an important role.

The Trans Mountain Pipeline Saga

Climate scientists tell us that, if we are to meet climate targets, most currently identified fossil fuel reserves need to stay in the ground.[7] Producing oil from the tar sands generates higher emissions than production of oil from conventional sources; this is one reason why oil produced from this project is sometimes referred to as "dirty oil."

The citizens profiled in this book took courageous stands in opposing the Trans Mountain Pipeline. The reasons for opposition described in their stories can be summarized into a few broad categories of perceived injustice: 1) the violation of First Nations rights and title; 2) the negative impact of this project on the climate crisis (the burning of fossil fuels and contributions to increased greenhouse gas levels in the atmosphere); and 3) the immense potential ecological and economic damage of the project beyond producing increased greenhouse gases (e.g., poisoning of drinking water, contamination of ocean habitat for whales and other creatures, devastating the local economy in the event of a major oil spill, or storage tank explosion). Many contributors articulate another deep motive: their love of the natural beauty of the lands and waters of their homeland. They are protecting what they love from perceived destruction.

Where do ideas about civil disobedience come from?

To understand the tradition from which the TMX resisters acted, let's look at one of the earliest articulations of the concept of civil disobedience. In 1849, Henry David Thoreau published an essay entitled "Civil Disobedience."[8] This work was influential for both Gandhi and Martin Luther King Jr. Thoreau asks: "Unjust laws exist: shall we be content to obey them, or shall we endeavor to amend them, and obey them until we have succeeded, or shall we transgress them at once?" If a situation is morally unjust, Thoreau counsels:

> If the injustice has a spring, or a pulley, or a rope, or a crank, exclusively for itself, then perhaps you may consider whether

the remedy will not be worse than the evil; but if it is of such a nature that it requires you to be the agent of injustice to another, then I say, break the law. Let your life be a counter-friction to stop the machine. What I have to do is to see, at any rate, that I do not lend myself to the wrong which I condemn.

On the question of punishment for civil disobedience, Thoreau states: "Under a government which imprisons unjustly, the true place for a just man is also a prison."

In one of Martin Luther King Jr's most influential works on civil disobedience, "Letter from a Birmingham Jail," dated April 16, 1963,[9] King states, "I am in Birmingham because injustice is here." King then notes the four basic steps of a nonviolent campaign: "collection of the facts to determine whether injustices exist; negotiation; self-purification; and direct action." In discussing preparation for civil disobedience, King emphasized, like Thoreau, the need to be able to accept retaliation to civil disobedience without resorting to violence. Further, he emphasized the need to accept legal punishment for civil disobedience:

> Mindful of the difficulties involved, we decided to undertake a process of self-purification. We began a series of workshops on nonviolence, and we repeatedly asked ourselves: "Are you able to accept blows without retaliating?" "Are you able to endure the ordeal of jail?"

Like many of the contributors to this book, King believed in the alternatives to civil disobedience—such as attempts to persuade wider publics through dialogue, negotiations with authorities, and participation in electoral politics—and pursued them. But he observed that there comes a time when decisions about particular issues of injustice need to be forced.

> You may well ask: "Why direct action? Why sit-ins, marches and so forth? Isn't negotiation a better path?" You are quite right in calling for negotiation. Indeed, this is the very purpose of direct action. Nonviolent direct action seeks to create such a crisis and foster such a tension that a community which has constantly

refused to negotiate is forced to confront the issue. It seeks to dramatize the issue so that it can no longer be ignored.

King talks about the tension that is typically associated with civil disobedience, and notes, "I have earnestly opposed violent tension, but there is a type of constructive, nonviolent tension which is necessary for growth." Later in the essay, he notes: "Actually, we who engage in nonviolent direct action are not the creators of tension. We merely bring to the surface the hidden tension that is already alive. We bring it out in the open, where it can be seen and dealt with."

These points relate to the larger issue of conflict in society. People may assume that conflict is bad and is to be avoided whenever possible. However, social scientists have observed that conflict is often a key driver of positive social change. Indeed, the lack of conflict between groups is sometimes a result of the overwhelming dominance of one group over another (such as the overwhelming dominance of non-indigenous people over Indigenous people in Canada during the majority of the twentieth century). In the case of the TMX pipeline, the contention generated in response to the project has changed the way in which many actors (the general public, governments, corporations) think about large fossil fuel infrastructure projects, and will likely limit the initiation of future projects of this type.

Some critics and other observers of civil disobedience question how and why protesters break or otherwise ignore certain laws and accept others. Indeed, in some instances, protesters seek legal remedies to particular conflicts. On this topic King observes:

> One may well ask: "How can you advocate breaking some laws and obeying others?" The answer lies in the fact that there are two types of laws: just and unjust. I would be the first to advocate obeying just laws. One has not only a legal but a moral responsibility to obey just laws. Conversely, one has a moral responsibility to disobey unjust laws. I would agree with St. Augustine that "an unjust law is no law at all."

King articulates the logic of accepting jail and other penalties for the act of civil disobedience:

One who breaks an unjust law must do so openly, lovingly, and with a willingness to accept the penalty. I submit that an individual who breaks a law that conscience tells him is unjust, and who willingly accepts the penalty of imprisonment in order to arouse the conscience of the community over its injustice, is in reality expressing the highest respect for law.

Most of the injunction-breakers featured in this anthology accepted the punishment meted out by the sentencing judge, including fairly lengthy jail terms. Many spoke of their deep respect for rule of law in their court statements.

Violent Direct Action and Related Phenomena

The contributors to this volume are all adherents of nonviolent civil disobedience, a practice they adopt for moral as well as practical reasons. And in British Columbia in the early 2000s, they could take this stand without fear of torture or death; in other settings, that assurance might not exist. However, some individuals and groups, including some environmental groups, such as the Sea Shepherd Society, have adopted violent tactics. Generally, violent tactics are directed toward equipment and property (e.g., sabotage of machinery, vandalism) rather than people. Some commentators have called for the use of more violent methods in the climate movement; one high-profile example is Andreas Malm in his recent book *How to Blow Up a Pipeline*. Kim Stanley Robinson also explores the potential future role of political violence in the context of climate change, in his outstanding novel *The Ministry for the Future*.

Some scholarship suggests that the use of violent tactics tends to have a negative effect on support for a social movement in terms of indicators like public opinion, and such actions sometimes increase support for opponents of a social movement.[10] However, the effect on public opinion also depends on a number of sociodemographic factors. Practitioners of nonviolent civil disobedience, such as the contributors to this book, tend to see the consequences of violence on public opinion as somewhat irrelevant and reject such tactics on moral grounds.

Why do people engage in civil disobedience?

In line with Thoreau and King, many of the contributors to this book saw the injustice that they acted against as simply unacceptable. They perceived normal legal and democratic processes as unable to address the problem. For many individuals, participation in civil disobedience is a deeply personal decision with significant moral dimensions. They see the need to act as a moral necessity, and the failure to take some sort of action as moral abrogation.

Sometimes what starts out as moral motivation turns out in practice to be good strategy. Civil disobedience is often perceived as an effective way of making change. In a mailed questionnaire survey I conducted in the 1990s, I asked members of a major organization involved in the Clayoquot Sound protests about their perceptions of the effectiveness of different tactics. About 50 percent indicated that they thought blockading logging roads "greatly helped the cause" while 42 percent thought it "somewhat helped the cause."

In separate interview research with Clayoquot movement leaders, I asked whether civil disobedience helped the cause. A typical response was: "Yeah. I do. Oh, I think for sure it did in Clayoquot. . . . If they [we] hadn't done it, I mean, there wouldn't be anything [any forest] left there." This resonates with what Martin Luther King Jr. himself observed: "My friends, I must say to you that we have not made a single gain in civil rights without determined legal and nonviolent pressure." By contrast (in the Clayoquot case), only 1.5 percent of activists who participated in the questionnaire survey thought that illegal protest involving property damage, such as vandalizing forestry equipment or bridges, "greatly helped the cause."

Injustice

In communication theory, "framing" allows individuals to perceive and label events in the world. "Frame alignment" that makes a connection between the ideology, activities, and goals of social movement actors and the values, opinions, and interests of potential supporters is seen as a necessary prerequisite to movement action. In "transformative frames,"[11] there is a change in the perceived seriousness of the condition such that what was previously seen as unfortunate but tolerable is redefined as inexcusable, unjust, or immoral.

In the case of the TMX protesters, the reframing of the relations between environment, economy, and society created a desire to advocate for a transformation in worldview, in particular the place of humans in nature, as passionately articulated in the writing of William Winder, Rita Wong, Rev. Emilie Smith, and Hisao Ichikawa.

This is coupled with a sense of deep injustice about what was happening. There is growing awareness of the rights of Indigenous Peoples and the violation of these rights, a theme that leaps out in virtually all of the resisters' statements. There is also a sense of injustice about the climate crisis and what it will mean to future generations. The narrative by Emily Kelsall laying bare her eco-anxiety and the letter from Ruth Walmsley's daughter embedded in Ruth's court statement relay the profound psychological impact that the climate crisis is having on young people now. Further, there is a sense of injustice about what things like oil spills will do to local human communities, as well as nonhuman life forms, such as orcas. On all of these topics, there has been a real shift in the past sixty years in how the issues are viewed.

Risks and Costs of Civil Disobedience

There is always uncertainty in the outcomes of protest actions, and in particular to civil disobedience. The act of civil disobedience really does take courage on the part of individuals. Participants do not know in advance exactly what their punishment will be, and they also don't know if their actions will positively effect change. Civil disobedience is perhaps made a bit easier when it is a group activity, and we can see from the stories in this book how "the Alouette Sisters," the tree-sitters, the T-Rex gals, and other groups helped and supported each other.

In the context of civil disobedience, cost refers to things like time and money. Risk refers to things like being subject to violence, harms to one's reputation, or the possibility of jail time. These things influence who is able and/or willing to participate in protest actions that are high-cost or high-risk, such as civil disobedience.

Many people were sentenced to jail time for the protests over clear-cut logging in Clayoquot Sound and in the protests against the construction of the Trans Mountain Pipeline.

Some people were the subject of civil lawsuits. For example, as Elizabeth May describes in her narrative, professors Lynne Quarmby and Stephen Collis had a SLAPP (strategic lawsuit against public participation) suit for $5.6 million filed against them by Kinder Morgan in 2014. This might have resulted in them both losing their homes; one can only imagine how nerve-racking it was. Fortunately, the suit was later dropped. Kinder Morgan tried that tactic again in the spring of 2018 against 168 arrestees, including many featured in this book, who had protested at the oil tank facility on Burnaby Mountain in March of that year.

From the stories of contributors in this book, it is clear there was unequal treatment of Indigenous and nonindigenous protesters, and that Indigenous protesters received harsher sentences at the hands of the courts. Prison can also place protesters' lives or health in jeopardy, as seen with Jim Leyden and Maya Laframboise, who were denied or given wrong medications, or Earle Peach, who was denied vegan meals and access to showers while in prison.

Having a criminal record for participating in civil disobedience can also have long-term consequences in terms of limiting employment opportunities and restricting one's ability to participate in international travel, among other things.[12] People who choose acts of civil disobedience are compelled to consider the possible consequences of any punishment they may endure.

Civil Disobedience as a Deliberative Act

In most instances, civil disobedience is a deliberative act, one that has involved a great deal of reflection, as in the case of the Brunette River Six, though in some instances people report that they were not sure they were going to go through with it until the last minute (see narratives by Robert Stowe and Robert Hackett). Organizations involved in these protests have frequently offered training in nonviolent resistance, and generally protesters take advantage of this training.[13]

The Resisters

In contrast to a common stereotype about activists (that activism can be explained by the impulses and exuberance of youth, and is something people grow out of), there is often a great deal of consistency in the commitment of activists over the course of their lives. We can see a few examples of this in the current volume; for example, the cases of Robert and Barbara Stowe, who were among the founders of Greenpeace in the early 1970s and are still involved in environmental activism. Ruth Walmsley was arrested at Clayoquot in 1993 and Burnaby Mountain in 2014 and 2021. Hisao Ichikawa has been arrested at least five times for civil disobedience. Another good example is Elizabeth May, who has tirelessly worked on environmental issues for decades, including as the executive director of the Sierra Club of Canada, and later as the first elected Green member of the federal parliament and the long-time leader of the Green Party of Canada.

My research has shown that participants in the environmental movement have higher levels of formal education than the general public does. The contributors to this book come from a variety of backgrounds, but as their biographies describe, many have achieved much in their lives outside of their participation in civil disobedience. Some have been involved in activism throughout their lives, and others came to it in later life, but for all of them their action emerged from a considered moral stance.

Outcomes and Impacts

Protests and legal challenges do seem to have slowed down the construction of the Trans Mountain Pipeline. For example, a CBC News report states that in 2018 "Kinder Morgan Canada . . . threatened to scrap the pipeline's planned expansion project in the face of environmental opposition, legal challenges and political risk."[14] If the company had scrapped the project it would have marked a major victory for First Nations communities and environmental activists. However, the project was purchased by the federal government that year and began again in 2020.

It is possible that the slowing down of the project will mean that the total amount of bitumen that passes through the pipelines will be less than it would have otherwise been. An overall assessment about this is yet to come.

Besides slowing down the project to a certain extent, civil disobedience over the Trans Mountain Pipeline garnered media (including social media) attention and, in turn, this attention likely had an impact on values and attitudes among the general public regarding the relevant issues and opinions about the project in particular.

Those who engaged in anti-TMX civil disobedience inspired others to undertake action in regard to this project, but also in regard to other industrial extractive developments that entail harms to the environment and violations of First Nations rights, such as the protests at Fairy Creek and against gas pipelines that pass through First Nations traditional territories.

Sometimes groups that engage in perceived radical actions, such as civil disobedience, create radical flank effects.[15] In some circumstances, a result is that authorities become more willing to negotiate with and meet the demands of groups that are seen to be more moderate.

On the other hand, the TMX resistance campaign also inspired a countermovement of sorts, with various groups opposing and mobilizing against the anti-Trans Mountain Pipeline protesters and the organizations that supported them. Most notable of these were the federal government of Stephen Harper and the Alberta provincial government of Jason Kenney, who created an entire government initiative to counter the environmental and First Nations TMX protesters. Several right-wing media outlets and high-profile journalists were also part of this effort.

At the completion of this essay, the Trans Mountain expansion was 98 percent built and oil was expected to start flowing sometime in late 2024. It seemed likely that the pipeline expansion would be completed. But partly as a result of the active resistance to the project by protesters, this is probably the last large-scale tar sands oil pipeline to be built in Canada. Since the Trans Mountain Pipeline project began, there has been significant change in natural resources development, environmental policy, and recognition of Indigenous rights.

The direct impact of the protesters on the outcome of this specific project may be modest, but in the long run the future of developing more fossil fuel infrastructure in Canada is not bright. In the words of George Hoberg of the School of Public Policy and Global Affairs at the University of British Columbia, in talking about the TMX protesters, "They . . . lost the battle but won the war."[16] And yet this is but one of many campaigns, and certainly will not be the last one, to oppose misguided actions that worsen the climate crisis.

Acknowledgements and Thanks

Contributor and arrestee Catherine Hembling first brought up with editor Rosemary Cornell the idea of chronicling the resistance to the Trans Mountain Pipeline Expansion by compiling the stories of those arrested in the resistance.

Mairy Beam generously shared the court statements she obtained for her play *Irreparable Harm?*

The Protect the Planet: Stop TMX website was a key resource in sharing information about arrests, and they continue to support us with publicity for the book and as a source of updated information.

Kris Hermes provided crucial information for contacting many of the contributors. Contributor Barbara Stowe describes Kris Hermes as a "true unsung hero of this movement, for his invaluable support to myself and other arrestees, including keeping statistics on arrests and incarcerations." We thank Barbara for her encouragement, advice, and enthusiasm.

Contributor Ruth Walmsley and Tim Takaro provided contacts with Indigenous contributors and others, and Ruth helped edit the background chapter.

Robert Hackett and Karl Perrin also helped with the background content and fact-checking.

Niamh Kelly read several of the contributors' pieces and offered helpful advice.

Siobhan O'Connor at The Writers' Union of Canada gave us advice on publication and agreements with contributors.

We are grateful to friends and family who offered their time and thoughtful critique during the journey from idea to book. We especially thank Rhea Tregebov and John Bechhoefer for their input and advice.

Finally, we thank our editors Amanda Crocker and Tilman Lewis, as well as Devin Clancy for book design and graphics, Jasmine Abdelhadi and Sara Swerdlyk for publicity and marketing, and all the team at Between the Lines, many of whom are part of a volunteer collective, for their dedication to social justice and for the skills needed to make this book a reality.

Notes

Introduction and Background

1 We prefer the term "tar sands" over another commonly used term, "oil sands," because the original term was "tar sands" and the substitution of "oils sands" is greenwashing.

2 "World of Change: Athabasca Oil Sands," NASA Earth Observatory, earthobservatory.nasa.gov; "Options to Cap and Cut Oil and Gas Sector Greenhouse Gas Emissions to Achieve 2030 Goals and Net-Zero by 2050—Discussion Document," Environment and Natural Resources Canada, 2022, canada.ca.

3 "Product," Trans Mountain website, transmountain.com.

4 "Project Benefits," Trans Mountain website, transmountain.com.

5 Tsleil-Waututh Sacred Trust Initiative website, twnsacredtrust.ca.

6 "Trans Mountain Market Insights," Trans Mountain website, transmountain.com.

7 D. Welsby, J. Price, S. Pye, and P. Eakins, "Unextractable Fossil Fuels in a 1.5 °C World," *Nature* 597 (2021): 230–40.

8 M. Jaccard and J. Hoffele, "Impact on GHG Emissions and Climate Targets of the Trans Mountain Expansion Project," report for the City of Vancouver, MK Jaccard and Associates, May 14, 2014, vancouver.ca; "Trans Mountain Expansion Project: Review of Related Upstream Greenhouse Gas Emissions Estimates," report from Environment and Climate Change Canada, November 2016, iaac-aeic.gc.ca.

9 "Options to Cap and Cut," Environment and Natural Resources Canada discussion paper, 2022.

10 "Greenhouse Gas Emissions from the Trans Mountain Project," Environment and Climate Change Canada, 2019, canada.ca.

11 Jaccard and Hoffele, "Impact on GHG Emissions and Climate Targets."

12 C. Nardi, "Canada's Environment Watchdog Blasts Government for Going from 'Failure to Failure,'" *National Post*, November 25, 2021, nationalpost.com.

13 B. Richter, "Oil Tankers Could Strike Ironworkers Bridge, Engineers Warn," *North Shore News*, November 22, 2016, nsnews.com.

14 "10 Largest Ports in North America," Shipa Freight, shipafreight.com.

15 J.W. Short, "Fate and Effect of Oil Spills from the Trans Mountain Expansion Project in Burrard Inlet and the Fraser River Estuary," appendix 3 of Tsleil-Waututh Nation's *Assessment of the Trans Mountain*

Pipeline and Tanker Expansion Proposal (2015) for the National Energy Board review, twnsacredtrust.ca.

16 "Burnaby Terminal," Trans Mountain website, transmountain.com.

17 "Westridge Marine Terminal," Trans Mountain website, transmountain.com.

18 "Trending Topic: Trans Mountain Pipeline," *Narwhal*, thenarwhal.ca.

19 "Coast Salish," *Canadian Encyclopedia*, thecanadianencyclopedia.ca.

20 "Kinder Morgan Pipeline Hearings a 'Farce,' Says Former BC Hydro Head," CBC News, November 3, 2014, cbc.ca.

21 *Report from the Ministerial Panel for the Trans Mountain Expansion Project* (Natural Resources Canada, 2016), natural-resources.canada.ca.

22 "The Dirty Dozen: 'Carbon Bombs' Threaten to Blow Up Canada's Climate Commitments," *Ricochet*, November 22, 2022, ricochet.media.

23 Michelle Bellefontaine, "Notley's Leadership, Climate Plan, a Factor in Pipeline Approvals, PM Says," CBC News, November 29, 2016, cbc.ca.

24 For an excellent dive into internecine conflicts between BC and Alberta over TMX, see chapter 6 of George Hoberg, *The Resistance Dilemma: Place-Based Movements and the Climate Crisis* (MIT Press, 2021), mit.edu.

25 N. Bulowski and J. Woodside, "What We Do and Don't Know about Chrystia Freeland's Trans Mountain Claims," *National Observer*, nationalobserver.com.

26 "Economic Benefits of the Trans Mountain Expansion Project," Government of Canada, canada.ca.

27 A. Ballingall, "Trans Mountain Pipeline Expansion Could Leave Canadians on the Hook for Billions of Dollars," *Toronto Star*, March 9, 2022, thestar.com; R. Allan, "Trans Mountain: Compromised Viability to Cost Taxpayers More Than $17 Billion," report for West Coast Environmental Law (October 6, 2022), wcel.org.

28 N. Bulowski, "Canada's Case for Trans Mountain Assumes the Pipeline Will Operate for 100 Years. PBO Disagrees," *National Observer*, June 24, 2022, nationalobserver.com.

29 B. Hill, "Liberals Say Trans Mountain Pipeline Could Stay Open until 2060," Global News, September 14, 2021, globalnews.ca.

30 A. Cruickshank, "Vancouver's Development Destroyed Burrard Inlet. Tsleil-Waututh Nation Is Determined to Save It," *Narwhal*, June 21, 2023, thenarwhal.ca.

31 Tsleil-Waututh Nation, *Assessment of the Trans Mountain Pipeline and Tanker Expansion Proposal*, assessment report for the National Energy Board review (2015), twnsacredtrust.ca.

32 D. Kresnyak, "Rueben George Blasts Pipeline Expansion Proposal

at Kinder Morgan AGM," *National Observer*, May 7, 2015, vancouverobserver.com.

33 "Rueben George Speaks at TD Bank AGM: Tsleil-Waututh Nation Does Not Consent to TMX," TWN Sacred Trust, April 20, 2022, twnsacredtrust.ca.

34 A. Stephenson, "'This Is Our Vatican': Trans Mountain Route Change Will 'Desecrate' Sacred B.C. Site, Says Secwépemc Knowledge Keeper," *Vancouver Sun*, October 8, 2023, vancouversun.com.

35 J. Woodside, "Trans Mountain Tries to Duck Fire Safety Standard for Burnaby Tank Farm," *Energy Mix*, January 3, 2022, theenergymix.com.

36 M. Hume, "Burnaby Fire Chief Warns against Expanding Kinder Morgan Tank Yard," *Globe and Mail*, May 14, 2015, theglobeandmail. com; *National Energy Board Report: Trans Mountain Expansion Project* (National Energy Board, 2016), iaac-aeic.gc.ca.

37 *NEB Report*.

38 R. Zussman and S. Boynton, "B.C. Government, Environmentalists 'Disappointed' over Trans Mountain Court Decision" Global News, January 16, 2020, globalnews.ca.

39 Conservation/environmental organizations with major campaigns in opposition to TMX include the Wilderness Committee, 350.org, Stand.earth, Dogwood BC, Georgia Strait Alliance, Sierra Club, Raincoast Conservation Foundation, Living Oceans Society, Leadnow, Greenpeace, West Coast Environmental Law, and Ecojustice. In addition, organizations like Protect the Planet: Stop TMX, BROKE, and Protect the Inlet have been focused solely on the TMX project.

40 *NEB Report*, chapter 10.

41 *NEB Report*, summary table, p. XIV.

42 Kinder Morgan dropped these suits against all five in 2015 and offered to pay their court costs rather than accept the consequences of the cases going to court. Jennifer Moreau, "Kinder Morgan Drops Multimillion-Dollar Civil Suit against Protesters," *Burnaby Now*, January 30, 2015, burnabynow.com.

43 "Kinder Morgan Burnaby Mountain Protest Injunction Granted," CBC News, November 14, 2014, cbc.ca.

44 "Kinder Morgan Loses Bid to Extend Injunction," CBC News, November 27, 2014, cbc.ca.

45 *Report from the Ministerial Panel*.

46 A. Cruickshank, "Supreme Court Rejects Trans Mountain Legal Challenges," March 9, 2020, thenarwhal.ca; "Challenging the Trans Mountain Pipeline Expansion," Ecojustice, ecojustice.ca.

47 "Good trouble" is a term made famous by civil rights icon and US congressional representative John Lewis.

48 Canada's laws do not have a formal notion of "criminal record." In practice, criminal convictions are stored in a database called CPIC (Canadian Police Information Centre). The offence of Criminal Contempt is an exception; it does not result in a CPIC record.

49 "Trans Mountain Pipeline Construction Ordered Paused in B.C. Bird Nesting Area," CBC News, April 26, 2021, cbc.ca.

50 R. Walmsley, "Why We Face Jail Time for Safeguarding a Livable Climate," *Vancouver Sun*, February 9, 2022, vancouversun.com.

51 In addition to their testimony within these pages, more information on these and other arrestees can be found on the Protect the Planet: Stop TMX website (stoptmx.ca).

52 C. Helgren, "UN Committee Criticizes Canada over Handling of Indigenous Pipeline Opposition," *Globe and Mail*, May 11, 2022, theglobeandmail.com.

53 "Amnesty International's 2022/23 Annual Report Denounces Canada's Record on Indigenous People's Rights, Climate Justice," Amnesty International Canada, March 28, 2023, amnesty.ca.

Part 1: Resistance from Turtle Island

1 On July 25, 2023, the prosecution dropped the charges against Jim pertaining to the 2019 arrest, realizing that their case would not stand in appeals court.

2 The Gladue guidelines recommend that sentencing of Indigenous persons consider their background including a history of trauma, Indigenous law, and alternatives to incarceration for relatively minor infractions.

3 "Allodial rights" refers to land ownership by virtue of occupancy and defence; wikipedia.org.

4 The charges against Lorelei Dick were later dismissed, as she had not breached the injunction area.

5 "Taking Accountability—and Asking the B.C. Supreme Court to Do the Same," *IndigiNews*, March 20, 2023, indiginews.com.

6 A. Hemes, "Secwépemc Matriarch and Hereditary Chief Head to Jail for Opposition of TMX Construction on Unceded Land," *IndigiNews*, November 15, 2023, indiginews.com.

7 The original people of the Shuswap Territory.

8 In the Oregon Boundary Treaty of 1846, Britain and the United States divided the territory west of the Rockies between themselves.

Part 2: Resistance from a place of spirit

1 "Witchita—A Lakota Women's Water Song," M'Girl Music, YouTube, youtube.com.

2 Convention 169 is the agreement that safeguards the rights of

Indigenous and Tribal peoples, guaranteeing their right to "prior and informed consent" regarding any megaproject that is planned on their land. Canada, shamefully, has not ratified this convention.

3   Maria Choc is a Guatemalan land defender who has been repeatedly incarcerated. Edwin Espinal is a Honduran community leader in a high-security prison in Honduras. Beatriz Barrios Marroquin, a Guatemalan human rights advocate, teacher, and mother, was Emilie's sister-in-law. She was kidnapped on December 10, 1985, and her mutilated body was found on the side of a highway four days later. The UN reported that during Guatemala's brutal civil war (1960–1996) an estimated 250,000 citizens were murdered or "disappeared," never to be heard from again.

Part 3: Resistance from a place of priviledge

1   Witt-O'Briens, "A Study of Fate and Behavior of Diluted Bitumen Oils on Marine Waters: Dilbit Experiments—Gainford, Alberta," report prepared for Trans Mountain Pipeline, ULC (Polaris Applied Sciences and Western Canada Marine Response Corporation, 2013).

2   T.L. King, B. Robinson, M. Boufadel, and K. Lee, "Flume Tank Studies to Elucidate the Fate and Behavior of Diluted Bitumen Spilled at Sea," *Marine Pollution Bulletin* 83, no. 1 (2014): 32–37.

3   P. Gosselin et al., Royal Society of Canada Expert Panel, *Environmental and Health Impacts of Canada's Oil Sands Industry* (December 2010).

4   "Properties, Composition and Marine Spill Behaviour, Fate and Transport of Two Diluted Bitumen Products from the Canadian Oil Sands," Technical Report from the Departments of Environment, Fisheries and Oceans, and Natural Resources, Canada (2013).

5   As predicted, projected costs for finishing the project rose to $31 billion as of June 2023. (D. Thurton, "Budget Watchdog Says Trans Mountain Expansion Is No Longer Profitable," CBC News, June 22, 2022, cbc.ca.) That figure was raised to $34 billion in February 2024. (Amanda Stephenson, "Trans Mountain's Latest Cost Estimate Climbs 10%, Regulatory Filing Shows," Canadian Press, February 27, 2024, cbc.ca.)

6   "Secretary-General Warns of Climate Emergency, Calling Intergovernmental Panel's Report 'a File of Shame', While Saying Leaders 'Are Lying', Fuelling Flames," United Nations press release, April 4, 2022, un.org.

7   "Climate Campaigners Call for Lawyers to Warn Clients of Environmental Risks," *Irish Legal News*, September 19, 2022, irishlegal.com.

8   Atmospheric CO_2 concentration is presently 420 ppm (December 2023), climate.nasa.gov.

9   Mary Eberts, Kim Stanton, and Lara Koerner Yeo, "RCMP Must Acknowledge the Force's Racist Underpinnings," *Policy Options*, July 28, 2020, irpp.org.

10 Paul Rogers, "UK Activists Keep Being Acquitted by Juries: What Does That Mean for Protest?," *Resilience*, January 31, 2022, resilience.org.

11 Robert Joseph Neubauer, "Moving beyond The Petrostate: Northern Gateway, Extractivism, and the Canadian Petrobloc," *Studies in Political Economy* 99, no. 3 (2018): 246–67, DOI: 10.1080/07078552.2018.1536369; William K. Carroll, ed., *Regime of Obstruction: How Corporate Power Blocks Energy Democracy* (AU Press, 2021); Kevin Taft, *Oil's Deep State: How the Petroleum Industry Undermines Democracy and Stops Action on Global Warming—in Alberta, and in Ottawa* (Lorimer Press, 2017).

12 E.P. Thompson, "Notes on Exterminism, the Last Stage of Civilization," *New Left Review* 121 (1980): 3–31; J.B. Foster, "Notes on 'Exterminism' for the Twenty-First-Century Ecology and Peace Movements," *Monthly Review* 74, no. 1 (May 2022): 1–17.

13 Arthur Manuel and Grand Chief Ronald Derrickson, *The Reconciliation Manifesto* (Lorimer Press, 2017).

14 Ta'ah George refers to Amy George, the daughter of Chief Dan George. Ta'ah means grandmother or Matriarch.

15 See part 4.

16 See unnaturalgas.org.

17 See doctorsforplanetaryhealth.com.

18 B.N. Madison, P.V. Hodson, and V.S. Langlois, "Cold Lake Blend Diluted Bitumen Toxicity to the Early Development of Japanese Medaka," *Environmental Pollution* 225 (2017): 579–86, DOI: 10.1016/j.envpol.2017.03.025.

19 M. Anderson, "Spill from Hell: Diluted Bitumen," *Tyee*, March 5, 2012, thetyee.ca.

20 M. Hume, "Burnaby Fire Chief Warns against Expanding Kinder Morgan Tank Yard," *Globe and Mail*, May 14, 2015, theglobeandmail.com.

21 A. Dew, A. Hontela, S. B. Rood, and G.G. Pyle, "Biological Effects and Toxicity of Diluted Bitumen and Its Constituents in Freshwater Systems," *Journal of Applied Toxicology* 35, no. 11 (2015): 1219–27, DOI: 10.1002/jat.3196.

22 Samuel J. Spiegel, "Climate Injustice, Criminalisation of Land Protection and Anti-Colonial Solidarity: Courtroom Ethnography in an Age of Fossil Fuel Violence," *Political Geography* 84 (2021): 102298, sciencedirect.com.

23 Kris Hermes, "Twelve People Sentenced by BC Supreme Court for Civil Disobedience against TransMountain Pipeline," Last Real Indians, July 12, 2018, lastrealindians.com.

Part 4: Resistance from high in the trees

1   The figure of $21 billion was raised to $31 billion in January 2023 and $34 billion in February 2024. Amanda Stephenson, "Trans Mountain's Latest Cost Estimate Climbs 10%, Regulatory Filing Shows," Canadian Press, February 27, 2024, cbc.ca.

2   "Climate Change: A Threat to Human Wellbeing and Health of the Planet. Taking Action Now Can Secure Our Future," IPCC news release, February 28, 2022, ipcc.ch.

3   Judge McEachern opinion in *MacMillen Bloedel Ltd v. Brown*, 1994 CanLII 3254 (BC CA), canlii.ca.

4   Several resisters chose to go by pseudonyms during their direct actions. We are respecting their choices here.

5   Story shared with Kukpi7 Judy Wilson's permission.

6   "IPCC Adaptation Report 'a Damning Indictment of Failed Global Leadership on Climate," UN News, February 28, 2022, un.org.

7   "Secretary-General Warns of Climate Emergency, Calling Intergovernmental Panel's Report 'a File of Shame', While Saying Leaders 'Are Lying', Fuelling Flames," UN press release, April 4, 2022, un.org.

8   A. Stephenson, "Trans Mountain Pipeline to Result in Net Loss for Ottawa: PBO," *Financial Post*, June 22, 2022, financialpost.com.

9   *Peter Kiewit Sons Co. et al. v. Perry et al.*, 2007 BCSC 305, bccourts.ca.

10 T.M. Lenton *et al.*, "Climate Tipping Points—Too Risky to Bet Against," *Nature* 466 (2019): 575, 592–95, nature.com.

11 Mark Poynting, "World's First Year-Long Breach of Key 1.5C Warming Limit," BBC News, February 8, 2024, bbc.com.

12 "Defendants Acquitted in Extinction Rebellion Trial," *Ekklesia*, April 25, 2021, ekklesia.co.uk.

13 Charles Denson, "Valve Turners to Present Climate Necessity Defense at Minnesota Jury Trial," Civil Liberties Defense Center, April 23, 2018, cldc.org.

14 Washington State Supreme Court, Docket number 97182-0, September 4, 2019, climatecasechart.com.

15 For more on the Ecological Footprint tool, visit the Global Footprint Network site: footprintnetwork.org.

16 "Secretary-General Calls Latest IPCC Climate Report 'Code Red for Humanity', Stressing 'Irrefutable' Evidence of Human Influence," United Nations press release, August 9, 2021, un.org.

17 "UN Report: Nature's Dangerous Decline 'Unprecedented'; Species Extinction Rates 'Accelerating,'" Sustainable Development Goals, United Nations, May 6, 2019, un.org.

18 Tsleil-Waututh Nation Sacred Trust Initiative, twnsacredtrust.ca.

19 "Federal, Provincial and Territorial Interpretation and Implementation

of Free, Prior and Informed Consent Must Be Aligned with Canada's Human Rights Obligations," Coalition for the Human Rights of Indigenous People, February 12, 2019, quakerservice.ca.

20 "IPCC Adaptation Report 'a Damning Indictment of Failed Global Leadership on Climate,'" UN press release. February 28, 2022, un.org.

21 R. Walmsley, "Why We Face Jail Time for Safeguarding a Livable Climate," *Vancouver Sun*, February 9, 2022, vancouversun.com.

22 For the story on the bear encounter, see Bill Winder's piece in part 4.

Part 5: Resistance through art

1 Donna Clark, "B.C. Imprisons People We Should Listen To," *National Observer*, October 18, 2023, nationalobserver.com.

2 M. Hume, "Burnaby Fire Chief Warns against Expanding Kinder Morgan Tank Yard," *Globe and Mail*, May 14, 2015, theglobeandmail.com.

3 B. Richter, "Oil Tankers Could Strike Ironworkers Bridge, Engineers Warn, *North Shore News*, November 22, 2016, nsnews.com.

4 *Force majeure* describes those uncontrollable events (such as war, labour stoppages, or extreme weather due to, e.g., global heating) that are not the fault of any party and that make it difficult or impossible to carry out normal business.

5 D. Boyce, M. Lewis, and B. Worm, "Global Phytoplankton Decline over the Past Century," *Nature* 466 (2010): 591–96, DOI: 10.1038/nature09268.

6 "Civil Disobedience," *Stanford Encyclopedia of Philosophy Archive*, Summer 2020 edition, stanford.edu.

7 To learn about Coast Salish laws, visit Tsleil-Waututh Sacred Trust Initiative, twnsacredtrust.ca.

8 "Joint Effort," Prison Justice website, prisonjustice.ca.

9 Brent Patterson, "Land and Water Defenders Criminalized, while Kinder Morgan Gets $920 Fine for Violating the Water Sustainability Act," Council of Canadians, July 5, 2018, canadians.org.

10 The Solutions Project website, thesolutionsproject.org.

11 "Greta Thunberg and George Monbiot Make Short Film on Climate Crisis—Video," *Guardian*, September 19, 2019, theguardian.com.

12 R. Wong, "Ethical Waters: Reflections on the Healing Walk in the Tar Sands," *Water* 103 (2013): 133–39, jstor.org.

13 Mountain Protectors, Unceded Coast Salish Territories, on Facebook, facebook.com.

14 Peace Valley Environment Association, peacevalley.ca.

Part 6: Resisters fighting for their future

1 During the sentencing, before my address, Judge Fitzpatrick

rhetorically asked: "Did they (meaning Maya and myself) miss civics class?" and suggested that becoming an MLA or MP was a better way of making change. I added this amendment to my speech at the last minute. It ushered a wave of cheers and applause from the gallery.

2 Emily published a three-part series of her time in the trees in *Canada's National Observer*: "My Year in the Trees," June 20, 2022, nationalobserver.com; "The Treesit 'Eagle' Was a Masterpiece with Four Walls, a Roof, Six Windows, a Bed and a Heater," June 22, 2022, nationalobserver.com; "TMX Can Tear Down Our Treehouses, but Not Our Mission," July 8, 2022, nationalobserver.com.

3 To be clear, none of the TMX arrestees, including Emily and Maya, have criminal records for their civil disobedience.

4 We had at least one slice of bread with every meal.

5 "Treaty Alliance Against Tar Sands Expansion Responds to NEB Decision to Restart Energy East Review, Union of British Columbia Indian Chiefs," January 27 2017, ubcic.bc.ca.

6 Clayton Thomas-Muller, "Tar Sands: Environmental Justice, Treaty Rights and Indigenous Peoples," *Canadian Dimension*, March 6, 2008, canadiandimension.com.

Conclusion

1 Aaron Hemens, "Regulator Approves TMX Plan to Trench through 'Extremely Sacred' Secwépemc Site," *IndigiNews*, September 26, 2023, indiginews.com.

2 George Monbiot, "Here's a Question Cop28 Won't Address: Why Are Billionaires Blocking Action to Save the Planet?," *Guardian*, November 29, 2023, theguardian.com.

3 Barry Hadden and Helena Alves, "Six Young Activists Devote Years to Climate Fight with 32 Governments. Now Comes Their Day in Court," City News (Kitchener), September 25, 2023, citynews.ca.

4 "State of the Netherlands v. Urgenda Foundation," *American Journal of International Law* 114, no. 4 (2020): 729–35, DOI: 10.1017/ajil.2020.52.

5 Kate Selig, "Judge Rules in Favor of Montana Youths in Landmark Climate Decision," *Washington Post*, August 14, 2023, washingtonpost.com.

6 "Youth-Led Climate Case in Ontario Heads Back to Court," Ecojustice press release, January 15, 2024, ecojustice.ca.

Appendix

1 David B. Tindall and Noreen Begoray, "Old Growth Defenders: The Battle for the Carmanah Valley," in *Environmental Stewardship: Studies in Active Earthkeeping*, ed. Sally Lerner (Waterloo: University of Waterloo Geography Series, 1993), 269–322.

2   D.B. Tindall, A.C. Howe, and C. Mauboulès, "Tangled Roots: Personal Networks and the Participation of Individuals in an Anti-environmentalism Countermovement," *Sociological Perspectives* 64, no. 1 (2021): 5–36.

3   In this essay the term "civil disobedience" implies "nonviolent civil disobedience." It is worth noting that use of this term varies among activists and commentators. Sometimes protest that goes beyond civil disobedience is described as direct action. However, some people refer to vandalism and other forms of property destruction as civil disobedience. The term "nonviolent civil disobedience" is sometimes used to distinguish from this and other forms of direct action.

4   T. Berman, "Takin' It Back," *BC Studies* 200 (2018): 81–86; P. Walter, "Adult Learning in New Social Movements: Environmental Protest and the Struggle for the Clayoquot Sound Rainforest," *Adult Education Quarterly* 57, no. 3 (2007): 248–63.

5   Richard Watts, "Environmentalists, Action Difficulties Surprised Cashore," *Victoria Times Colonist*, December 27, 1992, A13.

6   Keith Flemming, "'Socially Disruptive Actions . . . Have Become as Canadian as Maple Syrup': Civil Disobedience in Canada, 1960–2012," *Journal of Canadian Studies* 54, no. 1 (2020): 181–212.

7   C. McGlade and P. Ekins, "The Geographical Distribution of Fossil Fuels Unused when Limiting Global Warming to 2 Degrees C," *Nature* 517 (2015): 187–90.

8   Henry David Thoreau, *Civil Disobedience and Other Essays* (Digireads Publishing, 2017), Kindle edition 11–12.

9   Martin Luther King Jr., "Letter from a Birmingham Jail," 1963, African Studies Center, University of Pennsylvania, upenn.edu.

10   B. Simpson, R. Willer, and M. Feinberg, "Does Violent Protest Backfire?: Testing a Theory of Public Reactions to Activist Violence," *Socius* 4 (2018), DOI: 10.1177/2378023118803189.

11   D.A. Snow, E.B. Rochford Jr., S.K. Worden, and R.D. Benford, "Frame Alignment Processes, Micromobilization, and Movement Participation," *American Sociological Review* 51, no. 4 (1986): 464–81.

12   None of the arrestees featured in this book have criminal records as a result of their actions against TMX.

13   Walter, "Adult Learning in New Social Movements."

14   Kyle Bakx, "Why Canada Likely Won't Need Any More Big New Oil Pipelines after Trans Mountain," CBC News, March 16, 2023, cbc.ca.

15   H.H. Haines, "Black Radicalization and the Funding of Civil Rights: 1957–1970," *Social Problems* 32, no. 1 (1984): 31–43.

16   Bakx, "Why Canada Likely Won't Need Any More Big New Oil Pipelines."

Index

Page numbers in italics represent photos/illustrations.

Rosemary Cornell has been an activist for Nature conservation and regeneration since childhood as she watched in consternation and grief as the forest surrounding her home was converted into a housing subdivision. Speaking the uncomfortable truth is a value engrained into her by the religious community within which she was raised. She was a professor of Molecular Biology and Biochemistry at Simon Fraser University on Burnaby Mountain for 33 years, and for eight years collaborated in research with co-editor Adrienne Drobnies. She lives in a wonderful neighbourhood on the territories of the Musqueam, Squamish, and Tsleil-Waututh, and has two inspiring adult children, whose future is her prime concern.

Adrienne Drobnies is a PhD chemist and poet living in Vancouver, BC, on the territories of the Coast Salish people. She was a researcher at Simon Fraser University, and then project manager at the BC Genome Sciences Centre until 2013. In 2019, she published her first book of poetry, *Salt and Ashes* (Signature Editions), which won the Fred Kerner Award from the Canadian Authors Association. Her poem "Randonnées," won the Gwendolyn MacEwen Award and was shortlisted for the CBC Literary Prize. She is grateful to breathe the air, walk along the ocean, and wander through the forests of the lands where she resides, and seeks in whatever ways she can to sustain that abundance for future generations.

Tim Bray is a software engineer, writer, and environmentalist in Vancouver, BC, on the territories of the Coast Salish peoples. He is the founder of two companies, a major contributor to Internet Standards, and the author of a popular blog at tbray.org. In March 2018 he was arrested while protesting the TMX pipeline, and in May 2020 he made headlines by resigning from his position as VP/Distinguished Engineer at Amazon's cloud computing division in protest at the treatment of warehouse workers and whistleblowers.